Lilia Mironov

AIRPORT AURA

A SPATIAL HISTORY OF AIRPORT INFRASTRUCTURE

D1731802

v/d\f

Published with the support of the Swiss National Science Foundation.

This work is licensed under a creative commons licence:

Bibliographic Information published by Die Deutsche Nationalbibliothek
Die Deutsche Nationalbibliothek lists this publication in the Internet at
http://dnb.dnb.de.

An online version of the work is made available under a Creative Commons license
for use that is noncommercial. The terms of the license are set forth at
https://creativecommons.org/licenses/by-nc-nd/2.5/ch/deed.en.

© 2020, vdf Hochschulverlag AG an der ETH Zürich

ISBN 978-3-7281-3990-0 (Print version)

Download open access:
ISBN: 978-3-7281-3991-7/ DOI 10.3218/3991-7
www.vdf.ethz.ch
verlag@vdf.ethz.ch

Contents

Acknowledgements 5

Abstract 7

1 Introduction 9
  1.1 The Project 9
  1.2 Research 10

2 Travels through Airports: In Search of a
Narrative 13

3 The Architecture of Travel 23
  3.1 Mobility Culture 23
  3.2 The Aerotropolis 29
  3.3 Generic Junk 33
  3.4 The Beginnings of Mobility 39
  3.5 Railways and Vistas 40
  3.6 Railway Stations 48
  3.7 Grand Central Terminal 54

4 Airports! 61
  4.1 Where to place an Airport Terminal? . . . 61
  4.2 Airport Typology 68
  4.3 The Naked Airport 72
  4.4 Airports of the Jet Age 75
  4.5 Rounding up 80

5 Tracing the Architecture of Leisure and
Consumption in Airports 81
  5.1 Home 82
  5.2 The Interior and Exterior 86

5.3 Glass and Iron 91
5.4 Crystal Palace 96
5.5 Crystal Palaces of Aviation 103
5.6 Places of Consumption 109
5.7 From Non-Places into Places of
  Enjoyment 113

6 Architecture of the Senses –
Experiencing the Airport 121
  6.1 A Phenomenological Introduction of
  the Sensorial and Auratic in Airport
  Design 121
  6.2 Airport Empire – Crisis Heterotopia
  and Panopticon 129
  6.3 Event-architecture in Airports 138
  6.4 Performative Architecture 141
  6.5 Art in Airports 149
  6.6 The Airport is a Stage 158

7 Airport Aura 163

8 Illustration Credits 169

9 Bibliography 177

Acknowledgements

I wish to thank the following supporters, mentors and interview partners during my PhD research:

My parents, Prof. Dr. med. Angel Mironov and Dr. med. Nadja Mironov.
My sister, Katja Mironova. Daphne and Eliza.
The Swiss National Science Foundation SNF for offering me the doctoral grant.
My PhD supervisors, Professors Bernd Nicolai and Luis Carranza.
Professor Christine Göttler for instigating the SNF project.
Steve Swanson and Robert Bedrick of LAX, Curtis Fentress of Fentress Architects, David Loyola of Gensler, Paul Senzaki of The Jerde Partnership, Professor Anna Minta, Professor Philip Ursprung, Professor Marc Angélil, Professor Ákos Moravánszky, Roald Sand of Nordic Architects, Zahnarztpraxis Neuwiesen Winterthur, Nadia Wipfli and Manel Boulfernane from the University of Bern, Angelika Rodlauer of vdf Hochschulverlag an der ETH Zürich and many more individuals who provided me with information and input.

I gave my best to verify and confirm the image copyrights of this dissertation, should I have unwittingly omitted the correct designation, I apologize profoundly and am willing to have this rectified.
   The following people and companies have provided me with image rights permissions and I am deeply grateful to them:

Kate Igoe of the Archives Division of the National Air and Space Museum, Smithsonian Institution, Washington; Margit Millstein Moorhouse of Nordic Architects; Gordon Welters; Stephane Aleixandre at the Centre Canadien d'Architecture; Musei Civici e Pinacoteca Como; Richard Burton Archives at Swansea University; Margo Stipe at the Frank Lloyd Wright Foundation; Joe Wong of Foster + Partners; Argiñe Diana of the Norman Foster Foundation; Alanna Malone Murray of HOK Architects; Nadine Degen at ProLitteris; Richard Wilson; Ulrike Feucht at Spillmann Echsle Architekten; Dr. John D. Kasarda; Stefania Canta of Renzo Piano Building Workshop; Mathieu Pomerleau, Katherine Prater, Margaret Smithglass and Cristina Seghi of the Avery Library at Columbia University.

Abstract

Throughout the 20th century and into the 21st, the emergence of airports as gateways for their cities has turned into one of the most important architectural undertakings. Ever since the first manned flight by the Brothers Orville and Wilbur Wright on December 17, 1903, utilitarian sheds next to landing strips on cow pastures evolved into a completely new building type over the next few decades – into places of Modernism as envisioned by Le Corbusier and Frank Lloyd Wright (who themselves had never built an airport), to eventually turn into icons of cultural identity, progress and prosperity. In Europe, military aerodromes created during the First World War, such as Bourget and Croydon airports in France and Great Britain respectively, were transformed into civilian airport terminals.

Many of these airports have become architectural branding devices of their respective cities, regions and countries, created by some of the most notable contemporary architects.

This interdisciplinary cultural study deals with the historical formation and transformation of the architectural typology of airports under the aspect of spatial theories. This includes the shift from early spaces of transportation such as train stations, the synesthetic effect of travel and mobility and the effects of material innovations on the development, occupation, and use of such spaces. The changing uses from mere utilitarian transportation spaces to ones centered on the spectacular culture of late capitalism, consumption, and identity formation in a rapidly changing global culture are analyzed with examples both from architectural and philosophical points of view.

The origins of this glass and iron architecture can be traced to Joseph Paxton's Crystal Palace, built for the Great Exhibition of 1851. This was the first time that the exhibition venue itself took a backseat to its architecture. The composition of the interior and the perception thereof were of a fluid nature with myriads of possibilities for interior design. The crystalline exhibition and dwelling premises of the Crystal Palace were the idealized interiors where the enlightened citizens dwelled and strolled as analyzed in Walter Benjamin's Arcades Project. They were consequently recreated in arcades, tea rooms, cafés, and grand train stations at the turn of the century, setting the stage for what would become urban realm and airport architecture.

Much like ubiquitous modern day coffee shops, airports aim to be the third place as per Ray Oldenburg, but are rather a non-place according to Marc Augé and a Foucauldian interplay between heterotopias, utopias, and dystopias. Many have become nightmarish panopticons of migration, surveillance, and control, triggered by the events surrounding the terrorist attacks of the last two decades.

Current airport design puts an emphasis on the regional and anthropological place to counteract the dehumanization of mass transportation. Its transitory character is fused with art exhibition sites, culminating in airport-museum-hybrids, such as Mumbai and Doha airports. The future of airport architecture and design looks very much like the original idea of the Crystal Palace: to provide a stage for consumption, social theatre, and art exhibition.

1 Introduction

1.1 The Project

This dissertation has evolved from the Swiss National Science Foundation (SNSF) Sinergia funded Research Project *The Interior: Art, Space, and Performance (Early Modern to Postmodern)* at the Institute of Art History at the University of Bern. Within the subproject *Heterotopian Spaces: Public, Semi-public and Non-public Interiors in Contemporary Architecture, 1970–2010* the aim of my research was to explore the cultural and architectural evolution of airport interiors and airport designs as hybrid spaces during the twentieth and twenty-first centuries. These hybrid spaces encompass airports, railway stations, malls, public buildings as well as public squares and event spaces.

I use the term hybrid spaces specifically to describe newly emerged architectural creations of the late twentieth century that fuse retail, relaxation, dining, and entertainment as an actual amalgamation of architectural and societal spaces. Different spatial denominations define modernism and our cultural evolution as a society. The terms space, place, public, private, interior, exterior, and transitory permeate our lives and conspicuously appear in this thesis, culminating in my naming this work Airport Aura – the *auratic* being the capstone of my airport research.

My research project was initially titled Heterotopian Spaces in relation to Michel Foucault's term which describes real places and other spaces that exist as *counter-sites* to our everyday sites and applies to liminal spaces, especially so to airports because of their status as *other* and *hybrid*, with Foucault even speaking of the twentieth Century as the "epoch of juxtaposition".[1]

Another important discourse in this matter is Marc Augé's sociocultural study "Non-Places" that shows us the places that supermodernity has created as well as destroyed and that we peruse but cannot find a personal or emotional connection to – the places of our daily rat race towards our careers and tasks, namely train stations, malls, consumerist infrastructure such as supermarkets and gas stations – and ultimately airports.[2]

In our globalized world, heterotopias alienate us and non-places displace us of our anthropological origin, they make us lose our identities to the point that we turn into vapid consumers of a transitory system that dictates our behavior and consumption.

There is a counter-movement to oppose this loss of identity. The architecture of these hybrid spaces has evolved dramatically in the last few decades to create more meaningful buildings and places with the purpose of connecting to the emotions and ethnocultural origins of the people it addresses. New idioms such as the word *glocal*, a linking of the terms global and local, enhance the global and regional aspect of this system.

My dissertation aims to show the architectural and sociocultural process that airport typology has under-

---

1   Foucault's *heterotopian spaces*, which he describes in his works "Of other Spaces: Utopias and Heterotopias", are a treatise in understanding the concepts of our contemporary time, society, culture and the spaces as well as the rituals (habits) and rules that have been superimposed on its inhabitants (originally: Michel Foucault, Des Espaces Autres, 1967).

2   Augé raises the term postmodernity, which is the preeminent cultural denomination of our era beginning in the latter half of the twentieth century, to his superlative term *supermodernity* which he sees characterized by excess (especially so since the 1980s). (originally: Marc Augé, Non-lieux, introduction à une anthropologie de la surmodernité, 1992)

taken, particularly under the influence of globalization and politics.

Migration and world politics have tremendously changed the transitory places such as train stations and airports. In social sciences, both these infrastructures fall under urbanism studies as they are deeply tied to the theories of urbanization and transportation and the social production of space, the latter defined by Henri Lefebvre in a work of the same title, arguing that space is a social product. During the twentieth century, intellectuals and sociologists explore *space* as the signifying universe of modernity and especially so of late modernity with its roots in the nineteenth century.

Space has a distinguished connotation in the arts, beginning with the central perspective which was discovered at the onset of the Renaissance and allowed for more natural, realistic and three-dimensional artworks. The central perspective not only created scientifically accurate renderings in art and architecture but also opened the mindset beyond the two-dimensional philosophy of viewing and understanding.

Space also stands for interior design which flourished throughout the centuries since the Renaissance, such as in Palladian villas, Rococo furniture, court rituals, and eventually culminating into the exhibition-spectacle-leisure kind of spatial performance in gardens, greenhouses, orangeries, public places and museums. Space and the interiorization effect (the emphasis on the inside and outside of the home and consequently the need for dwelling spaces in the city realm) during and after the industrialization set the tone for this thesis. The advancements in technology and society, the onset of modern transportation via railways, the surge of retail and consumption all stand in reciprocal connection to space and all contribute to a newly constructed social space for humans. The history of airport architecture is evidently a history of our society and culture.

1.2 Research

How have history and mobility affected airport design? How do tourism and politics influence travel and infrastructure? Are there specific design paragons for airport architects? How can airport architecture contribute to and represent a city or region?

This dissertation will reassess the given theories about airport architecture and interior spaces and discern new ways of spatial design in airports. As the number of airplanes will more than double within the next decade, there will be numerous transformative effects on the infrastructure of airports. Will there be many new greenfield (built from scratch) airports or will there be mostly expansions of existing terminals? If so, the latter proposal will reach its limits. How then can an existing airport in a dense urban area such as in Northern Europe or North America handle the double amount of airplanes in the coming years? I aim to follow up on all these questions and trace the origins and cultural implications of this architectural phenomenon by establishing that the current global trends and developments in our society are creating new architectural paradigms. Changes are happening to airports that are hard to pinpoint in their genre. Mumbai airport's new terminal wants to compete with the Louvre museum in matters of art exhibition, at Singapore Airport the *Jewel* project will be a new crystalline event space that will connect the three terminals together; it will add new retail space, new transitory space and offer one of the biggest indoor gardens in the world, including a giant waterfall. How can this possibly be an airport if not a whole new cityscape? The research of both urban studies and airport architecture will lead to an understanding of what the current state of airport affairs is now but it will also be able to show what lies ahead in aerial mobility.

The various members of the SNSF Sinergia project The Interior at the Institute of Art History at the University of Bern have been collaborating in joint workshops, symposiums and colloquiums in Bern, Zurich and Cologne on their perspective of the interior phenomenon and spatial theories in their respective fields, be that women's interiors in paintings, Jesuit chapels, performance art, or in the case of the subproject "Heterotopian Spaces", airports. It has been a transdisciplinary journey throughout different fields of art history with international experts and guest speakers contributing to a puzzle-like foundation that I want to present in this thesis.

For research I have travelled extensively to airports throughout the world to gather material and also to "experience" the airport and its infrastructure as well as gain emotional sensations, both positive and negative, from the point of view of the traveler and employee who peruses that hybrid space.

I have connected with airport architects and attended conferences designed to cater to aviation developers and builders. An immeasurable gain was getting to know and collaborate with international airport designer Curtis Fentress who has built so called iconic airports on three continents. He also bestowed a keynote lecture on our project during our project's architectural conference Hybrid Spaces in Bern in November 2014.

Another research highlight was meeting airport architect Meinhard von Gerkan at a Roundtable discussion with the renowned airport engineer Werner Sobek (a frequent collaborator of architect Helmut Jahn) at the University of Munich in 2013. Von Gerkan's company has built many mid- to late century German airports but he is mostly known as the architect of the much maligned and never activated Berlin Brandenburg Airport which was supposed to open for operation in 2012 but has since been indefinitely postponed, if not abandoned, due to constructional and political discrepancies.

Other architectural firms that I visited and interviewed were Gensler in Newport Beach, California and The Jerde Partnership in Venice Beach. Jerde and Gensler specialize in interiors, retail and office design and have worked on many airports, respectively public plazas on the architecture of consumption and the public realm.

I gatecrashed the offices of Jahn Architects in Chicago during a conference I attended in the city, because they are renowned for their archi-engineering process of design and I needed research material on their Bangkok airport.

In 2017 I coincidentally flew to New York with Pierre de Meuron, who after a spirited conversation told me he would wish to build an airport with his partner Jacques Herzog one day; so far, their museums excel globally as cultural and architectural places of art and gathering.

My American co-supervisor Professor Luis Carranza, who teaches architecture at Columbia and Roger Williams University, has been a constant mentor since attending our conference Hybrid Spaces and we have kept busy architectural exchanges on both sides of the Atlantic ever since.

My Master thesis supervisor Professor Philip Ursprung, who has the chair of the History of Art and Architecture at ETH Zurich, has encouraged me throughout this journey with thoughts and feedback.

These encounters with the – still living – artists behind my dissertation topic were very prosperous for my progress and very special to me as a form of direct and original oral history research.

A research stay at the Getty Research Institute Library further deepened my progress and enabled me to look into archival collections of early twentieth century airport designing competitions, sketches and studies. A pioneering spirit of adventure and competition had leading architectural designers of that time participate in the brainstorming of new airport designs for postwar America that was deeply influenced by the Wright Brothers, Charles Lindbergh, Le Corbusier, and even the Ford automobile industry.

My research methodology includes an iconological approach of classic art-historical methods, interviewing the architects and artists involved, and surveying spatial, architectural, and postcolonial discourses. The Architectural Biennales in 2016 and 2018 in Venice were a storehouse of information about the current social and cultural themes of migration and globalization, as well as the re-appropriation of social space. Prestigious architecture firms took upon themselves to present architectural solutions to the refugee crisis which would benefit the region receiving the refugees.

A challenging aspect of this dissertation is the fact that the topic is situated in an ever changing, still evolving field in contemporary history. This dissertation will be an interdisciplinary study on airport architecture and will take into consideration architectural and spatial theories as well as research from art history and from theatre, performance, culture, and globalization studies.

My background is art and architectural history, meaning that my research approach is based on literature theories about the iconology and iconography of art and architecture. This includes many cross-comparisons between multiple fields of cultural studies. Consequently, this dissertation is loaded with philosophical detours on spatial, architectural and philosophical theories, and my aim is to simultaneously show their effect on airport design.

Even though I am writing about the development of railway stations, I mean to show the reference to airports. Even though we are reading about the Crystal Palace, which Queen Victoria inaugurated in 1851, there are consequences to current airport designs.

The necessity of a place of one's own, where one dwells and thrives, the importance of home and social places outside of home, as well as conspicuous consumption further describe the transformation of the architecture of public and transitory places. We are architecturally moving throughout three centuries – with the onset of industrialization to present time supermodernism. However, not only airports are presented here, but rather cityscapes (Paris, Shanghai, New York …), buildings, atriums, performance and land art, and ultimately museums, which set the paradigm for airport architecture. This interconnectedness is the quintessence to show how airport aura came to be.

2   Travels through Airports: In Search of a Narrative

"Airplanes and airports have my favorite kind of food service, my favorite kind of bathrooms, my favorite peppermint Life Savers, my favorite kinds of entertainment, my favorite loudspeaker address systems, my favorite conveyor belts, my favorite graphics and colors, the best security checks, the best views, the best perfume shops, the best employees, and the best optimism."[3]

Andy Warhol

Andy Warhol epitomizes my fascination with airports.

As an adult I turned my love of traveling and aviation into a part-time hobby: Whilst studying art history at the University of Zurich, I flew around the world as part of the Swissair cabin crew. I consider my flying career as my own personal *Bildungsroman*, fortunately not as dramatic as Goethe's tragic Figures and their fateful self-realization, but rather as my cultural for-mation through the means of travel and aviation. My own *Grand Tour* through world history via aviation was filled with a great spirit of adventure; with inspiration from Jules Verne to Jack London in my mind, I set off with an explorer's spirit of foreign cultures and civilizations and boldly went where I had never gone before (Figure 1).

Figure 1: Kona International Airport, Big Island, Hawaii: A view from the plane onto the open-air terminal design with Mauna Loa Volcano in the background. Typical Hawaiian/Polynesian thatched architecture. Photograph taken by Lilia Mironov

3   Andy Warhol, The Philosophy of Andy Warhol (From A to B and back again), p 160

I began seeking out airports via my airline work and in my free time, being able to travel at reduced rates, I practiced something similar to Lucius Burckhardt's *Strollology* which I will present later on in this thesis – namely taking in the aesthetic and historical aspects of airports and foreign cities on a sensorial and emotional level by the means of research and leisure trips.

As part of my preparation for this dissertation I flew to Incheon Airport (Seoul) in 2013 and spent 24 hours there, immersing myself into the airport experience of what was then repeatedly awarded with the best airport in the world honors.[4] I did not leave the airport to seek out Seoul; I truly only stayed inside, that was the purpose of my trip. Similar travels brought me to Denver and Kona Airports, albeit I left the premises eventually to interview the respective architect and see an exhibition on van Gogh in the city (Denver, 2012) or to enjoy the actual island (Hawaii). Many more airports I have experienced on work duty as well as a tourist. There are different perceptions for each of the airports – either as a traveler or as an employee. I got the dual experience.

The theme of the *Benjaminian flâneur*, of passageways and non-places not only permeated my part-time hobby but also defines my dissertation.[5] It also traces the cultural genesis of the airport building type and its subsequent use by the flâneurs and travelers, thus addressing the feelings it evokes: I myself am spellbound and alienated at varying stages when traveling through airports and when traveling in general.

In the 1950s' song popularized by Jo Stafford, "You belong to me", the lyrics go like this: "See the pyramids along the Nile, watch the sunrise on a tropic isle … ." As a lover of old movies and songs, I felt particularly incited by this song; it was the quintessential wander-

lust song to me even before I joined the airline business. Accordingly, I was utterly disenchanted when I found myself on a tour of the Great Pyramids of Gizeh during a Swissair layover in Cairo at the turn of the millennium and found the pyramids' aura tarnished with a Pizza Hut fast food restaurant.

Globalization gives us strawberries in December, but coincidentally takes away from the aura of uniqueness. The big alienating factor of contemporary travel is the ubiquity of globalized brands which are found in the most exotic places. The travel industry destroys the local idiosyncrasy and uniqueness through its mere presence and the travelers' consumption of global brands in the most remote of places. But the travel industry – tourism – has always been cut both ways.

It attributes to the economic progress of a region and it alienates. In E. M. Forster's Edwardian novel "A room with a view", the English tourists who partake in the *Grand Tour* in Italy are depicted as a Baedeker-reading elite who exist within their own English bubble in a foreign country. They stay in English-run pensions, eat food prepared to please the English palate, have their high tea, travel in groups with English chaperones and English tour guides. They marvel at the beauty and art of Florence, yet they are detached from the local people. They are like consumers in a department store, picking out what suits them in a transitory space.

The culmination of this bubble travel is to be found on cruise ships: They invade places like Venice and let their customers swarm out like bees for a few hours, running havoc with consumption, upon which the bees return to their hive.

There's a strong interlink between tourism and retail by all means. A chapter in this dissertation is dedicated to conspicuous consumption and its fallout. We can-

---

4   Skytrax World Airport Awards, 2012

5   During my travels I was a flâneur in airports and foreign cities, exploring museums and phantasmagorias, much like Walter Benjamin's description of the modern city dwellers in the age from enlightenment onwards in his Arcades Project (Benjamin, The Arcades Project 1982).

not imagine aviation without retail nowadays. To stroll through the duty-free shopping while on our way to the airplane is a rite of travel.

Within the last twenty years major changes in aviation occurred, triggered by 9/11. An increase of security checks and complete rethinking of the airport experience was challenged by the simultaneous contradiction of having fewer passport control checkpoints (within the European Union). Face recognition software tracks us in most modern airports. Travel agencies have virtually disappeared in favor of online bookings. Retail is taking on a paramount role in these spaces. It is hard to discern the mall from the actual airport nowadays. When researching this thesis, questions arose about the challenges airport designers face with the above-mentioned topics. In a way, airport architecture reflects any other architecture of our times – it is becoming more modern and technically advanced by the decade and has a strictly functional task to fulfill. And yet, airport architecture stands out in ways that surpass other urban architecture. Airport architecture both defines and is defined by mobility. It also aspires to define identity through the use of symbolic architecture. Symbolic or contextual airport architecture found its apotheosis in postmodernism. This is the era of the event architecture airports.

Mobility is defined by politics, economy, and society. Ultimately, airport architecture aspires to be *hybrid*, a term that will be evaluated in depth.

When I was a child and living in Western Germany during the 1980s, a trip to my native Bulgaria encompassed flying from Hanover into West Berlin either to Tegel or Tempelhof airport, which were serviced by only three airlines of the Western Allies: Pan Am, Air France and British Airways. And then changing to East Berlin's Schönefeld Airport on the Eastern side of the iron curtain, where Interflug, the airline of Eastern Germany, serviced the Soviet Union and Eastern Bloc countries. As a child I found this endeavor enormously adventurous and romantic.

In preparation for this dissertation I learned that Rudolf Nurejew, the great Soviet male ballerina, defected to the West during a tour of the Kirov Ballet of all places at Paris' Bourget airport in 1961! An airport which made history in 1927 when American aviation pioneer, Charles Lindbergh, first landed there after his sensational Atlantic crossing. Airports truly are a place of ritualistic transformation.[6]

When our relatives came to visit us by train from Sofia via Yugoslavia and Austria, it was not an un-dangerous journey of three days for them. We would hold our breath until they made the journey unscathed, facing random displays of power and control from the then Soviet controlled Eastern Bloc countries, facing dangerous and haphazard checks on a scheduled train service in and out of Bulgaria and Yugoslavia, facing criminal gassings in the sleeping wagon of the train at night to be robbed of their valuables, facing tedious and random customs and border controls into Western Europe at the Austrian border. And these were just regular relatives coming to visit family in Western Germany, not refugees, not migrants and not defectors.

In 2016, world politics was dominated by the refugee- and migration crisis in Europe and by terrorism linked to the Syrian war and Middle Eastern conflict around Islamic fundamentalism. To top it off, in November 2016 the new American president was elected, who had boasted during his candidacy with his intentions of building a border wall of gigantic proportions between the United States and Mexico. In a nutshell, our current state of affairs is defined by migration, terrorism and the fear of "otherness", leading to a dangerous emergence of new nationalism by literally building walls at borders that were previously torn down during the onset of globalization and the abolishment of the iron curtain.

---

6   Alastair Gordon, Naked Airport. A Cultural History of the World's most Revolutionary Structure, p 8

As I just mentioned politics and our current world affairs, where else do they coalesce with art and architecture then at the *Biennale Architettura di Venezia*?

The Architectural Biennale in Venice from May until November 2016 was aptly titled *Reporting from the Front* and dealt with the divergence between architecture and civil society. The Architettura Biennale in 2018 was titled *Freespace*, dedicated to the sense of humanity and quality of space itself. Once again, *space* is the great human denominator of our society. Housing, migration, refugee housing, economy, community, quality of life, sustainability, traffic, waste, and pollution were the core themes of the various exhibitions on display during both exhibitions. They were also focus themes in the diverse pavilions in the *Giardini* location[7] (Figures 2 to 10).

Figure 2: "*Reporting from the Front*", Biennale di Architettura 2016, Venezia, Photograph by Bruce Chatwin, Travillion Images, photograph by Lilia Mironov

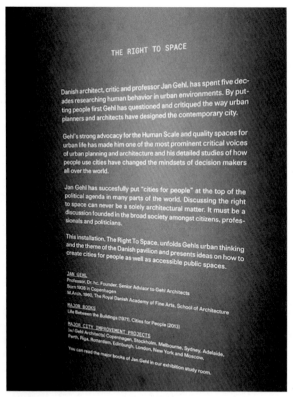

Figure 3: Impressions from "*Reporting from the Front*", Danish Pavilion, Biennale di Architettura 2016, Venezia, photograph by Lilia Mironov

7   http://www.labiennale.org/en/architecture/exhibition/national-participations/

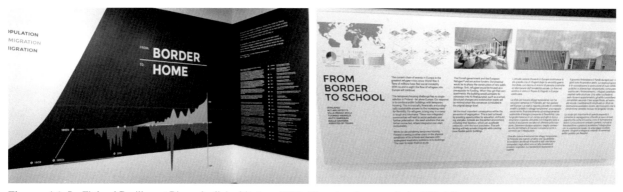

Figures 4 & 5: Finland Pavilion at Biennale di Architettura 2016, Venezia, photographs by Lilia Mironov

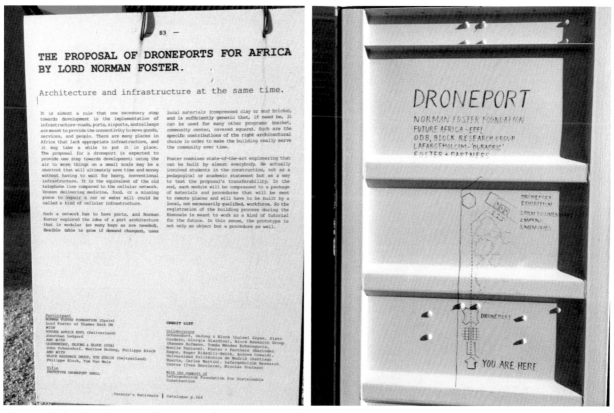

Figures 6 & 7: "The Proposal of Droneports for Africa by Lord Norman Foster", Biennale di Architettura 2016, Venezia, photographs by Lilia Mironov

Figures 8 & 9: *"The Proposal of Droneports for Africa by Lord Norman Foster"*, Biennale di Architettura 2016, Venezia, photographs by Lilia Mironov

Figure 10: *"The Proposal of Droneports for Africa by Lord Norman Foster"*, Biennale di Architettura 2016, Venezia, photograph by Lilia Mironov

Standing out during my visit in 2016 were the spirited exhibitions of Finland and Denmark. The Danish Pavilion housed an exhibition which offered two complementary spatial installations: "The Right to Space" by Jan Gehl was dedicated to improve living- and dwelling space in human-friendly cities, a life task in the work of architect and urban planner Gehl. "The Art of Many" was dedicated to the creative Danish welfare institutions such as hospitals, social housing, and public spaces (institutions that Michel Foucault calls Heterotopias). The Finland Pavilion with its theme "From Border to Home: Housing Solutions for Asylum Seekers" addressed the current refugee crisis which it called the "greatest refugee-crisis since World War II" with innovative, modular, temporary and ephemeral housing solutions. In a visionary leap of faith, Finland would first provide refugee housing in newly constructed public buildings funded by the Finnish government and the European Union (or its Refugee Fund). These temporary dwellings for refugees would later be repurposed into much needed new public buildings such as schools. There were further proposals of refugee housing in tents and containers which are stackable and modular.

"Start with a Roof" proposed using roof structures of future housing as temporary shelters for refugees in Finland, and after the crisis, when the asylum seekers have found permanent housing and legal residency, moving them to new constructions as permanent roofs. It shall be a financially and economically sustainable solution.

The latter is comparable to the other big attraction of the Architectural Biennale, namely the *Droneports Project* by Norman Foster (in collaboration with instigator Jonathan Ledgard). "The Proposal of Droneports for Africa" by Norman Foster borrows on similar principles as the Finland roof project – a network of drone airports throughout developing countries (initially Rwanda) to help set up an infrastructure of humanitarian support and aiding in local businesses. The droneports too, are modular and flexible and use local materials such as compressed clay and mud bricks. Each module will be compressed to a package of materials and procedures that will be sent to remote places and can be built by a local and not necessarily trained workforce.[8]

The pervading architectural theme of the mentioned examples is repurposed and re-appropriated social space with an architecture of temporary character that can be modified into permanent architecture. It poses the question as to what the Architectural Biennale and the topic of migration and refugees contribute to airport architecture.

As an initial answer I can give the example of Berlin Tempelhof Airport which was permanently shut down

Figure 11: Temporary Refugee Housing at Berlin Tempelhof Airport, 2016, photograph by Gordon Welters ©

in 2008, and has been housing around 3000 refugees since the refugee and migration crisis in Europe from 2015 onwards. (Figure 11)

I want to emphasize the interconnectedness of society and globalization which defines architecture and ultimately airport architecture. Migration, displacement, and transition are the hot topics that permeate our society and culture right now. One cannot only look at airports to understand them. We see the manifestation of these topics in any transitional and transitory place such as airport, train station or even state border. To interconnect these threads and see the greater and historical aspect is what I have learned to do as an architectural historian.

Eventually, this dissertation centers around two ideas of performance – the airport as a modern day social theater and the airport as the derivative after the white cube.[9] The latter deals with the overall trend of fus-

---

8   Notes from the Biennale visit in October 2016 taken by the author

9   Meaning that after different forms of exhibition settings, such as the emergence of museums during the eighteenth century which displayed private and state art collections; during the twentieth century the term "white cube" was borne out of the modernist influences that especially De Stijl and Bauhaus evoked: preferring to exhibit works of art against white walls in mostly cubic rooms in order to emphasize the individual work of art and prevent distraction. This was a countermeasure to the horror vacui room full of paintings, one such example being J.W.M. Turner's artworks displayed at the Royal Academy.

ing art and exhibition spaces into airport designs. Both ideas are based on social space and spatial function.

In order to cover a valid assemblage of data and material, more than just airports will be explored, beginning with modes of transportation and places of society, especially so the importance of the city center.

The genesis of airport architecture can be traced back to the early transitory spaces that sprung up with the advent of the Industrial Revolution and the discourse of the private interior versus public space. The need for social congregation within a society can be traced back to prehistoric times when people would gather around the fireplace or get together at places of devotion or trade their wares in the center of villages or in open-air market squares such as the Greek *agora*. The industrialization in the nineteenth century, especially in Great Britain and Continental Europe brought advances in cities through improvements in science and technology like gas lighting, electrical engineering and the steam engine, which also created steady work in factories and government offices and a whole new awareness of

home (interior) and work (outside/public). Thus, a third place was created – the place of pleasure and leisure next to the world of home and work.

It is in these (post-)industrialized new cityscapes that the individual could unfold and dwell. The most relevant of these cities, Paris, set a paradigm with its shopping arcades and passageways which stem from the early nineteenth century. Walter Benjamin devotes a magnum opus to the social analysis of this time by using the Parisian glass arcades as a research object. This is where he comes up with the term *flâneur*, an enlightened individual dweller who leaves his interior and strolls through these exterior, public city galleries of consumption and phantasmagorias.

These glass arcades were recreated in Joseph Paxton's Crystal Palace for the World Fair in London in 1851; they can be found in train stations old and new and most interestingly they are an important architectural theme in airport terminals. The glass arcades of Walter Benjamin's opus are metonymical of our society and therefore a valid research tool of architecture and culture.

"Like the great railway stations, airports are also the contemporary equivalents of gateways – very often they represent your first experience of a city or country. In that sense, they have the potential to excite and inspire. An airport should be a celebratory structure. It should combine a strong visual identity with a humanistic sense of clarity so that the experience of air travel is uplifting, secure, welcoming and efficient." [10]

Norman Foster

Norman Foster's vision of airports, as captured in an interview with the architecture magazine Icon in 2011, pretty much sums up the purpose of airport architecture. It is about providing a grand entrance, a unique

sensorial experience and ultimately smooth flight operations. (Figure 12)

---

10   http://www.iconeye.com/architecture/features/item/9300-interview-norman-foster

Figure 12: Grand Entrance (by car, what else in LA) to Los Angeles International Airport, LAX, with the iconic Tom Bradley International Terminal by Fentress Architects (2013) in the background, evoking the crashing waves of the Pacific Ocean. Photograph by Lilia Mironov

3　The Architecture of Travel

3.1　Mobility Culture

Mobility is the actual physical travel, the ability to travel from one point to another. Culture is the definition of a set of values, conventions, social practices, and rituals. *Mobility Culture* is accordingly the "set of values, conventions, or social practices associated with the ability to travel from one point to another and with actual physical travel."[11]

In modern society though, physical travel is not always a choice. It is the dependence on infrastructure and the availability of technology as well as the presence of an operator or pilot of the vehicle, making our ability to travel a societal achievement that is being shaped through these practices and framework conditions.

"Mobility Culture is the entire set of symbolic and physical social practices that relate to the ability to travel. This includes the design of infrastructure and public spaces, transport policy role models and associated public discourses as well as individual travel behavior, including the mobility and lifestyle orientations which shape it."[12]

John Kasarda, an academic specialized in the economics of aviation and instigator of the *Aerotropolis* model, estimates together with journalist Greg Lindsay that the number of city-dwellers will rise to more than six billion by 2050 with the number of megacities (10 and more million inhabitants) increasing to 27. Around USD 37 Trillion are expected to be spent globally on infrastructure and transport in the coming two de-

cades. By 2016, 7 billion plane trips were already taken by passengers annually.[13]

In this thesis we are mostly interested in the socio-economic, socio-spatial and historical conditions of mobility culture and ultimately mobility architecture. The term mobility behavior concerns the individual social practice regarding long-term and everyday mobility decisions. Long-term decisions include the

---

11　Tobias Kuhnimhof, Irene Feige: "What is Mobility Culture?" in: Megacity Mobility Culture, p xvi.
　　Kuhnimhof und Feige cite Götz und Deffners "Eine neue Mobilitätskultur in der Stadt – praktische Schritte zur Veränderung): Researchers from the Institute of Mobility Research in Munich, a Research Facility of the BMW Group in Germany, pin down the mechanisms of mobility culture to *actors* and *actions*.
　　Actors are the individuals or groups whose values, conventions and social practices constitute mobility culture. The actions are the social practices which enable travel and they include innovation, communication, technology, and infrastructure. They are all contained by framework conditions which present physical or social constraints for mobility, such as the built environment in cities, transport networks, topology or climate, and socioeconomic conditions of the growing and ever changing urbanization.

12　Ibid., p xvii

13　John Kasarda, Greg Lindsay: Aerotropolis. The way we'll live next, p 10

choice of workplace and location of residence (which is influenced by urban topography), whereas everyday mobility includes the choices about which activities to engage in, and destinations and modes of travel, such as railway, car or plane. Mobility is strongly tied to migration. Migration is not only the result of governmental politics encompassing refugees and economic migrants, but also entails the highly-educated global and mobile expatriates who are on a quasi-pilgrimage of high-profile (yet often temporary) jobs between the global financial and economic centers.

Mobility culture is thus not static but rather a fluid development which entails many factors. It also varies geographically and culturally. Mobility culture determines the future as well as the past of urban and international transport systems.

In 1995, Beijing was still classified a non-motorized city with about a fifth of the vehicle ownership rate of London. In just two decades this balance tipped: Beijing today has a vehicle ownership rate (around 5 Mio) of roughly two thirds of that in London, much of which is attributed to the cultural and economic progress of China since the 1990s.[14]

As a further example, Shanghai's urban landscape completely reinvented itself during the past two decades, as it arose from an ancient Chinese town and former imperial and colonial outpost in the Yangtze River Delta to one of the most populated financial centers with the most futuristic, high skyscrapers. Part of this urban development is due to the infrastructure of transportation and aviation. Shanghai's downtown area is linked to the Pudong International Airport by a magnetic levitation train, named Maglev, which conquers the 30 km distance in mere eight minutes.

A worthy representative of China's economy and progress, the Maglev train was inducted in 2004 and is a valuable alternative to the otherwise congested hourlong drive into the city. Shanghai Pudong Airport, built in 1999 by French airport architect Paul Andreu as a symbol of the rising economic power that emerged from China, especially from Shanghai at the onset of the millennium, is the catalyst that enabled the rise and power of the Metropolis Shanghai. Its winged appearance and linear steel and glass building show the design vocabulary of postmodernism: The quasi-sculptural, aesthetically pleasing building has been constructed with technically state-of-the-art materials and designs, such as glass footbridges, elevated roadways, and short walking distances to the embarkment area, and plays a representational role for the region. The smooth high-tech architecture of the Shanghai skyscrapers already starts at Pudong Airport and continues via Maglev train into the city center (Figures 13 & 14).

---

14   Tobias Kuhnimhof, Gebhard Wulfhorst: "The Reader's Guide to Mobility Culture" in: Megacity Mobility Culture, p 58–59

Figures 13 & 14: Maglev Train entering Longyang Road Station in Shanghai; Shanghai Pudong Airport, as seen from the Maglev Train. Photographs by Lilia Mironov

Similar infrastructure that was involved in airport masterplanning was created by Ove Arup Engineers in collaboration with Norman Foster's Hong Kong International Airport, Chek Lap Kok, which opened on a man-made island in 1997: The Airport Express is a high-speed rail line that links Hong Kong International Airport Chek Lap Kok with downtown Hong Kong (which is on another island). Passengers can check in at downtown check-in terminals which are connected to this airport train (Figure 15).

The actors which denominate mobility culture are consequently the travelers and commuters perusing the infrastructure that will transport them either from the mobility hub of the airport via train to the city center or from home to work. Their actions influence the framework conditions for travel, including airports.

Figure 15: Hong Kong International Airport Chek Lap Kok, photograph courtesy of Foster+Partners ©

The mobility culture around airports is summed up by airport architects such as Curtis Fentress as the Heroic, Golden, Democratic and Optimistic Ages of Aviation:

The Wright Brothers and their contemporaries (around the 1910s) originated the beginnings of aviation, the so-called Heroic Age. The 1940s were considered the Golden Age: The beginning of commercial aviation, still exclusive to the elites of society. By 1958 there were already 58 Mio people traveling around the world. In 1962, Eero Saarinen's TWA building became the first iconic symbol of the Jet Age, so called after the jet engines that arose in the 1950s (Figure 16).

The democratization of air travel came to its fulfillment in the 1970s when airports began growing into much bigger sizes than before. The newly introduced Monorail system (people mover system) in Tampa Airport was the first such system in an airport.

In 1973, Dallas Fort Worth Airport was completed, yet upon construction began a whole new remodeling process because HOK's initial design wrongfully promised the shortest distance between car and plane. Since then, remodeling has become a fate that accompanies basically every big airport project. [15]

---

15   Curtis Fentress, keynote lecture "The Architecture of Flight" at The Interior – Hybrid Spaces, Symposium, University of Bern, November 7, 2014

Figure 16: TWA Flight Center, Eero Saarinen, photograph by Nick Sherman

Figure 17: Kansai International Airport, Osaka, Renzo Piano. Photograph courtesy of Sky Front's © RPBW – Renzo Piano Building Workshop Architects © Fondazione Renzo Piano (Via P. P. Rubens 30A, 16158 Genova, Italy)

Figure 18: Denver International Airport, Fentress Architects, photograph courtesy of Denver International Airport. To the left is the newly erected Westin Hotel which upset the original architect Curtis Fentress

Figure 19: Incheon Airport, Seoul, photograph by Lilia Mironov

Dallas Fort Worth Airport was initially masterplanned for four terminals with the option for continuous expansion up to 13 terminals, though as of today there are five terminals interconnected by a people mover. The car-to-plane idea proved a hindrance for connecting passengers who had to walk long distances.

Other innovative changes which influenced airport design were the invention of the roller bag in the 1970s whose noisy wheels proved exasperating on the tile floors, forcing airport designers to rethink interior design and flooring. Ticketing areas began shrinking due to automatisms behind the scenes. Trains and people movers began appearing, like the underground trains connecting the concourses at Atlanta Airport. Airfare became more affordable due to the mass transportation aspect of the democratic age.

This period was called the big shed architecture and produced many international airports in the same concrete and utilitarian style. The democratic age lasted from the 1970s to the 1990s. Those enormous structures involved the economic and technical collaboration of a whole region. During this time, basic principles in air travel were established: Self-check-in kiosks came up in 2000, as well as e-tickets on mobile devices, full body scanners, and new forms of behind the scenes security and detection as a consequence of 9/11.[16]

The age of optimism (and supermodernism) followed with many architectural masterworks or magna opera of contemporary "starchitects"[17]: In 1994 Kansai Airport was erected on an artificial island off the coast of Osaka by Renzo Piano (Figure 17). Denver International Airport by Curtis Fentress opened that same year with a unique tensile roof structure, alluding to the snowy Rocky Mountain hilltops (Figure 18). Hong Kong Airport by Norman Foster followed in 1997 on an island off Hong Kong. Incheon Airport, erected in 2001, as already mentioned, came to be called the fairest of them all (Figure 19). These are some of the paragons of postmodernist mobility architecture.

3.2   The Aerotropolis

Incheon Airport in Seoul (2001, Fentress Architects) presents a small-scale Korea inside the airport. This airport was masterplanned to be the prototype of an *aerotropolis* around the area of Songdo, 65 km south of Seoul – a planned city built around a planned airport to perform as an urban mobility concept. A quarter of the world's population lies within three-and-a-half-flight hours of Incheon's periphery. While construction on the various economic, commercial, and entertainment infrastructure in Songdo is still underway, with the economic crisis of 2008 putting a damper on the development, the airport caters 62 million visitors per year.

Cities have always formed around transportation hubs such as ports and harbors and later on railways, and as air travel connects globally, cities will grow around airports.

The evolution of airport mobility moved the city gate towards the airport. Entering the city *begins* at the airport. In fact, John Kasarda and his *Aerotropolis* co-author Greg Lindsay write about Amsterdam Airport, the world's first aerotropolis-by-design: "The air-

---

16   Curtis Fentress, keynote lecture "The Architecture of Flight" at The Interior – Hybrid Spaces, Symposium, University of Bern, November 7, 2014

17   The term "starchitect" is closely affiliated with the rise of postmodern architecture where the architect expressed his personal style in his buildings, creating extravagant architectural blockbusters with metaphorical and deconstructivist structures which took on his trademark name. A logical consequence of globalization, starchitecture tries to put its mark on repetitive global architecture with cities, regions, and airports fighting to differentiate themselves from the homogeneity of ubiquitousness. From an academic standpoint, however, it is a pejorative term associated with celebrity culture and superficiality.

port leaves the city. The city follows the airport. The airport becomes the city."[18] (Figure 20).

The emergence of the railroad produced cities like Kansas City, Omaha, and the stockyards of Chicago. It connected two oceans by an array of infrastructure, but most importantly re-created (sub)-urban space. It created terminals and ports and the first "Terminal City" in Manhattan's Grand Central Station at the beginning of the twentieth century.

Economics professor John Kasarda coined the term *Aerotropolis* in the late 1990s as a sustainable and smart-growth planned city surrounding an actual airport hub. Even though there are examples of already existing aerotropolises, such as Amsterdam, Dallas Fort Worth, Memphis (the headquarters of FedEx) and New Songdo City, Kasarda's proposal for the future of the aerotropolis lies mainly in the concept of "greenfield airports" which are newly masterplanned airports outside of city centers.

Some of his thoughts for the aerotropolis are:

— Aerotropolises of the future can be thoroughly planned through strategic infrastructure and urban planning despite organic and spontaneous growth to date;

— Airport suppliers and businesses shall be located in proximity to the airport based on the frequency of their use;

— Cluster development should be encouraged along airport transportation corridors such as to allow green spaces;

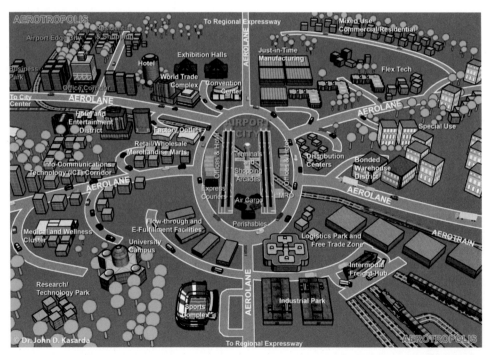

Figure 20:
Drawing courtesy of
Dr. John Kasarda

18 John Kasarda, Greg Lindsay: Aerotropolis. The way we'll live next, p 20. This is an unsourced Dutch quote that Kasarda and Lindsay have picked up.

— Place-making and wayfinding shall be emphasized through architectural features and public art, iconic structures should re-interpret the place.[19]

This concept experienced international exposure during the last decade through Kasarda's publication about the aerotropolis and his appearances on television programs and the academic circuit. Kasarda's concept is mostly feasible in Middle Eastern and Asian locations and in rising economies such as India and China, where greenfield airports are a booster to the economy and the region. As such, there are currently 18 greenfield airports being planned in India.[20]

An aspect of the aerotropolis that is hardly imaginable in India is the smooth connectivity to the city center and region by a reliable network of transportation, be it rail, monorail or magnetic rail. This kind of transportation works very well with European airports such as Zurich, London, Amsterdam. In Japan, as well as in Chinese megacities such as Shanghai and Hong Kong, the airport connectivity via rail and road is just as reliable. But regions and countries such as India, Africa and even the United States lack the evidence of reliable, safe, and continuous public transport between airport and city. As a matter of fact, when Denver International Airport opened in 1995 as a newly erected greenfield airport, there had been plans for a rail connection towards the city center, situated roughly 40 km away. This railway was only put into service in 2016, over twenty years later.

When Hong Kong International Airport Chek Lap Kok was masterplanned in the early 1990s, not only was a whole artificial island erected with its connecting railway and motorway infrastructure to downtown, including suspension bridges, but a whole planned city as well. Tung Chung is a suburban new town built on the periphery of the airport. It primarily houses airport workers and airline personnel but also includes shops and outlet centers as well as airport hotels.

One of the earliest aerotropolis models might have sprung up from the industrious mind of Henry Ford (1863–1947). The inventor of the assembly line and of the famously successful *Model T* automobile (1909) aimed to expand his mobility enterprise into aviation. For his subsequent Tri-Motor airplane he hired Charles Lindbergh as his test pilot and had an airport built on the grounds of his factory in Dearborn, Michigan. Ford Dearborn Airport, completed in 1926 by Albert Kahn, who had also designed Ford's factories, was the first airport built with permanent concrete runways, flood light, a restaurant and hotel.[21]

At Dearborn, the entrepreneur Ford not only built cars and planes but also provided their stage – an airport!

The aerotropolis bears resemblance to Manuel Castell's *technopole*. The technopole as a planned development of technology and industry is tied to the *new economy*, which is itself based on productivity, knowledge and innovation, all of which distribute knowledge back into the system. Technopoles are the mines and foundries of our information age – they are "quarries" of raw materials such as technology and information, but those products are also designed and manufactured

19   John Kasarda, aerotropolis.com
20   http://timesofindia.indiatimes.com/india/govt-nod-for-18-greenfield-airports/articleshow/57789788.cms
21   Hugh Pearman. Airports: A Century of Architecture, p 48

within.[22] Examples of technopoles are Silicon Valley, Cambridge in Massachusetts with MIT and Harvard, as well as The Research Triangle in North Carolina (Raleigh-Durham-Chapel Hill).

Technopoles, science cities, smart cities, aerotropolises, and the global village are all part of the mobility culture of globalization. Half a century ago, Marshall McLuhan meant something completely different by *global village* than what it has come to be understood in the current zeitgeist, namely the relative closeness and proximity globalization provides through technology, mobility, infrastructure, and communication.

In *The Gutenberg Galaxy: The Making of Typographic Man*, McLuhan investigates the impact of the printing press and mass media in Western history, instigated by Johannes Gutenberg's invention of printing, and how much more in common we have with pre-literate societies and their oral cultures through the newly developed audio-tactile (typography and electronic communications) and diminished visual senses. To McLuhan, we, our modern culture, are akin to tribal people living in a village.

Electrical light literally changed our vision and perception and lessened our primal senses. "The medium is the message", McLuhan says, "the content of writing is speech, just as the written word is print".[23]

McLuhan's musings on the impact of different new media types on our senses and the synesthesia is a theme taken up in the following chapter about railways and panoramic vision, as well as the phenomenological perception and Merleau-Ponty's themes on the visible and invisible. McLuhan's theses on the oral history and village tribes also draw parallels to Bruce Chatwin's

Songlines, which in turn amplify Michel de Certeau's discerning between space and place, a discourse of superior importance in this dissertation. In *The Songlines*, nomadic travel writer Chatwin takes us on a journey of Aboriginal history and mysticism and the Aboriginal Australians' tradition of mapping their culture through dreaming tracks, so called songlines (footprints of the ancestors). Songlines are a labyrinth of invisible pathways which meander all over the Australian continent. While they traversed the land by foot, the Aborigines would sing every rock and stream into being. These songlines have been handed down through generations and contain the oral history of their people.[24]

These philosophic excursions shall demonstrate the importance of society's village or city center. We shall see how this translates into airport architecture, as airport architecture in turn seeks to translate the city center within its premises.

The concept of the aerotropolis is tied to the ubiquity of transport infrastructure. Kasarda's model shows a generic outline with the various functional and economic clusters surrounding the aerotropolis. In 1995, Rem Koolhaas developed his Generic City theory as an example of rapidly growing Asian metropolises. Growing urban development led to the reproduction of cultural identity out of itself, thus these cities have no recognizable connection to their own history and identity. For Koolhaas, a connection to place as an expression of tradition, cultural identity, and history is irrelevant in contemporary architecture. Instead, he is outspoken in favor of dynamic modernism or modernization.

---

22   Manuel Castells and Peter Hall. Technopoles of the World: The Making of Twenty-First-Century Industrial Complexes, p 2
      Castells discerns between six groups for his 20 case studies of technopoles with differing emphasis on pure science cities without direct connection to regional industries but with synergies between universities (such a modern example would be the ETH Science City on Hönggerberg in Zurich, which at the time of Castells' publication did not yet exist).

23   Marshall McLuhan, The Gutenberg Galaxy: The Making of Typographic Man, p 8

24   Bruce Chatwin, The Songlines

3.3 Generic Junk

"Is the contemporary city like the contemporary airport – all the same?" asks architect and theorist Rem Koolhaas in Generic City, a theorem about ubiquity and what he calls XL-Architecture. "And if so, what ultimate configuration is it aspiring?" Convergence, he claims, is only possible with the shedding of identity. "And what is left after identity is stripped? The generic?"[25]

Identity is constructed from the physical and historical, from context and experience, but they will all be surpassed by human growth. They will become obsolete. Identity as a form of sharing the past is a losing proposition, as history has a half-life that is watered down exponentially with population growth and mass tourism. One such example Koolhaas gives is the polished caricature of Paris which has become hyper-Parisian, whereas London is becoming less and less London and evolving through modernization. Another example: *The Singapore Songlines – Portrait of a Potemkin Metropolis*, an essay in Koolhaas' *S, M, L, XL* in which he shows Singapore to be the quintessential generic city, if not *Potemkin Village*, with its colonial history basically erased and a new city built from scratch.

Koolhaas especially deconstructs the importance of the city center. The center which has to be "constantly maintained" and modernized has been perceived as the most important place throughout centuries but is now in a flux of constant adaptation. Koolhaas praises the city center of Zurich which he finds "radical and innovative by not being in-the-eye and discreet", by existing through many layers underground and skyward, even toward the earth.[26]

I do not necessarily concur on Zurich's "underground" center but instead think of the underground infrastructure in cities such as Montreal where a network of passageways, shopping centers, and metro stations connects the city center below ground. These underground pedestrian systems were developed to connect buildings and nodes of transportation especially during the harsh Canadian winters. Conceived by urbanist Vincent Ponte in Montreal during the 1960s as *Réso*, a play on the French word for network, réseau, it found its parallel in Toronto's *Path* underground system which emerged during the construction of Mies von der Rohe's Toronto Dominion Centre design.[27] As a city dweller in winter one need not emerge to the sub-zero temperatures above, as everything the city center offers can be found underground. It is a wondrous experience to be there in winter, reminding me of the science-fiction movie *Logan's Run* from the 1970s which depicted an underground society sheltered from the evils above ground – which turned out to be none, just nature having taken over the remnants of a previously highly developed civilization.

Koolhaas navigates through modernization to understand the tremendous changes of architecture in the last century and to find orientation within modern architecture. It is his cultural analysis of this globalized city "without history" that continues the thoughts of Theodor Adorno on tradition. [28]

"Once tradition is no longer animated by a comprehensive, substantial force but has to be conjured up by means of citations because 'It's important to have tradition', then whatever happens to be left of it is dissolved into a means to an end." Adorno writes in his *Prisms*.

25 Rem Koolhaas, S, M, L, XL, p 1248

26 Ibid., p 1249

27 Michelangelo Sabatino & Rhodri Windsor Liscombe, Canada: Modern Architectures in History, p 260

28 Rem Koolhaas, Lecture „Navigating Modernization", 2010, American University Beirut: http://oma.eu/lectures/navigating-modernization

Citations here are to be understood as architectural applications, in order to create a museal showpiece of tradition where tradition has been destroyed.

The German word *museal*, which means museum-like, has negative overtones as it describes objects to which the observer no longer has a vital relationship. Museums testify to the neutralization of culture. This is the fatal situation of what is called "the cultural tradition".[29]

For Adorno, tradition (the idiom stemming from Latin *tradere* – to hand over) is a craft that is handed down from generation to generation, not a superimposed aesthetic which functions as a surrogate. This surrogate without tradition, origin, nor history translates smoothly into Koolhaas' depiction of junkspace.

Junkspace or junk-space is Koolhaas' pun on space-junk, which is the debris from the space missions that litters earth's orbit. (Figure 21) In the Pixar movie "Wall-E", there is a striking scene of deep visual impact, which has stuck in my mind ever since and which depicts space-junk: It is when the spaceship, to which the little robot of the titular name has attached himself, breaks through earth's atmosphere on its way towards outer space and traverses this junkyard of debris that is orbiting our atmosphere – the disposed-off space-junk as in discontinued satellites, pieces of old space stations, various scrap metal and so on. It is the great Pacific garbage patch, but in space.[30]

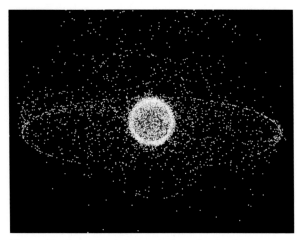

Figure 21: Space debris / space-junk, as simulated in a computer image by NASA, courtesy of the NASA Orbital Debris Program Office

Junkspace is modernization's fallout, the residue mankind leaves on the planet. Junkspace is the side-dish or rather leftover of modernization and modern infrastructure, it is the sequence of consumerist brands which render city centers ubiquitous and continuity is their essence: air-conditioning, escalators, hot air curtain. It is feigned, simulated order.

"I really believe in empty spaces, although, as an artist, I make a lot of junk." – confesses Andy Warhol in his philosophical musings. Empty space is never-wasted space. Wasted space is any space that has art in it:

---

29   Theodor W. Adorno, "Valery Proust Museum", in: Prisms, p 175:
"Anyone who thinks that art can be reproduced in its original form through an act of the will is trapped in hopeless romanticism. Modernizing the past does it much violence and little good. But to renounce radically the possibility of experiencing the traditional would be to capitulate to barbarism out of devotion to culture. That the world is out of joint is shown everywhere in the fact that however a problem is solved, the solution is false."

30   Created by Pixar and directed by Andrew Stanton, Wall-E deservedly won the 2008 Academy Award for best animated feature. The story of the little waste collecting robot with personality is not only a funny romance but a reproach of our consumerism and disposable society, ending with humanity obese, immobile and daft in comfortable spaceships away from earth, which has perished with pollution with only Wall-E and a cockroach left behind to sort the garbage.

"So on the one hand I really believe in empty spaces, but on the other hand, because I'm still making some art, I'm still making junk for people to put in their spaces that I believe should be empty ..."[31]

Junk has become colloquial for any kind of superfluous material possession of ours. Architectural junk thus is the quintessential material obscenity we create. And architectural junk comes with the excesses of supermodernism.

Koolhaas even mocks the exaggerated branding of airports, such as the billboard of Boston's airport: "Logan Airport: A World-Class Upgrade for the Twenty-first Century", and makes about Los Angeles Airport this snarky remark: "LAX: welcoming – possibly flesh-eating orchids at the counter ... identity is the new junk food for the dispossessed, globalization's fodder for the disenfranchised ..."[32]

Brands in junkspace are adequate to black holes in the universe – they are essences through which meaning disappears.

Architectural branding is the measure of our society: I still laugh at Tom Wolfe's expression of "row after Mies van der row of glass boxes" when decrying the cold, ubiquitous International Style of skyscrapers on Manhattan's Avenue of the Americas in his ingenious treatise on American architecture, *From Bauhaus to Our House* (1981).[33]

Airports are brands. Thus their meaning and their identity disappear, they are part of the "sparkling infrastructures of light" and superstrings of graphics and emblems in an authorless world beyond anyone's claim. According to Koolhaas, architects thought of junkspace first and named it *megastructure*.

"Through junkspace, old aura is transfused with new luster to spawn sudden commercial viability: Barcelona amalgamated with the Olympics, Bilbao with Guggenheim, 42nd (Street, Broadway) with Disney. Masterpiece has become a definitive sanction, a typology: it saves the object from criticism with qualities unproven, its mission is precarious with its exterior surfaces bent and too much of its square footage dysfunctional, with centrifugal components held together by the pull of the atrium."[34]

---

31   Andy Warhol, The Philosophy of Andy Warhol, p 143–144
32   Rem Koolhaas, "Junkspace", in: October. Obsolescence, Vol 100, p 175
33   Tom Wolfe, From Bauhaus to Our House, p 4
     Note: the International Style, as incepted by Ludwig Mies van der Rohe, attempted to break completely with the past, to fashion a new aesthetic that was simple and "pure", lacked any references to classical antiquity, and was completely devoid of ornamentation.
34   Koolhaas, "Junkspace", in: October. Obsolescence, Vol 100, p 178–190

Masterpiece invokes the notion of the *aura* on which Walter Benjamin bestowed utmost importance. The auratic effect – the uniqueness of the building instead of its generic architecture and ubiquity – is the essence of this thesis.

Airports as bygone manifestations of ultimate neutrality are now some of the most characteristic elements of the generic city, a key denominator. Airports are the grand entrance to the generic city because they are all the average person experiences of a particular city.

Airports become emblematic signs imprinted on the global collective with spectacular spatial qualities, such as places for consumption and entertainment.[35]

In regard to iconography and performance, the airport is the concentrate of both the hyper-local and hyper-global – meaning that you can get goods there that you cannot get elsewhere or that are not even available in the city (only in global duty-free).

The *airport gestalt* tends toward ever greater autonomy and is sometimes not even related to a specific generic city, as it is in itself replacing the city.

Shanghai Pudong Airport, Beijing Capital Airport, Mumbai, Osaka airports are accordingly megastructure, masterpiece airports in places where modernization has performed a quantum leap and the generic is taking over the vernacular. Modernization in these Asian cities has left only a few historically preserved enclaves with a theme-park-like atmosphere in their city centers, such as the French Concession area in Shanghai (Figure 22).

What used to be the traditional is now the spectacular. The same goes for Beijing – The Forbidden City now being the spectacle of old tradition in a postmodern generic city.[36]

Figure 22: French Concession Area in Shanghai: http://www.chinahighlights.com/travelguide/china-hiking/shanghai-hiking.htm, retrieved February 12, 2017

The rulership of the French Concession existed from 1849 until 1943. It is now a sightseeing attraction in Shanghai, a historical reminder of colonialism.

Nowhere is the process of enclave formation stronger than in the field of airport architecture, writes architectural theorist Hans Ibelings. The world's major airports have grown into mega-structures that accommodate a growing number of functions that have little to do with aviation, but which make a bigger contribution to airport turnover. Since the 1990s, airports have become what museums were to the postmodern 1980s: The arena where contemporary themes converge and all kinds of interesting developments happen.[37]

In their megastructure iconicity airports seek to recreate lost history and emotions; these airports are a branding device just as the skyscrapers in the city centers. Their brand is modernization and being able to

---

35   Rem Koolhaas, S, M, L, XL, p 1251

36   Ibid., p 1254

37   Hans Ibelings, Supermodernism: Architecture in the Age of Globalization, p 78

afford a Western starchitect to build their megastructures.

Koolhaas states that 51% of the generic city consists of atrium. He deems the atrium the "diabolical device" in its ability to substantiate the insubstantial, with its Roman name promising architectural class where there is none, and as such the atrium accommodates the cave-dweller in a void space with repetitive interiors, interchangeable, cold, ubiquitous. Where does Koolhaas' disdain for the atrium stem from? After all, its original meaning meant the gathering place of the Roman household, the centerpiece, the anthropological place. But in modernist architecture, the atrium became quite the non-place. In the Industrial Style architecture it became a mundane yet transitory emblem of affluence and power of the working and financial classes. Skyscrapers, hotels and malls had atriums, and they somehow all looked the same.

John Portman (1924–2017), an architect of hotels and skyscrapers, created a brand out of the atrium. It was his architectural branding device. In his hotel complexes since the 1960s, he has created his trademark atrium lobbies with skylights soaring above dozens of stories in hotels from Shanghai to San Francisco.

Incidentally, my favorite hotel lobby is the one of Portman's Hyatt Regency San Francisco by the Embarcadero (1973, the whole retail and office complex was masterplanned by John Portman), because at Christmas time they would set up an elaborate winter wonderland around the central lobby sculpture and even make it snow from the upper floors down onto the lobby level (Figures 23 & 24).

Figure 23 & 24: Atrium lobby of the Hyatt Regency San Francisco by the Embarcadero. Figure 24 depicts the winter wonderland decorations around Christmas time 2011, photographs by Lilia Mironov

During my airline Grand Tour, that hotel was our San Francisco base and I have witnessed its atrium being re-appropriated in different seasons during many conferences, fairs, and even Star Trek conventions. It performed very much like a village market place. No wonder, the Guardian would call Portman's hotel lobbies and atriums the "Disneyland for adults".[38]

Every modern airport terminal has an atrium. It is called the Great Hall or the Main Hall and it represents the microcosm of its corresponding generic city – a recreation of its ubiquity with the usual chain brands of fast food, sushi and fancy coffee, and handbag outlets.

There is an abundance in the iconography that the generic city and generic airport atrium adopt. If it is close to water, then water-based symbols such as ships and sails are distributed over its entire territory. If it is Asian, then delicate women appear in sensual poses, suggesting sexual and religious submission and cultural appropriation there.[39]

It is this fact about the absence of history in the generic city that makes for cultural appropriation and patronization. A façade of icons is being created to evoke feelings of authenticity, history, and tradition. It is a modern day Potemkin Village.[40]

The Great Hall of the Tom Bradley International Terminal at Los Angeles International Airport was inaugurated in 2013 (Figure 25). The Great Hall is the signature of every Fentress terminal and in LAX it is a soaring public place that extends over one hundred thousand square foot with ceilings that are ten stories high. Three tiers break up the verticality to give it a human scale. Passenger shops on the main level evoke the

Figure 25: Atrium / Great Hall of Tom Bradley International Terminal, Los Angeles International Airport, photograph by Lilia Mironov

feeling of a piazza while second and third tiers house fancy restaurants and exclusive lounges.[41]

The Fentress terminal at LAX invokes the crashing waves of the Pacific Ocean in its roof structure, and on giant screens in the atrium there is a nonstop-loop of a neo-black-and-white cartoon depicting the golden age of cinema with characters resembling Harold Lloyd. An imposing clock tower with high definition projections of ballerinas dancing to the rhythm of the dials purports the place as the entertainment capital of the world, where dreams are created. This is the sense of place design of the terminal, evoking the history of Los Angeles.

A Disneyland for adults?

"Walt Disney World is a post-modernist utopia of happy consumerism, a pre-emptive heterotopia of

---

38   Rowan Moore, "Disneyland for Adults: John Portman's dizzying interior legacy", in The Guardian

39   Koolhaas, S, M, L, XL, p 1262–1263

40   Prince Potemkin built these mock-up villages along the route Empress Catherine the Great would take on her journey to the Crimea in 1787 in order to impress her – he was the region's governor and Catherine's lover.

41   Curtis Fentress, Now Boarding: Fentress Airports and the Architecture of Flight, p 92

deviation, both of illusion and compensation."[42] The philosopher Christophe Bruchansky picks up the Foucauldian terms of the heterotopia of deviation and compensation in his depiction of this illusionary place, and in fact sums up any event space where we dwell to escape reality – the experience for which we pay to escape reality is in fact a commodity.

This atrium terminal, on the other hand, is an example of the architectural efforts of recreating the urban public realm within the airport. Because the generic is also the cause of destruction or as Koolhaas names it, the "evacuation" of the public realm, the urban plan now primarily accommodates mobility, particularly that of the car, facilitated by highways which take over more and more of the urban space. The generic city is always founded by people on the move, they are all about moving on, and this explains the insubstantiality of their foundations (e.g. lack of a center).

As such, digital infrastructure in its omnipresence becomes more obscure. Infrastructural space is regarded as a hidden substrate, a binding medium between objects. Repeatable formulas for spatial products like resorts, malls, IT campuses or free zones, as well as airports, manifest in gigantic world city formations (such as aerotropolises); many such infrastructures are the urban formula and the very parameters of global urbanism.[43]

Koolhaas' theories stand in stark contrast with the identity-seeking airport architecture that is presented here. He is correct about the generic aspect of megacities in the Far East and Middle East that have sprung up during the development boom of the last decades. Coincidentally, those cities try to recreate their loss of historic city center within their airport designs.

In the same decade as Koolhaas (1990s), ethnologist Marc Augé argued that modernism is accompanied by loss and destruction of place. His conclusion is that supermodernism creates non-places which as spaces are not anthropological places. Supermodernism is the excess of postmodernism. Non-places have lost contact with history and therefore do not generate place-related identities. This can be counter-acted by an architecture of the sense of place, meaning the return to the original and vernacular.

3.4 The Beginnings of Mobility

The evolution of our civilization is strongly tied to different modes of transportation. On foot and on horseback have been the earliest means of movement throughout the continents. The domestication of pack animals enabled prehistoric societies to transport goods on animals and in animal carts for longer distances with the invention of the wheel some 4000 years ago.

The ancient Silk Road and its ramified Eurasian network of transport routes, which were interconnected to roads, rivers, shores and other natural formations such as mountains and lakes was the first conceptualization of a highway. The ancient Romans had a sophisticated system of highways, leading to the saying that all roads lead to Rome. Transport routes evolved from trade routes and not only allowed for the travel and exchange of wares between civilizations and cultures, but also for a cultural transfer of knowledge and science.

Preempting Marshall McLuhan's term of the global village in the 1960s, globalization can be linked to the beginnings of the physical movement of these early civilizations, even though when we speak of globalization in the context of this thesis we are talking about the advancements of travel, trade, and migration of the

---

42   Christophe Bruchansky, The Heterotopia of Walt Disney World, conference talk at Philosophy for All

43   Keller Easterling, "The Action is the Form", in: Sentient City: ubiquitous computing, architecture, and the future of urban space, p 154

nineteenth and twentieth centuries up till the present and into the future.

Seafaring is the second oldest form of transportation.[44] The development of seaports is closely linked to the continental trade routes connecting to the Silk Road and historical ports in and near cities such as Athens, Lisbon, and Venice. Seafaring not only enabled trade but also advancement in sciences, navigation, cartography – and colonization. Seafaring for the common person also enabled emigrating to the New World or the colonies, pilgrimages to the Holy Land, and to the affluent upper class and aristocracy it allowed partaking in the Grand Tour.

Since the Renaissance and during its heyday in the eighteenth and nineteenth century, the Grand Tour has been the term for the formative cultural experience of the young and coming of age aristocrats and privileged society from England, Scandinavia, Germany, and even America. For the British, it involved the crossing of the Channel, mainly between Dover and Calais, and the subsequent cultural travel through Continental Europe as an early version of a tourist. The voyage would almost certainly pass through the Netherlands, France, Germany, Switzerland, and culminate in Italy. The Grand Tourist was typically a young man and his tutor or entourage, with a classical education of Greek, Latin, and the arts that needed refinement through visiting the cultural sites in Continental Europe. But as we have learned from the Edwardian writer E.M. Forster in his book *A Room with a View*, also affluent young women were sent on the Grand Tour for refinement.

Once on the continent, the voyage would continue in a coach and later by railway.[45] Railways connected cities with transport nodes like seaports and other cities and spread across every continent in the nineteenth century.

3.5 Railways and Vistas

The Industrial Revolution at the onset of the eighteenth century brought tremendous societal and manufacturing changes to the cities. A whole new living standard allowing steady work was created through the invention of electricity, gas lighting, and manufacturing machines. The steam engine was initially invented to power factories, and consequently pumped water to move the locomotive. New ways of building emerged, such as cast iron and glass paneling and allowed for new building types in the cities and countryside: Factories, galleries, train stations, warehouses, bridges, and viaducts.

One of the most famous paintings and emblems depicting the advent of industrialization and modernity is J.M.W. Turner's *Rain, Steam and Speed – The Great Western Railway* (1844), a synonym of modernity which was akin to the age of the railway.[46]

This painting captures the fascination and thrill that emanates from the steam locomotive approaching the viewer, and simultaneously depicts a subliminal danger that this new technology might bestow upon mankind. A bridge or viaduct can be discerned in the

---

44 http://www.dovermuseum.co.uk/bronze-age-boat/bronze-age-boat.aspx:
One of the oldest boats ever known stems from the Bronze Age some 3000 years ago and is displayed in the Dover Museum and Bronze Age Boat Gallery. Discovered in 1992 by Kent construction workers, this wooden canoe offered archeologists a glimpse into the development of seafaring. Speculation goes that the earliest seaworthy boats might stem back to forty thousand years ago to the age of Neanderthals who hunted marine animals. Around that age seafaring was strongly tied to the history of whaling.

45 The Grand Tour, Metropolitan Museum: http://www.metmuseum.org/toah/hd/grtr/hd_grtr.htm

46 https://www.nationalgallery.org.uk/paintings/joseph-mallord-william-turner-rain-steam-and-speed-the-great-western-railway: The painting shows an approaching train, most probably near the Maidenhead Bridge, designed by Isambard Kingdom Brunel between 1837 and 1839.

background, the new iron-engineering attribute of the railway age.[47]

While the European city remained in its medieval layout until the late eighteenth century, at the onset of the industrial revolution it dramatically transforms due to new means of transportation – the railway.

Cultural critic and historian Wolfgang Schivelbusch recounts in his "Geschichte der Eisenbahnreise" ("Railway Journey") the impact of the age of the railway on industrialism and space and time as a new mode of perception or sensation. Annihilation of space and time has been a characteristic of the railway journey, he writes, based on the notion of speed which railways were able to achieve. By reducing the old spatial distance with a fraction of that time, the rail journey meant shrinking of space.[48]

The railway produced a new landscape, with the movement of the train creating a whole new perception of the landscape. Until the beginning of modern transportation, goods and commodities remained part of the local identity of their place of production. Only when modern transportation – the railway – created a definite spatial distance between the places of production and consumption did the goods become global commodities. This created a locational movement – the transporting of the product to the market and turning it into a commodity. In a way, such a product lost its local identity and spatial presence. The railways joined the metropolis with the regions and caused a loss of their spatial-temporal presence, a loss of their uniqueness and "aura" that Walter Benjamin attributed to the "original" work of art.[49]

The detachment from its original place and the alienation of the process of traveling not only takes away from the aura of the product that is being transported but also has an alienating effect on the voyager himself. Schivelbusch speaks of a devaluation of the outlying regions by their exploitation for mass tourism, not only during the inception of the railway voyage but especially well into the twenty-first century. In a way, the tourist destroys what he actually seeks – the originality and local sense of place. The railway's transportation of products and people hence attributed to mass tourism.

The first mass tourism was the conquering of seaside towns of Southern England in the nineteenth century, which for decades and centuries were citadels of the aristocracy until the middle classes arrived in hordes via the railway. The affluent aristocracy then retreated to different parts of Great Britain, such as the Lake District, in an effort to remain amongst their exclusive peers. Similarly, airline travel further devalues formerly exclusive and remote regions by making them accessible to everyone.

The destruction of the aura by means of reproduction of which Benjamin speaks and by means of traveling of which we here speak, brought the masses closer to outlying regions and their desire to bring things closer spatially diminished the value of the original product or location.

In the 1840s, the English railway companies were behind the standardization of time in order to accommodate the different time zones crossed by railway travel, and so Greenwich Time was introduced as a standard valid on all lines throughout the Kingdom. The Unit-

---

47 Rolt, https://www.britannica.com/biography/Richard-Trevithick: Mining engineer Richard Trevithick invented the steam locomotive in 1804, an advancement from James Watt's low-pressure type.

48 Wolfgang Schivelbusch, Geschichte der Eisenbahnreise: Zur Industrialisierung von Raum und Zeit im 19. Jahrhundert, p 33: The average traveling speed of the railways in England was twenty to thirty miles an hour.

49 Walter Benjamin refers to the loss of the "aura" (essence) of a work of art or product through the various reproduction techniques of the nineteenth and twentieth centuries in his much revered work "The Work of Art in the Age of Mechanical Reproduction" from 1936.

ed States had a more difficult task of railway timing as each private railway company had its own time – the local time of its headquarters – until 1889, when they, too, adapted the time zone system.[50]

The railroad reorganized space and time and introduced glass and steel, which were both expressions of the accomplishments of the industrial revolution.[51]

When watching a movie, the viewer in a way detaches himself from reality, at least to a certain point, while trying to compartmentalize and analyze the action on the screen. The drama on the screen makes the viewer create an imaginary space, he participates in the story, yet is detached from it (and in a safe space). This is part of the aesthetic experience of movies. The viewer knows it is not reality, he knows that it is only two dimensional, yet the power of the visual imagery helps him create his own imaginary space. The same power took place when first experiencing the railway journey, it set the stage for the architecture of viewing. [52]

In *Eye and Mind*, Maurice Merleau-Ponty analyzes the complexity of vision through painting. He argues that we do not only see the things that the world presents us, but that we see ourselves in the world. This is part of Merleau-Ponty's phenomenology, namely that the reflexivity between what we see and ourselves produces our ambiguous vision of things. Merleau-Ponty gives the example through viewing art, in particular a painting by Paul Cézanne which deceives our perception as there is no third dimension. The third dimension is perceptible to the viewer only through the distance between the object and the eye. Consequently, depth in

Figure 26: "Vista" – view onto Downtown Chicago from the window of a Swiss Airbus 330, photograph by Lilia Mironov

seeing, especially in the metaphorical sense, is part of the viewer's actions within this space.

The body sees and is seen. It is within this merging between the perceiver and the observer that distinctions break down between the subject and the object, the real and the imagined, and the space between them all.[53]

The increased velocity of railway travel introduced a great number of visual impressions and the development of an urban perception. It certainly did so for air-

50   Schivelbusch, Geschichte der Eisenbahnreise: Zur Industrialisierung von Raum und Zeit im 19. Jahrhundert, p 43–44: Greenwich time is the time kept at the Royal Observatory in Greenwich, founded in 1675.

51   Ibid., p 45

52   Nathalie Bredella, Architekturen des Zuschauens, p 20

53   Maurice Merleau-Ponty, „Das Auge und der Geist", in: Raumtheorie. Grundlagentexte aus Philosophie und Kulturwissenschaften, p 184

line travel (Figure 26). The intense experience of traversed space incurred into a loss of landscape, a condition that "mechanized the traveler's perceptions", the "synesthetic perceptions" that had defined physical travel so far, disappeared, and the stimulus increase overwhelmed passengers. Synesthesis as an artistic design ideal describes the Hegelian notion of the historical process of the idea (*thesis*) being argued by another idea (*antithesis*) which then resolve into the third, complete solution of the *synesthesis*.

The travel in a railway carriage (and airplane) and the gazing outwards was a complete new mode of "Weltanschauung", a new kind of perspectivism that interprets the world seen through subjectively (*perspectiva* literally meaning "seeing through" in Latin) and creates a self-determined apperception of the world (in this case rather the landscape seen outside).

I captured Beijing Capital Airport from the cockpit window on a flight returning from Shanghai and was enthralled by the perspective I got. My passion is airport architecture. This was a unique chance to view this airport, which I have been writing about, from the airplane perspective at 33,000 feet or 11 km above and which I have only once visited so far, right upon its completion (Figure 27).

Beijing Capital Airport was built in 2008 by Foster and Partners just in time as the gateway for the Olympic Games. It was at the time the biggest airport building in the world and functioned in Norman Foster's much coveted single-shed airport architecture, which he follows through in all of his airport designs and which stems from Le Corbusier's theories of the naked airport.[54]

It celebrates the sense of place through the traditional Chinese colors red and yellow within the terminal – and even from 11 km above one can discern the brick red roof of the building, which symbolizes the mythological Chinese dragon, a reference to China's imperial heritage and a bearer of luck, protection, and wealth in Chinese culture. The roof structure is composed of

Figure 27: View onto Beijing Capital Airport from the cockpit of a Swiss Airbus 340, photograph by Lilia Mironov

---

54   David Jenkins, Foster 40 / Norman Foster, p 296

skylights which resemble the scales of a dragon's skin and are a source of daylight.

Perspectivism since the Renaissance also means relativism and literally seeing things from a specific point of view, based on the linear perspective. The "perspectival" view, according to Panofsky, did not mean the "foreshortening" of houses and objects in a painting, but rather transforming the entire picture into a "window" when we are meant to believe we are looking through this window into a space.[55]

Art historian Erwin Panofsky called the pictorial perspective a symbolic form because it is an abstraction of reality, a form of thought that is bound to a place and time. In a nutshell, Panofsky suggests that the perspective is a change of view of the world, the change that the Renaissance brought after the Middle Ages, away from the infinity of religion that put the earth and God at the center of the universe.

Perception does not know the concept of infinity, he writes, it is confined within spatial limits:

"[...] The view that had been blocked since antiquity, the vista or 'looking through', has begun to open again [...] and the painted picture will once again become a section cut from an infinite space."[56]

A Room with a View by E.M. Forster is not only a classic reading in English Studies, it is considered a tongue-in-cheek *Bildungsroman* as well. Bildungsroman because it tells of the Grand Tour a young English woman partakes in around 1910 and consequently of her humanistic awakening, just as the purpose of this tour is. This book with the Grand Tour as a setting tells of the sophistication of a young woman and her putting such great importance on the *vista*, the view. I deliberately traveled to Florence when I was an art history student with this book in tow. I wanted to experience the contemplating effect of the views just as the protagonist Lucy does. On the other hand, I wanted to take in the views and various artworks and architecture as an art historian. To consciously view and inspect Masaccio's Trinità in Santa Maria Novella, which is considered the breakthrough of painting the central perspective, and to consciously take in sights and vistas as an emancipated spectator were the purpose of my Florence journey.

---

55   Erwin Panofsky, Die Perspektive als „symbolische Form", p 99: Panofsky here cites Leon Battista Alberti und Leonardo, who both mentioned the perspective view from outside a window.

56   Ibid., p 101–116: Panofsky further specifies the perspective:
"At this point we can almost predict where 'modern' perspective will unfold: namely, where the northern Gothic feeling for space, strengthened in architecture and especially sculpture, seizes upon the architectural and landscape forms preserved in fragments in Byzantine painting, and welds them into a new unity. And in fact the founders of the modern perspectival view of space were the two great painters whose styles, in other ways as well, completed the grand synthesis of Gothic and Byzantine: Giotto and Duccio. Closed interior spaces reappear for the first time in their works. These interiors can in the final analysis only be understood as painterly projections of those 'space boxes' which the northern Gothic had produced as plastic forms [...] It signifies a revolution in the formal assessment of the representational surface. This surface is now no longer the wall or the panel bearing the forms of individual things and figures, but rather is once again that transparent plane through which we are meant to believe that we are looking into a space, even if that space is still bounded on all sides. We may already define this surface as a 'picture plane', in the precise sense of the term. The view that had been blocked since antiquity, the vista or 'looking through', has begun to open again [...] and the painted picture will once again become a section cut from an infinite space."

The panoramic, three-dimensional (seeing things live and not in a catalogue) and the gazing view of the traveler, both during the journey inside a railway wagon or airplane cabin as well as at the destination of choice is one of the most important aspects of a journey.

The difference between real and imaginary spaces of our mind is that the latter make us rather passive and incapacitated.[57] The challenge is to discern between illusion and reality.

The window "vista" is one of the key elements of the perspective seeing in Renaissance art. The perspective seeing of things which are no longer recreated from ideals but from reality empowers the viewer. This self-determined and sophisticated viewing is the running theme throughout A Room with a View.

Spectatorship is the focus in Jacques Rancière's understanding of the arts and theater. In his *Emancipated Spectator* his thoughts about active and self-determined spectatorship against passive consumption-viewing are valid for the aesthetics in general, especially so for art and performances on display. Thus, Rancière assesses that emancipation begins when we challenge the opposition between viewing and acting; when we understand that the relations between saying, seeing, and doing themselves belong to the structure of domination and subjection; and when we understand that viewing is also an action that confirms or transforms this distribution of positions. The spectator also acts, and observes, selects, compares, interprets.[58]

Rancière gives credit to the emancipated (not passive!) spectator and her/his intellectual and self-determined observational viewing. It is not the idea that the viewer needs to be educated and inspired by the artist as the genius, which would be an antiquated assumption. Active spectatorship leads to emancipation and vice versa. The meaningfulness of viewing lies also in the distance between artist and spectator, as well as the distance as an autonomous thing that defines the sensation or comprehension of the spectator as his perception of what the artist intends to say.[59]

The active spectator forms an opinion based on his viewing of things. This is the translation of the artwork or performance for the spectator. A very "auratic" experience happens to the spectator, in the sense of Benjamin's definition of the aura of the original work of art and its loss through reproduction. The spectator reappropriates and translates the "original" view into his own intellectual realm and makes this a very personal experience. To further demonstrate this, one might consider the passivity of today's cinemagoers who are satisfied with serialized franchises of movies that are easy on the eyes and easy on the brains. This also includes reality television programs where spectators are neither intellectually stimulated nor have a choice to change the point of view or perspective. Of course people choose to watch movies of their free will, but once inside this mechanism there is no way out. The emancipated spectator Rancière talks about consciously chooses to view things, autonomously so. Choosing to view Masaccio's Trinità from many different angles and distances, gazing away, wandering away and returning to view it again. Viewing it with accompanying literature in hand that further describes it. And creating a personal contemplative experience through this viewing translation, this is emancipated viewing.

---

57 Bredella, Architekturen des Zuschauens, p 20

58 Jacques Rancière, The Emancipated Spectator, p 13: Rancière does not write about railways though; his theories are about spectatorship and participation in regards to the theater and the arts. I deem his ideas as valid for the newly emerged emancipated spectatorship of traveling since the Grand Tour.

59 Ibid., p 15

Travelers of the new mode of railway transportation experienced traveling altogether as a boring experience due to the initial inability to adapt to this new mode of perception, depriving them of the contemplation of travel. But a new awareness formed through this new mode of rapid travel – the velocity that initially destroyed the classic perception of landscape now made the objects of the visible world attractive, by sitting comfortably in the train carriage and turning the traveler's eyes outward.[60]

The traveler gazed through the compartment window, where the motion of the train through the landscape appeared as the motion of the landscape itself, the railroad choreographed the landscape. The immediate succession of objects and scenery was likened to that of the panorama apparatus. This concept of the panoramic serves as a description of European modes of perception in the nineteenth century: To see the discrete indiscriminately – the railroad transformed the landscape and seas into a panorama and diorama that could be experienced. Even though this experience was very individual and no two travelers would have the exact same emotional response or translation of the seen, the scenery could become generic to the viewers, rendering them passive, or making them oscillate between active and passive spectatorship. Dioramic and panoramic shows would take on the subject of the train journey and provide the audience with distant landscapes and exotic scenes as a substitute for the expensive and onerous journeys[61] (Figure 28).

For Wolfgang Schivelbusch, the main sensorial impact of these new modes of perception meant that the panoramic, intensive experience of the sensuous world

Figure 28 Diorama of a Buffalo in Nebraska, Durham Museum, Omaha, photograph by Lilia Mironov

that was terminated by the industrial revolution experienced a resurrection in the institution of photography. The foreground enabled the traveler to relate to and identify with the landscape through which he was moving, joining him in the landscape. Panoramic perception became a sensual and phenomenological experience.

Those railway voyages were being celebrated as an event of the senses, to experience the panoramic landscape from the comfort of the train wagon. Alas, the speed of the railroad also destroyed the close relationship between the traveler and the traveled space and landscape became geographical space.

The loss of landscape affected the senses, while the railroad created conditions which mechanized the trav-

60   Wolfgang Schivelbusch, Geschichte der Eisenbahnreise: Zur Industrialisierung von Raum und Zeit im 19. Jahrhundert, p 60

61   Schivelbusch, Geschichte der Eisenbahnreise: Zur Industrialisierung von Raum und Zeit im 19. Jahrhundert, p 60: Schivelbusch quotes Hans Buddemeier's "Panorama, Diorama, Photographie: Entstehung und Wirkung neuer Medien im 19. Jahrhundert" (1970): A diorama is a full-sized or miniature model of a three-dimensional landscape recreation, popular at museums and later in department stores in the nineteenth century. Invented by Daguerre and Bouton in 1822 in Paris, diorama literally means "through that which is seen", it was first used for theatrical effect as kind of an early "cinema" experience where the entire audience would be rotated to view a second scenery. It is similar to the panorama, meaning the "all-encompassing view".

eler's perceptions and contributed to the loss of spatial awareness. Smells and sounds and the outside temperature disappeared; those senses and the synesthetic perceptions though were all of what travel was about in earlier times and in Goethe's grand travel writings.[62]

The participatory aspect of this viewership was indeed rather passive; Rancière writes of the power of associating and dissociating that makes the emancipation of the spectator. Being a spectator is not a passive condition that shall be transformed into activity, it varies and changes, just as we learn and teach. Every spectator is already an actor in her / his story.[63]

That is part of our emancipation, to decide if we want to be passive or active in the perception of our surroundings and our viewing and ultimately form our opinions.

During the early train journeys it became customary to pass the time with reading, which encouraged bookstores at railway stations and travel guides such as the popular Baedekers to meet the general demand for literature while traveling. Reading while traveling was part of the panoramic perception of the voyage and created an imaginary surrogate landscape of the book.[64]

The situation during present day airline travel is similar and yet different. In general, travelers seem immensely bored throughout the automated processes and long queues at airports. Alienation and the transitory status of this space further enhance the feelings of unease or boredom. They too, read or watch movies on their devices to pass their time and beat boredom. But they have not necessarily had the choice to participate in active viewing during their plane ride. For one thing, 90% of their plane journey consists of travel at 30,000–40,000 feet (10–11 km) height with little to see outside and only around 30% of passengers sitting at windows. Their vistas are totally different from the contemplative landscape viewing of the railway traveler. The whole travel process through airports leaves little to personal emancipation or autonomy. The panoptical passage through the terminal with its various security and passport controls and mandatory run through its shopping mall is psychologically unsettling. Airport design strives to recreate vistas, panoramas, and dioramas in order to placate the harassed travelers.

This chapter about the travel experience in railways and spectatorship of travel shall be concluded with a quote from avid world traveler and author Rudyard Kipling, who in 1907 remarked about airplanes:

"The time is near when men will receive their normal impressions of a new country suddenly and in plan, not slowly and in perspective; when the most extreme distances will be brought within the compass of one week's – one hundred and sixty-eight hours – travel; when the word 'inaccessible', as applied to any given spot on the surface of the globe, will cease to have any meaning."[65]

---

62   Schivelbusch, Geschichte der Eisenbahnreise: Zur Industrialisierung von Raum und Zeit im 19. Jahrhundert, p 53

63   Rancière, The Emancipated Spectator, p 17

64   Schivelbusch, Geschichte der Eisenbahnreise: Zur Industrialisierung von Raum und Zeit im 19. Jahrhundert, p 64: The reading public on the railway voyage was almost exclusively bourgeois. According to an English survey of 1851, instead of the usual trashy mass literature in regular bookstores, railway bookstalls in both France and Great Britain carried respectable literature and non-fiction, as well as travel guides.

65   Rudyard Kipling, "With the Night Mail", McClure's Magazine, November 2015, 23–25, quoted in: Alastair Gordon, The Naked Airport, p 8: Kipling apparently expressed this quote with regard to the novelty of airplanes yet it fully purports on the experience of traveling either mode.

3.6   Railway Stations

David Lean's 1945 movie *Brief Encounter* is a cinematic classic. A romantic drama by playwright Noel Coward, Brief Encounter is the doomed love story of two married British train commuters which mostly plays out in a train station waiting room somewhere in the periphery of London. Interspersed with Rachmaninov's Piano Concerto No. 2, the movie is a character study of suffering, love, adultery, longing, and loneliness in the backdrop of the transitory place of the train station. This non-place enhances the movie's post-war setting of displacement and alienation. The waiting room of the train station is metonymous of life. One waits, bearing a burden or an anxiety, for a connection to somewhere better or somewhere home. The railway station has been given great importance in culture and literature. Painters such as JMW Turner and Claude Monet captured the progress and perils of modernization within their railway subjects. In literature, scenes from Anna Karenina, from various Agatha Christie mysteries and Brief Encounter found their climactic scene in a train station and cemented the railway journey and railway station as an important setting of the drama of life.

The newly industrialized city in the 1800s was for the first time divided into residential, industrial and leisure districts, based on the changes brought on by railways and railroads. The construction of infrastructures and cityscapes as well as railroads involved architects, engineers, developers, and urban planners, but from the second half of the nineteenth century, a new building type emerged – the train station.[66]

The vanguard of airport terminals is the classic train station. The railway station had become the characteristic of modernity, just as much as the railway itself stood for progress and prosperity. And, consequently, the airport terminal has become the characteristic of postmodernity and globalization in our day and age.

Train stations were the first transitory spaces of our society. Ever since the beginnings of the railway, similar to what we will see happens with airports, train stations needed to morph their identity from mere shelters to modern gateways to the city. As a consequence, the station had to be reinvented from a utilitarian piece of engineering into an architectural theme for the city. It became a representative building for the city, where economical activities concentrated around a central node of public transportation.[67] Hence, the railway takes a leading position in urban development of the twentieth century.

After comparing Aldo Rossi and Kevin Lynch's writings on the perception and construction of the city, Roberto Cavallo concludes that "the architecture of the railway could be understood as the making of the entire range of buildings forming the physical body of the railway yard in the city, all of them being part of a primary element."[68]

---

66   Roberto Cavallo, Railways in the Urban Context, p 70: Architects such as Robert Owen, Tony Garnier and Ebenezer Howard took on the task of studying and planning for the growing modern city. Their utopian models were based on philosophical and sociological studies – especially Howard succeeded in creating reality out of utopia with his garden city movement which greatly influenced housing and town planning for all social classes. Viennese architect Otto Wagner wrote in his study *Moderne Architektur* in 1896 that a modern city needs means of expansion by a series of districts which themselves radiate away from the city center and that it needs a functional public transportation system on rail. An architect had to harmonize the monumental engineering facilities of this railway transportation within the city (iron bridges and viaducts). Wagner won the competition for a Stadtbahn in Vienna in 1893 and by 1898 the first of these metros circulated through the city. The Stadtbahn metro systems in Vienna and Berlin were the earliest of the emerging city metros of that period.

67   Ibid., p 4

68   Ibid., p 18: By primary element he refers to Aldo Rossi's three principal functions in respect to the city – the housing, fixed activities, and circulation and concludes that the railway is an infrastructure which belongs to the fixed activities and as such is a primary element.

By being such primary elements, railways were the catalysts of city development.

At the inception of the railway, stations were merely collecting points of postal and utilitarian wares on the outskirts of cities. Railway historian Carroll Meeks calls this period between 1830 and 1850 the "functional pioneering" and "standardization"; later periods he names as "sophistication", "megalomania" and "twentieth century style" (much as airport architects named the different design periods of the twentieth century).

The first train stations were built at transportation nodes that would transfer passengers from central locations within the city to outside the city where they would connect onto the railway system. The Swansea and Mumbles Railway was initially a horse-drawn iron carriage line on tracks built to transport limestone from Mumbles to Swansea in Wales around 1800 (Figure 29). "The Mount" in Swansea is considered the first railway station serving passengers. While this was a horse-operated railway before the steam locomotive, its serving purpose was the same – offering a transportation system for paying passengers and operating from a shed-like building with the form of these early stations varying from case to case.[69]

In Europe, the railway emergence was a direct consequence of the industrial revolution and industrial production (the railway took over from pre-existing modes of transportation of industrial products, such as the cotton industry, which transported the imported cotton from Liverpool to manufacturing sites in Manchester). In the United States, the railway was primarily incepted to conquer the Wild West. The legendary Wells Fargo Mail service on carriage, which was based on the banking and financial institution of the same name, expanded into the railway business to gain access to the Pacific West around the 1860s and bought the Central Pacific Railroad which operated out of Omaha towards

Figure 29: Photograph of horse-drawn train, the first Mumbles Railway, Wales, photograph courtesy of the Richard Burton Archives, Singleton Park Library, Swansea, Wales

the West Coast. It is now known as the Union Pacific (Figures 30–33).

In 1862, President Abraham Lincoln signed the Pacific Railway Act, creating the Union Pacific Railroad with its eastern terminus at Council Bluffs, Iowa, just opposite the Missouri from Omaha. In 1869 the First Transcontinental Railroad came into being in Promontory, Utah, when the Union Pacific and Central Pacific railways from the eastern and western coast merged.[70]

---

69   Stephen Hughes, The Archaeology of an Early Railway System: The Brecon Forest Tramroads, p 333

70   https://durhammuseum.org/our-museum/history-of-union-station/

The First Transcontinental

On May 10, 1869, two railroads—built with haste, hope, and aspiration—joined in the lonely desert of northern Utah, at a place called Promontory.

At a small ceremony that day, dignitaries from both railroads—the Central Pacific, which had built from California, and the Union Pacific, which had built from the east—gave speeches and installed ceremonial last spikes.

The ceremonies were meant as a moment of self-congratulation, but the significance of the day's events is far broader. In the ensuing decades, railroad after railroad proposed new, competing transcontinental routes—and sometimes completed them. Their construction swept away the dominance of native

tribes, ended the open range, and restructured the West into a network of resources and industries connecting and feeding clusters of urban centers.

It was a change that photographers were on hand to depict. Both technologies, the railroad and the photographic camera, emerged in the early nineteenth century and found wide application across the West by the 1860s. One hundred and fifty years later, this exhibit looks back on how photographers, both past and present, have responded to the transcontinental project and its continuing legacy.

Constructing Railroads and Reconstructing the West

To build the transcontinentals, investors unleashed tens of thousands of laborers—mostly non-citizen immigrants. They constructed the railroads and in the process reconstructed the West itself.

The transcontinentals were Manifest Destiny writ in steel, the conversion of wilderness into an urban-centered, industrialized empire. The plow, the mineshaft, and the irrigation ditch extended from this network. In the words of historian Donald Worster, this was the birth of the "engineered West."

The project depended heavily on manual labor, with the bulk of early routes built by former slaves from the defeated Confederacy, refugees from Ireland, and workers recruited from China. After the racist policies of the Chinese Exclusion

Act of 1882, railroads began to employ workers from other countries, including Japan, India, and Mexico. Foreign labor was cheap and readily available, helping to ensure profitability.

To make way for development, the federal government pushed out existing First Nations peoples. In some cases, the transcontinentals directly assisted with the removal of tribes. In others, railroad managers appropriated native figures as ceremonial props, an attempt to depict the transcontinentals as a natural part of the western landscape.

Figures 30 & 31: Photographs from the exhibition about Promontory, Utah, where the Union Pacific and Central Pacific railway lines met to form the First Transcontinental Railroad in the United States in 1869. Exhibition at Durham Museum, Omaha, Nebraska, photograph by Lilia Mironov

Figure 32: Union Pacific "4-6-0 Ten Wheeler Steam Locomotive" built in 1890, Durham Museum, Omaha, Nebraska, photograph by Lilia Mironov

Figure 33: Wells Fargo Mail Service Carriage, Durham Museum, Omaha, Nebraska, photograph by Lilia Mironov

The Durham Museum in Omaha, Nebraska is situated within the premises of its old railway station and is dedicated to preserving the history of the "Wild West". The original Union Station of Omaha is a magnificent art deco building and firsthand testimony of the golden age of railway travel. It ceased rail service operations in 1971 after the National Railroad Passenger Corporation, Amtrak, took over from Union Pacific. The decline of the American railroads can be attributed to the automobile industry and lack of infrastructure upkeep. The present-day Amtrak station of Omaha, opposite the previous Union Station, is a shabby shed on the outskirts of the tracks and in service for the only scheduled Amtrak train that passes there once per day, often times with many hours of delay: The California Zephyr, which connects Chicago and San Francisco via Omaha and Denver. I took that train once, out of nostalgia and spirit of adventure. The voyage to Chicago took me 12 hours (including a four-hour delay) as opposed to the one-hour plane ride. Passenger trains in the US regularly get sidetracked to give precedence to freight trains which are more profitable and because there are not enough cross-country track lines.

The original Union Station of Omaha, nowadays the Durham Museum, is in my humble opinion one of the most magnificent railway stations I have ever seen. It was completed in 1931 as a remodeling of the Burlington Depot by the architect Gilbert Stanley in his finest art-deco style which was then pervasive to American architecture. The terra cotta exterior with its abundant decorations took on the form of an ancient temple (Figures 34 & 35).

Art Deco was a very popular and defining architectural style of the 1920s and 1930s. It came to prominence at the 1925 Paris exposition of Modern Decorative Arts and the 1933 Century of Progress Exposition in Chicago, with influences from Art Nouveau. In the United States, Art Deco progressed into a distinguished style of neo-gothic and ornamental buildings and skyscrapers with columns, spires, and applications of ancient Greek, Mayan, Aztec and Egyptian origins. In a way, the American Art Deco was the most creative of

Figures 34 & 35: Durham Museum (Union Station), Omaha, Nebraska, photographs by Lilia Mironov

all architectural styles, allowing for majestic-looking buildings and interiors.

The Durham Museum/Union Station of Omaha is relevant in this discussion as it shows what American railway terminal buildings looked like at the beginning of the twentieth century and how they influenced airport design.

The regional airport of Dane County in Madison, Wisconsin was extensively remodeled in 2001 to replicate this past era's look – if one compares the terracotta tiles and chandeliers of the Omaha Union Station with the Dane County Regional Airport, there is a distinct analogy, despite the nearly 60 year difference between the buildings (Figure 36).

It is not only the Art Deco style that is recreated in this airport terminal – the architects of Alliiance paid homage to Frank Lloyd Wright's *prairie style* of architecture which was popular in the area; after all, Lloyd Wright's Taliesin estate and studio were situated in Wisconsin. The prairie school, with influences from the Arts and Crafts Movement, put emphasis on the indigenous, local, and vernacular in the American North-/Midwest architecture and crafts. Lloyd Wright propagated for an organic architecture, using natural resources and a horizontal orientation. The sense of place is emphasized by the colors of the region: terracotta and earthen tones for the mosaic floors and wood paneling on the counters and bannisters, as well as a low-slung flat roof.[71]

Comparing these two distinguished buildings shows the interconnection between railway stations and airport terminals throughout the decades and how current airport designers try to capture aspects of the golden era of railway travel.

Figure 36: Madison Wisconsin Dane County Regional Airport, arrivals hall, courtesy of Alliiance Architects

The railway station finds its perfection under Queen Victoria's reign. St Pancras Railway Station was commissioned by the Midland Railway System in London and had become famous for its grand Victorian architecture in the Italian Gothic style. It was constructed in 1868 by William Henry Barlow with an adjacent hotel by George Gilbert Scott (Figure 37). It was a head type (terminus) station that housed diverse infrastructure functions such as retail, dining, and a hotel and became a prototype for many train stations on different continents.[72]

The terminus type railway station dominated the European cities from the mid-nineteenth century onwards as opposed to the "Anhalter"-Bahnhof such as Cologne (a drive-through for the railway). It was usually situated on the periphery of the city center and received

---

71 Steve Thomas-Emberson, Airport Interiors: Design for Business, p 60
http://www.alliiance.us/our-work/aviation/dane-county-regional-airport/

72 Carroll Meeks, The railroad station: The oldest purpose built train station is Manchester's Liverpool & Manchester Railway Station, built in 1830.

Figure 37: St. Pancras Station, London, present day, photograph courtesy of Hugh Llewelyn
Figure 38: Chhatrapati Shivaji Terminus, formerly Victoria Station, Bombay, photograph courtesy of Francesco Bandarin, ©UNESCO

the railway traffic from one transport node or direction which it redistributed into the city center.

St Pancras was at its time the largest passenger train station, followed by the Gare du Nord and Gare de Lyon in Paris; they all combined classical terminal buildings (mainly representative stone buildings) with iron and glass sheds (the new materials) in the rear. This was the standard typology of railway stations, a total juxtaposition of building materials – the stone main building and the cast-iron columns and soaring arches of the railway hall conveyed a sense of the beginning of the machine age.[73] For the approaching voyager a classical building with a façade similar to a museum or government office presented itself.

St Pancras Station served as the prototype for the revered Victoria Terminus in Bombay, which has since been renamed into Chhatrapati Shivaji Terminus (as is named the newest and biggest airport terminal of the city). Constructed in 1888 by British architect Frederick William Stevens in the Victorian Neo-gothic style, Chhatrapati Shivaji Terminus is a cathedral of the colonization of India. It was not only the most important British colonial building in India, but also the first truly public building in Bombay[74] (Figure 38).

---

73   Kurt Schlichting, Grand Central Terminal, p 34
74   Srinath Perur, Chhatrapati Shivaji Terminus, Mumbai's iconic railway station – a history of cities in 50 buildings, The Guardian

In 2014, another Chhatrapati Shivaji terminal opened in Mumbai – the striking Chhatrapati Shivaji International Airport Terminal 2 by Skidmore, Owings and Merrill (SOM). With regional patterns, columns and textures integrated into its architecture, it aspired to be the world's first integrated museum-airport with its own art history curator[75] (Figure 39).

Figure 39: Chhatrapati Shivaji International Airport, Mumbai, India, photograph by Lilia Mironov

The building type of the train station emerged from a shed into a representative place for transport and gathering in the city. Vast roofs spanned over multiple bays reminiscent of cathedrals. Translucent or transparent roofs with iron and glass frameworks created an impression of openness and light.

The roof of Paddington Station (1854) in London by Isambard Kingdom Brunel and Matthew Digby Wyatt was one of the first wrought-iron frames with arched ribs. The "style architecture" of the railway station which enabled it to harmonize with the surrounding city architecture was the task of the architect, but the engineer was responsible for the loadbearing structure. These mid-nineteenth century grand railway terminals were of prestigious and almost palatial architecture and extended the platform concourse as a transition into the cityscape.[76]

Motifs in station architecture were neoclassicist and historicist, and given their character of a gateway to the city, they were adorned with representative attributes such as the portico, triumphal arch, or propylea.[77]

3.7 Grand Central Terminal

The Grand Central Terminal in New York must be mentioned here for its uniquely hybrid infrastructure that linked the subway system to the railway and served as a public place and gateway for the city. The train

---

75   During English colonization the city was called Bombay and was renamed Mumbai only in the 1990s.

76   Staib, Glass Construction Manual, p 18:
     The Wiegmann-Polonceau system dominated the French train stations. Its loadbearing construction consisted of metal sheets and simple sections whose form derived from the structure. Such an example was the Gare d'Austerlitz (1847) with intricate trussed girders of the Wiegmann-Polonceau system. It had generous glazing in the roof, front, and sides to enhance the lightness inside.

77   Meeks, The Railroad Station, p 117: The Cologne Train Station (1889–1894 by Georg Frentzen) was a so called "Anhalter Bahnhof" which allows for railways approaching from opposite sides (as opposed to the head station or terminus station), with soaring glass cages that made them instantly recognizable as stations. Between elevated tracks and the cathedral square it required a raised shed and a station at the lower level. Completed in the Romanesque style, the visual effectiveness was increased by its elevated position. Stairs and elevators connected passengers to a central platform. The Central Station at Antwerp (1900) was defined by a glass and iron dome reminiscent of the Crystal Palace, with the shed extending back from a high-shouldered pyramidal head-building on the plaza. The glass having been replaced since World War II.

terminus on 42nd Street, as we know it, opened in 1913 after ten years of construction which had replaced the Grand Central Depot from 1871, the original Grand Central Station.

The American industrialist and railway magnate, Cornelius Vanderbilt, owned the New York Central Railroad which competed with the Pennsylvania Railway and Pennsylvania Station on 34th Street, being the rival "train hub". Pennsylvania Station had been opened two years earlier, in 1911.

Vanderbilt chose to unify the passenger operations of his railroads in the city within an appropriate passenger terminal and bestowed this task on the architect John Butler Snook who had specialized in cast-iron buildings. Snook created the Grand Central Depot with an iron and glass train shed and classical station building which represented the classical style for railroad stations during Europe's railway station boom of the mid-nineteenth century. The soaring iron arches supporting the train shed were fabricated in England and constituted the largest arches erected in the United States to date. By contrast, according to Kurt Schlichting, the station building with its stone and brick ornamentation and the mansard roof with five domes, mirrored the classical tradition, particularly the classi-

cism of the Second Empire of Napoleon III. This juxtaposition of the classical and the machine age created a stark contrast.[78]

Modeled after the Louvre and a number of European train stations such as St Pancras in London, Gare du Nord and Gare de Lyon, the Grand Central Depot, too, combined the classical terminal building with the glass train sheds in the rear. On the other hand, the rival Pennsylvania Station's original structure from 1910 was modeled after the Beaux-Arts style of Gare d'Orsay.

At the beginning of 1900, after a fatal train crash proved the old building antiquated, railway engineer William J. Wilgus had a flash of genius when faced with spatial constrictions in expansion – he proposed expanding vertically and not horizontally and not up but down, by building two terminals, one on top of the other.

In 1902 Wilgus created a plan with a complex of buildings around the Grand Central Terminal and its adjacent surroundings which was later named "Terminal City".[79]

The architects Reed & Stem and Warren & Wetmore won the design competition which honored Wilgus' abstract outline for the new Beaux-Arts Building. Wilgus

---

78 Schlichting, Grand Central Terminal, p 34

79 Ibid., p 60: Wilgus' multifunctional "Terminal City" plan which he proposed to the board of the New York Central directors incorporated:
   1. a double level, underground terminal with a loop track at the suburban (lower) level
   2. an elevated driveway around the twelve-story building connecting Park Avenue north and south of the new terminal
   3. the elevated driveway carried on an arch bridge over 42nd Street connecting with Park Avenue south to the street
   4. north of the terminal from 45th to 48th streets, over the underground train yard, provision made for a "grand court or park" over the train yard and for future development of revenue producing buildings
   5. a new hotel on Madison Avenue between 43rd and 44th streets to be "run on first class lines, similar to the Waldorf-Astoria"
   6. a waiting room eighty feet in width extending across the entire station
   7. the main concourse, sixty feet in width, with direct connections to Vanderbilt Avenue on the west and Depew Place on the east
   8. from the concourse, ramps leading down to the long-haul train platforms
   9. ramps from the concourse, along with stairs and elevators, to the lower concourse, where ramps would lead to the suburban train platforms
   10. a direct connection with the IRT subway at the suburban level
   11. north of the station between 45th and 48th streets, construction of a separate baggage facility connected to the tracks below by elevators and "endless belts"

also persuaded the board of directors to switch to electrical trains in lieu of the steam locomotives as those would be of hazardous nature in an underground train station.[80]

By separating the station's activities in his Terminal City masterplan, Wilgus' design brought order and set a precedent to the functionality of modern day airport terminals. He planned the lower level of the two-story underground facility exclusively for commuter service and the upper concourse for departing long-distance trains. For the heart of the Grand Central Terminal he planned a central concourse for the more popular and famous trains.[81]

Grand Central Terminal had 46 tracks and 30 platforms. It had diverse halls and waiting rooms for all kinds of comforts – ladies' rooms, dressing rooms, barber rooms, the Vanderbilt Hall (which used to be the main waiting hall and now is used for special events), the Grand Central Zone, the famous Oyster Bar and various restaurants and shops and even art galleries which were established by John Singer Sargent.

The magnificent twenty-six stories high Biltmore Hotel, a landmark of steel frame and masonry cladding designed by Warren & Wetmore, offered a private arrival station at Grand Central Terminal with elevator access to the lobby.

Grand Central still is the largest train station in the world by number of tracks and platforms. It was built as a stairless station with all levels and platforms reachable by ramps or lifts, a progressive design for the traveling passenger. The astronomical mural on the ceiling

of the main concourse shows the Mediterranean sky and features 2500 stars. After a decade long renovation in progress, Grand Central Terminal reopened to its full splendor in 2013 (Figures 40 & 41).

Grand Central stood in direct competition with Pennsylvania Station, which opened 2 years prior in 1911 on 33rd Street to serve the Pennsylvania Railroad. McKim, Mead and White's Pennsylvania Station (1901–1911) offered a Beaux-Arts design as well.

During the prosperous period after the Civil War, American architectural art of important public and private buildings developed heavily in the Beaux-Arts style, something that architectural critic Lewis Mumford referred to as "imperial".

Pennsylvania Station and Grand Central Terminal both epitomized this monumental style as gateways to the most important city of the country.[82]

The original Pennsylvania Station, which the Pennsylvania Railroad tore down in 1965 in favor of the new Madison Square Garden, was a classical head and shed station – head house being the American synonym for station building. A separate train shed housed the incoming trains. Pennsylvania Station separated the arriving and departing passengers via two concourses. When demolished in 1963, it became an underground station below the modernist and multipurpose Madison Square Garden arena and its accompanying infrastructure. But before that it served as one of the two railway gateways to New York City and its neoclassical structure was famously based on the Caracalla Ther-

80   Schlichting, Grand Central Terminal, p 93

81   Ibid., p 62: New York Central's famous passenger trains had exciting names such as the Twentieth Century Limited (which was a Pulman-only carrier connecting NYC with Chicago), the Empire State Express and the Wolverine.

82   Ibid., p 130: The lack of a long collective history of architecture in America created the search for a usable past, a vocabulary with which to express the American experience, for which the Beaux-Arts style fitted perfectly. The Beaux-Arts style takes its name from the Ecole des Beaux-Arts in Paris which practiced an academic neoclassical revival. At the end of the nineteenth century and into the beginning of the twentieth, the Ecole's influence reigned supreme in American architecture. The rebuilding of Paris from 1853 to 1870 took place under Napoleon III by the Prefect of the Seine, Baron Haussmann, whose monumental, classically inspired buildings defined the age.

Figures 40 & 41: Grand Central Terminal, Manhattan, present day, photographs courtesy of Professor Luis Carranza

Figure 42: Pennsylvania Station, 1962, photograph by Cervin Robinson, Library of Congress

mal Baths in Rome with an almost uncountable number of columns and pilasters[83] (Figure 42).

The completion of Grand Central marked the emergence of distinctive building art in the United States – the combination of innovative engineering and imaginative architectural design. The so called "American Renaissance", which had already produced the Brooklyn Bridge in 1883 and the first skyscrapers in the world

---

83   Meeks, The railroad station: An architectural history, p 131

in Chicago, also produced the largest subway system in the world in the New York area, comprising both Pennsylvania Station and Grand Central Terminal as the gateways to the city of Manhattan.[84]

The newest addition to Manhattan' railway system is Santiago Calatrava's long delayed railway station for Ground Zero, popularly called *Oculus* (2016). Following a masterplan by Daniel Libeskind for the redevelopment of Ground Zero after the attacks on September 11, 2001, *Oculus* at the previous World Trade Center site is a cathedral-like ribbed structure, typical of Calatrava's formulaic designs. Its sculptural form does not fit the grid of the city and is in contrasting angle to neighboring buildings, designed to let light fill the massive space as a memorial for the attacks on the twin towers, envisioned by Calatrava to symbolize a dove released from a child's hand. Built as a subterranean subway station with a mall on top, it serves as the third biggest railway station in the city of Manhattan.

The white tinted steel ribs soar to a height of 48 m and curve out and continue skyward to create asymmetric fins sheltering the Great Hall below[85] (Figures 43 & 44).

On a subjective note, the whole building evokes the motif of a skeleton with its ribs, much more so in relation to the terror that took place there on 9/11, with the images of the molten steel trusses of the Twin Towers burnt in one's head, hence I felt quite uneasy there.

To end this chapter about railway stations let us sum up their precursor role for airports:

During the nineteenth century, following the industrial revolution, the European city changed its medieval character. New technologies such as steel and electricity as well as the incorporation of railways led to an unprecedented expansion.

The terminus station would never be in the city center due to its size and infrastructure of multiple rail lines and sheds, but rather at the periphery. Nowadays, terminus stations in London, Paris, and Zurich are still within the approximate city center because those cities have grown around and beyond the terminus stations. It is the aerotropolis model, but projected onto railway stations: Infrastructure and social spaces grew around these early train depots into city centers. Local train and metro stations link to the bigger terminus stations, creating a network, as seen in the example of Tokyo Station which links transnational Shinkansen trains with the local and regional subway system across the city. Tokyo Station has increased to five platform floors below ground and two above. In its bustle it is a city in itself, consisting of various buildings and high-rises and offering a multitude of retail and dining venues. Its main building from 1914 still keeps its original historical brick façade reminiscent of a European train station building.

The multifunctional use of these stations, as already exemplified in both Pennsylvania and Grand Central terminals, has been extended incessantly since, combining retail, dining, leisure, and hotel business within these spaces. The fact that Pennsylvania Station was modeled on the ancient Caracalla Thermal Baths in Rome traces an arc to Henri Lefebvre who saw the first multifunctional entertainment and leisure place in these Diocletian Baths in Rome, a peculiarity which will be further examined later on in this thesis as the architecture of leisure.

---

84   Schlichting, Grand Central Terminal, p 115
85   Patrick Lynch, http://www.archdaily.com/795158/santiago-calatravas-oculus-opens-to-the-sky-in-remembrance-of-9-11

Figures 43 & 44: Oculus, Santiago Calatrava, Ground Zero, New York (2016), photographs by Lilia Mironov

4 Airports!

4.1 Where to place an Airport Terminal?

The architectural evolution of the airport terminal takes place within a time frame of roughly one hundred years. It is thus a very young field of research. It is closely bound to the evolution of flight. Flying itself has been a motif in cultural history that has permeated Greek mythology and art – from Pegasus to Leonardo da Vinci, who in the fifteenth century was working on designs and models of a winged self-propelling aircraft.

The first free human flight in a hot air balloon – the Montgolfière, named after the two brothers who invented it, took place in 1783 on the outskirts of Paris. In 1893, German Otto Lilienthal took to the air in a glider that he launched from a hill. In 1900, at the age of 62, Ferdinand Graf von Zeppelin flew five passengers for several miles at an impressive height in his first rigid airship, the Zeppelin. His base in Friedrichshafen by Lake Constance is considered to be the world's first passenger air terminal. It now serves as a regional airport and houses the Zeppelin museum.[86]

The 17 December 1903 was an exceptional day for aviation:

Orville and Wilbur Wright successfully flew the first motorized aircraft above the dunes of Kitty Hawk, North Carolina (Figure 45). The Wright Brothers were the first to fly in so called heavier-than-air machines which required airstrips for takeoff and landing – which

Figure 45: First flight of the Brothers Wright, in Kitty Hawk, North Carolina, December 17, 1903, photograph by John T. Daniels

in the beginning happened to be cow pastures. Around that time those rural airstrips and airfields would be serviced by a hangar, and many of them were remodeled with evened out farmland serving as a landing strip. American journalist Lowell Thomas even called them "cow-pasture aerodromes". As to the term "port", that one is attributed to an eyewitness who viewed Wilbur Wright's air show in Paris in 1908: "These ports will be squares erected in the forms of cones and surrounded by hangars."[87]

---

86   Hugh Pearman, Airports: A Century of Architecture, p 31. Developed in 1874 after ideas by Zeppelin, these aircraft with a fabric-covered rigid metal frame operated on gas and were widely used for passenger transport beginning in Continental Europe and later the United States. The fatal fire and crash of the then largest airship, the Hindenburg in 1937 in Lakehurst, brought an abrupt rift in the era of passenger zeppelin flights. Nowadays zeppelins are mainly operated for publicity, as done e.g. by the company Goodyear.

87   François Peyrey, "Les Premiers Hommes-Oiseaux." In Robert Wohl, A Passion for Wings Aviation and the Western Imagination, 1908–1918 (New Haven, Conn.: Yale University Press, 1994), 40. As quoted in: Alastair Gordon, The Naked Airport, p 11

At their time, these ports would alternatively be called aerodromes. They were to be found on farmland, far away from the confines of the city, or like the Wrights chose, in the dunes of North Carolina – if only because of the dangers of early flying.

A year after their inaugural flight the brothers Wright moved back home to Dayton, Ohio, where they practiced and perfected their flying machines on a repurposed pasture called Huffman Prairie. Years later that airfield would be renamed into Wright Field for military purposes and is now part of the Wright-Patterson Airforce Base.

The original pasture was located eight miles east of Dayton, Ohio, and belonged to a local banker named Torrence Huffman. It offered the main characteristics of an early aerodrome in the United States: Large stables that could be remodeled into offices and hangars and an endless prairie without obstructions, which allowed for landings from all sides.[88] This is a very similar development to the early railway stations which were mere huts and sheds and located on the outskirts of the city.

Airport construction experienced a boost after World War I when geographical lines were redefined. Airports became symbols of progress and utopian planning. Former war aircraft and bombers were converted for civilian use, airfields built during World War I, like Bourget outside of Paris and Croydon outside of London were converted into civilian aerodromes.

As a result, the first international airline service began in 1919 between Hounslow Aerodrome in London (the present-day Heathrow) and Paris.[89] Various passenger airlines were founded throughout Europe in the following years. The Treaty of Versailles had decreed the destruction of all German aircraft and airfields after World War I. The Allies lifted restrictions on aviation in 1925 and the Germans caught up quickly – within three years, the Deutsche Luft Hansa Aktiengesellschaft was founded, the predecessor to the current Lufthansa. As Germany was not allowed to build for war, it put its resources and engineering toward the development of civil aviation.[90]

The advent of aviation and its logistics would inspire futurists, urbanists, and visionary modernist designers such as Antonio Sant'Elia, Erich Mendelsohn, Le Corbusier, and Frank Lloyd Wright into toying with the public aspect and placement of such architectural constructs within the periphery of a city.

The Italian Futurist Sant'Elia proposed a gigantic aerodrome-train station in the city center of Milan in 1912. In his vision of the *Città Nuova*, Sant'Elia believed that every generation shall build its own city based on futurist architecture that is comprised of art, synthesis, and expression. At the center of this futurist city a *stazione aeroplani* (train station) with multilevel plazas would be linked to railways and highways by elevators, metal gangways, and moving pavements[91] (Figure 46).

Sant'Elia's sketches for this first hybrid between central train station, airport terminal, and public square can be considered one of the first planned airport terminals by an architect. It had, according to architecture critic Hugh Pearman, an "astonishingly prescient design for its time."[92]

---

88   Pearman, Airports, p 8: The Wright Flyer III from 1905 was the first fully functional aircraft and a prototype for military aircraft. After the death of Wilbur Wright in 1912, Orville retired from airplane constructing and sold his shares to his competitor Glenn Curtiss.

89   Gordon, Naked Airport, p 13

90   Ibid., p 19: Luft Hansa developed the F-13 Junkers, which was the first civilian airplane in Europe.

91   Antonio Sant'Elia, "L'architettura futurista: Manifesto", p 199–200

92   Pearman, Airports: A Century of Architecture, p 85

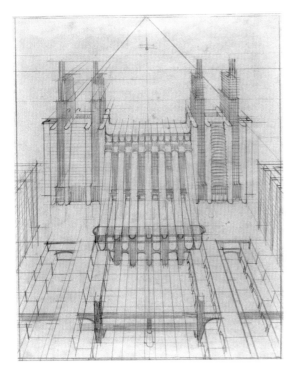

Figure 46: Stazione Aeroplani nella Città Nuova, Antonio Sant'Elia, 1912, photograph courtesy of Musei Civici di Como

Sant'Elia understood the importance of verticality in city planning, as did Rem Koolhaas much later in his essay on the generic city: "the Generic City is on its way from horizontality to verticality. The skyscraper looks as if it will be the final, definitive typology. It has swallowed everything else …"[93]

Erich Mendelsohn's never realized vision of an airport of the future were sketches of a dream city with drawings for a large-scale airport to be built from cast concrete with rounded corners and flowing surfaces over a skeletal steel frame. He called this drawing *Skizze für einen Flughafen für Luftschiffe und Aeroplane*.[94]

Sant'Elia was supposedly inspired by New York's Grand Central Terminal, where the sophisticated layering of transport and pedestrian routes were integrated. Unfortunately, the *Stazione Aeroplani* was never realized as Sant'Elia fell in battle in the Italian army during World War I.[95]

Also not realized were sketches and visions by architects such as Erich Mendelsohn's airplane sketch and Frank Lloyd Wright's *Broadacre City*. A counter draft to Sant'Elia's and Le Corbusier's visions of skyscraper cities, Frank Lloyd Wright's idyllic utopia model is called Broadacre City and which he first introduced in his book "The Disappearing City", a treatise on the effect of mobilization on urban society in 1932.

Even though Frank Lloyd Wright (1867–1959) did not envision an airport as such, his utopian thought experiment of the city of the future was based on the individual person and on decentralized infrastructure with no obscuring skyscrapers, on a kind of self-sufficient agricultural-urban existence where every person should have an automobile and flying machines, so called "aerators"[96] (Figure 47).

---

93   Rem Koolhaas, S, M, L, XL, p 1253

94   Gordon, Naked Airport, p 11: Even Bruno Taut toyed with ideas for airports, and proposed a giant aerial theatre-carousel that would be propelled by airplanes, "Das Karussell". Other futurists even considered sketching airports up in the air between skyscrapers, such as depicted in a cartoon sketch in the magazine *Aerial Age Weekly* in 1921.

95   Ibid., p 70

96   Frank Lloyd Wright, The Disappearing City, p 43

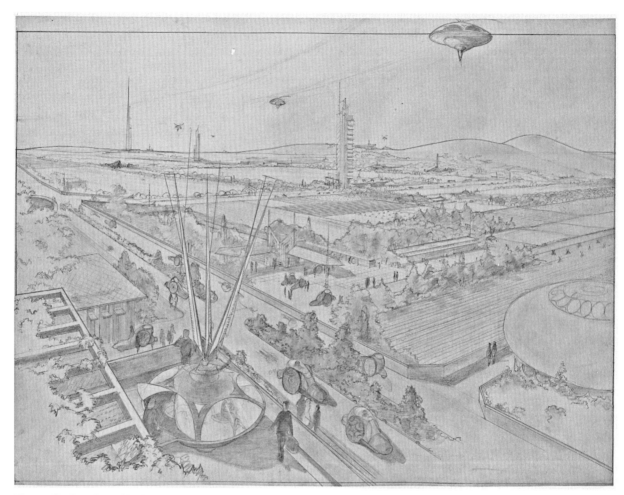

Figure 47: Broadacre City, Frank Lloyd Wright 1932, Drawing 5825.004, drawing Copyright © 2019 Frank Lloyd Wright Foundation, Scottsdale, AZ. All rights reserved. The Frank Lloyd Wright Foundation Archives (The Museum of Modern Art | Avery Architectural & Fine Arts Library, Columbia University, New York)

"[...] it is in the nature of universal or ubiquitous mobilization that the city spreads out far away and thin. [...] It is in the nature of flying that it disappears."[97]

---

97   Ibid., p 32

His term "aerator" only appeared in a subsequent version of his thesis from 1935, four years before Igor Sikorsky made the first successful helicopter flight.[98] These aerators were to be strapped onto the body according to the travel and flying needs of each individual citizen.

Frank Lloyd Wright, appreciated as one of the defining architects of the twentieth century, with an emphasis on natural and organic architecture detached from the centralized urban setting, never built an airport. His oldest son Lloyd Wright (1890–1978) witnessed Louis Blériots flight premiere across the English Channel in 1909 and became an enthralled flight enthusiast. The younger Wright later worked for Curtiss Aircraft.

Combining his aeronautical and architectural background, he sought out to sketch airport designs based on his father's organic architecture, in which form grew out of the specific conditions of the site and its needs.[99]

Wright Jr. entered the Lehigh Airport Competition – the first national contest for the design of modern airports held in the United States by the Lehigh Portland Cement Company, in 1929.[100] The competition's purpose was to "suggest practical airport designs of value to municipalities and other organizations which are today creating America's future airports."

It is notable to see what the requirements of airport building were some 90 years ago, not unlike those of our present day airport designs:

"[...] provisions shall be made for future expansion which will at least double the capacity of all such units without requiring the removal or abandonment of the original elements. [...] among the buildings called for in the program was a passenger terminal with complete facilities to the public, the transportation companies and the pilots using the field, with provision for immigration and customs offices and for complete traffic control facilities. [...] other buildings included hangars, repair service stations, a hotel of small size, various concessions from which income for the airport shall be derived ... ".[101]

Wright Jr.'s contribution to the competition, which was ultimately dismissed, showed the sketch of a lasso-shaped structure that encircled a field. Hangars and all other terminal facilities were integrated into semicircular buildings. Regrettably, Wright's proposal was not even merited with a comment by the Lehigh jury[102] (Figures 48 & 49).

The proposal did, however, show the trend for large-scale semicircular terminal buildings that half embraced the tarmac, as most prominently accomplished in Ernst Sagebiel's new terminal building for Berlin Tempelhof Airport in 1934. Tempelhof Airport set a paradigm as a city airport of gigantic proportions in Europe and was one of the Third Reich's most recog-

---

98   Pearman, Airports: A Century of Architecture, p 78

99   Gordon, Naked Airport, p 52

100   Archibald Black, Lehigh Portland Cement Company, American airport designs: containing 44 prize winning and other drawings from the Lehigh airports competition, the first national contest for designs of modern airports held in the United States, p 10

101   Ibid., p 10

102   Gordon, Naked Airport, p 52–54

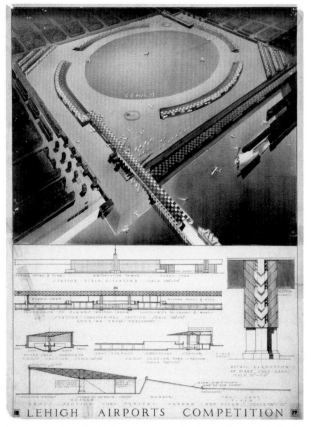

Figure 48: Lloyd Wright's entry contribution to the Lehigh Portland Cement Company's competition on American Airport Designs, 1929. Sketch courtesy of Eric Lloyd Wright.

Figure 49: Cover of the book

nized edifices. Norman Foster called it "the mother of all airports."[103]

Its sternly classical façade at a length of 1.2 km complimented other Berlin buildings by Sagebiel and those planned and commissioned by Generalbauinspektor Speer for the Reichshauptstadt Berlin/Germania. Coincidentally, architect Ernst Sagebiel worked in Erich Mendelsohn's office at the time, the latter having had to step down due to his Jewish roots.[104]

Sagebiel's design of Tempelhof is based on an expressionist sketch by Mendelsohn from 1914, which he had envisioned with a semicircular reinforced concrete terminal building of 400 to 600 m in length (Figures 50 & 51).

103 Helmut Trunz, Tempelhof Flughafen im Herzen Berlins, p 64

104 Elke Dittrich, Ernst Sagebiel: Leben und Werk, p 14–99. The early German airports were highly linked to both World Wars.

Figure 50: Architectural model of Zentralflughafen Tempelhof, Ernst Sagebiel, photograph ca. 1937, courtesy of Library of Congress
Figure 51: Flughafen Berlin Tempelhof in operation in 1984 during show day, photograph courtesy of Jose Lopez Jr.

The massive limestone walls and monumental re-inforced concrete façade of Tempelhof airport were a metaphor of power of the NS regime. This historicizing neoclassical design towards the landside and the city versus the steel and iron designed technical airside (towards the airfield) was a typical building modus for airport terminals and railway stations up until that time, with the intention of showing the city the representational (classical) architecture of the building façade which served as an identifying landmark.

It also adhered to the guidelines of the NS regime for representative buildings which required a rigorously stern façade in the classicist style. The modernist style of New Objectivity totally opposed the previous expressionism for industrial and technical buildings.[105] Nonetheless, that kind of stern and monumental con-crete architecture stood in stark contrast to the upcoming glass pavilions of modernist airport architecture that will be presented further down.[106]

Only 70% of the planned Zentralflughafen Tempelhof were completed during the reign of the NS regime. By 1940, the Weser Flugzeugbau GmbH manufactured the Junkers military aircraft in its subterranean production halls. At the end of World War II, in 1945, the airport had suffered astonishingly little damage, in part thanks to its bombproof ceiling.[107]

Berlin Tempelhof was the quintessential city airport. Situated literally within the city of Berlin, it was run by the allies after World War II and performed an important humanitarian task during the *Luftbrücke* 1948–1949, when the "Rosinenbomber" of the allies supplied the people of Berlin with food packages.[108] It was the

105 Gaby Dolff-Bonekämper, Berlin-Tempelhof, Liverpool-Speke, Paris-Le Bourget: Années 30 Architecture des aéroports, p 59
106 Ibid., p 55
107 Trunz, Tempelhof Flughafen im Herzen Berlins, p 78
108 Gordon, Naked Airport, p 159

American military that built the first concrete runway there in 1948. But its unique position within the city forbade a further expansion of the runways to develop into a big international airport, even though the terminal infrastructure would have allowed so. Thus it performed as a city airport for regional flights until its final closure in 2008.[109]

Since then it has become the setting for political occupy-movements: First, supporters fought to preserve its green spaces in order to re-appropriate its premises into a place of leisure.[110] Then came the refugee crisis of 2005 and that place was transformed into a humanitarian cause.

For a few decades in the last century, Berlin Tempelhof Airport was one of the most iconic entrances from above to a city, a paradigm for city airports and city entrances, as the passenger approaching that airport could see the city unfold from beneath. Even though it was the "architectural brand" of the NS regime, its later symbolic function as a savior in regards to the Luftbrücke and commercial city airport has turned it into one of the main gateways to Berlin.

Berlin Tempelhof Airport is still unique for its central setting within the city. It was the pinnacle of the urban studies and sketches of the early artists and visionaries presented above. City Airports such as London City are still on the peripheries of the big urban centers and strictly limited in their aircraft capacity. Airports have since moved their premises away from the city centers, so much so that they have become cities of their own. In that way they can be adjusted to passenger flows and future expansion.

4.2 Airport Typology

A distinct airport typology had solidified in the 1920s and 1930s both in Europe and in the United States. Whereas up until the 1930s airport terminals resembled early railway stations with the basic shed model, the various functional attributes of the airport infrastructure would now be housed within one big terminal, separated from the hangars. Being a completely new type of building, there was no precedent and no formula for airport building other than that the buildings should be attractive and dignified, corresponding to railway buildings. Though the passenger terminals should have been the most prominent structures, they were often overshadowed by hangars and maintenance sheds.[111]

The airport of Königsberg (1922) in then Eastern Prussia (now Kaliningrad in Russia) is considered the first modernist airport terminal. Its architect Hans Hopp had designed one single stepped building which housed all the main and administrative passenger functions, while the hangars for technical maintenance stood separate. He called it an airport station.[112]

On the other hand, in the United States, commercial airlines had remained in private hands and airport building was left up to municipal initiatives. The federal government stayed clear of commercial aviation. Aviation was dominated by the US Airmail Service which had been established in 1918 and operated on modest airfields across the country.

When Charles Lindbergh had returned from his flying shows in Europe, he toured the continental United States by plane, being sponsored by the Daniel Guggenheim Fund for the Promotion of Aeronautics on a

---

109 Dolff-Bonekämper, Berlin-Tempelhof, Liverpool-Speke, Paris-Le Bourget: Années 30 Architecture des aéroports, p 59

110 Ulrich Best, The Debate about Berlin Tempelhof Airport, or: A Lefebvrean Critique of Recent Debates about Affect in Geography, p14

111 Gordon, Naked Airport, p 43

112 Dolff-Bonekämper, Berlin-Tempelhof, Liverpool-Speke, Paris-Le Bourget: Années 30 Architecture des aéroports, p 23

mission to improve the ground facilities and to raise interest in airport infrastructure. But Lindbergh was apparently embarrassed by American airfields, finding the buildings shabby with shoddy hangars and shacks made for servicing mail planes. This highly publicized tour of his set in motion a wave of airport construction. Politicians who had shunned the airplane as an expensive and passing fad now embraced it as a patriotic symbol of the American way of life.

In the 'Roaring Twenties' aviation and airport building boomed, for which Lindbergh was the catalyst. Between 1927 and 1929 close to a billion dollars were invested in aviation and more than sixty different passenger lines were operating in the United States alone. Buffalo, New York developed an airport which was the result of eight years of exemplary planning. Buffalo was the seat of the Curtiss Aeroplane and Motor Company which had delivered planes for World War I allied pilots. Neighboring the Lehigh Valley Railroad, the airport was constructed with the farsighted vision and support of Henry Ford who needed new destinations for his new transport company in Dearborn, Michigan (where as we read in the Aerotropolis chapter he had already established factories for cars and airplanes as well as an airport). Two hard-packed runways, hangars, and a terminal were erected in the first phase of construction, which cost a million dollars.[113]

Albert Kahn's Ford Airport in Dearborn, Michigan, built in 1927, was one of the first realized architect-designed commercial airports in the United States. Built for automobile industrialist Henry Ford on his airplane factory grounds, Kahn, who had also designed the Ford hangars, airplane factory, and airport hotel, created the terminal in a modernized Spanish style with white brick walls as uniform pilasters and

Figure 52: Ford Dearborn Airport, Michigan, by Albert Kahn, 1927. Photograph courtesy of Don Harrison

offered a spacious waiting area, an observation deck, and other attributes to enhance passenger comfort.[114]

The automobile was conceived on the same principle of the steam engine as the locomotive, but proved unsuccessful until the German Karl Benz powered it with gasoline in 1885. The automobile became the definition of success and freedom in the United States and next to the railway is one of the most groundbreaking inventions of the nineteenth century. Henry Ford democratized the initial status symbol of the affluent class by his automated mass production in 1914 and use of the conveyor belt. The cost of his Ford Model T was fair enough that even the Ford Motor Car workers could afford to buy one. Henry Ford stood not only for the democratization of the car but also of the mass-produced airplane, his Ford Trimotor.

Most of the American terminals built after 1927 followed the Ford airport model of a symmetrical façade and depot-style interior with a waiting room and ticketing office.

Juan Trippe, the brilliant founder of Pan Am, had understood the symbolic importance of airport termi-

---

113 Gordon, Naked Airport, p 23–25
114 Timothy O'Callaghan, Henry Ford's Airport and Other Aviation Interests, p 51–59

nals as the stage for the adventure of flight.[115] In 1928, he hired the famed New York architects William Adams Delano and Chester Aldrich to design Pan Am's Miami terminal. As its paragon, the Ford Airport, Pan Am's terminal was noticeably positioned at one end of the airfield, while the hangars were removed to the other side. This was a concrete building with a vaulted roof reminiscing of the shape of the airplanes. A balcony allowed for spectators to watch the action on the airfield. Porters and pilots were dressed in white uniforms and a brass bell was rung to announce departures. The distinctly nautical theme was continued inside the terminal with metal railings and wicker furniture. Large windows at either end flooded the waiting room with natural light[116] (Figure 53).

There was still no defined style for airport architecture in the 1920s. First-generation airports in Europe were created to be national gateways. Historical themes alluded to a dignified continental building history, but were inconsistent with aviation itself. A Palladian manor style airport terminal was created for Croydon, a Petit Palais for Bourget and a Renaissance palazzo for Littorio airport in Rome. In the United States, American designers outdid each other with classical gateways or temples to evoke the ceremonial sense of arriving and departing at an airport and enhanced the buildings with propylaea.

Could the form of the Athenian propylaeum possibly bring a more humanist and representational element to the realm of the flying machine? Porticos, Greek pediments and other temple imitations were suddenly all the rage.

At Fairfax Airport in Kansas City, landscape architect Ernest Herminghaus extended the axis of the main runway with a 45 m long reflecting pool filled

with water lilies and fountains. Designed by architect Charles A. Smith in 1929 in the Art Deco style, the terminal building of Fairfax Airport was an impressive temple-like structure with two stepped-back wings that spread out from the center building (Figure 54).

Architectural historian Alastair Gordon calls this temporary trend of applying classical veneers and mixing styles of different eras a historical pastiche.[117]

It was not only the style of Art Deco that inspired airport architects at that time, but also

Figure 53: Pan Am International Airport, Miami, Delano & Aldrich, 1929. Photograph courtesy of Florida Memory

Figure 54: Fairfax Kansas Airport, Kansas City 1929, vintage postcard

115 Gordon, Naked Airport, p 44
116 Ibid., p 45–47
117 Ibid., p 47–48

building in the modernist (the first airport of Washington, 1930, designed by Holden, Scott and Hutchinson), the neocolonial (the first airport of St. Louis, 1931) as well as the Spanish-pueblo style on the West Coast (San Francisco, 1937, by H.G. Chipier).[118]

The Los Angeles area airports notably vied with one another with an architecture straight out from the movie sets: The airport in Van Nuys had a Moorish Revival Style terminal which was even used in movies as an exotic setting location. The Boeing Airport in Burbank was built in this style, too, with three levels stacked symmetrically like the Court of Lions at the Alhambra; the Grand Central Airport in Glendale (1928) had very similar architecture. Only the beacon on top of the roof would bespeak it of twentieth century architecture. The observation deck made a perfect platform for watching people[119] (Figure 55).

Speke Airport in Liverpool was built in the late Art Deco style at the same time as Sagebiel's Tempelhof Airport and Le Bourget in Paris, 1937–1938. Art Deco style airport architecture was an attraction in the United States but not so much so in Continental Europe. Speke's architect Edward Bloomfield had studied in Charles Rennie Mackintosh's Art Nouveau Glasgow School of Art.

Speke Airport sits on a levelled patch of land in the Mersex estuary a few miles south of Liverpool. Its steel-framed, brick-clad building with a tall, central, octagonal control tower flanked a pair of large hangars. Nowadays, that building has been converted into an airport hotel. Bloomfield had disengaged his control tower, wrapping the terminal around it and stepping it down from the center to the ends. A similar concept, by the way, as in Hamburg Fühlsbüttel Airport.

Liverpool Speke Airport wanted the same kind of representative airport building as Tempelhof had been

for Berlin, given that Liverpool was the last port between Europe and the United States and an important gateway into Europe[120] (Figure 56).

Many of the early airport building types had a stepped design structure, as seen above. This was according to the architectural style at the time a very representative and majestic kind of architecture.

Figure 55: Grand Central Terminal, Glendale, California (1928), photograph courtesy of San Diego Air and Space Museum Archives

Figure 56: Liverpool Speke Airport, now the Crowne Plaza Liverpool John Lennon Airport hotel. Photograph courtesy of Chris J. Wood

118 Pearman, Airports: A Century of Architecture, p 66

119 Gordon, Naked Airport, p 56–60

120 Pearman, Airports: A Century of Architecture, p 66

Rem Koolhaas attributes airport types to respective decades: The hexagonal plan (as well as penta- or heptagonal) is deemed typical for the 1960s. The orthogonal plan and section is the style of the 1970s, the collage city is purely 1980s. A single curved section that is endlessly extruded in a linear plan is a product of the 1990s (Kansai Osaka Airport being an example, presented later on).[121]

Yet the architect whose airport sketches and ideas had the most significant impact on future airport designs was Le Corbusier.[122]

4.3   The Naked Airport

As one of today's most prolific and well respected airport designers, Norman Foster has created groundbreaking and iconic airports such as Stansted Airport (1991), Hong Kong Chep Lap Kok Airport in 1997, Beijing Capital Airport in 2008, and unveiled masterplans for future airports of Kuwait and Mexico City. In an interview with the architecture magazine *Icon* from 2011 he laments that most airports are depressingly detached from the experience of flying and that one barely sees the aircraft when in today's multi-themed, retail-heavy airports. For Foster, an airport should be a celebratory structure with a strong visual identity that creates an uplifting experience of air travel. He aspired to embody all these values in his first airport, Stansted, and his subsequent ones. Foster drew inspiration from early airport buildings like Tempelhof which celebrated and revered the act of flying. Beginning with Stansted, he aspired to recapture the clarity of the first airfields from a hundred years ago.[123]

The one dominant influence on Foster's airport design has been Le Corbusier's *Naked Airport* theory. Like Foster, who also happens to be a certified private pilot, Le Corbusier was an aviation enthusiast, yet he never actually built an airport. He proclaimed the airplane to be the symbol of the new age, whose eye (meaning view) reveals the spectacle of decay and collapse:

"Cities, with their misery, must be torn down. They must be largely destroyed and fresh cities built [...] The airplane is an indictment. It indicts the city. It indicts those who control the city."[124]

Le Corbusier "accused" existing and decaying architecture which for the first time ever was seen from the airplane's view and needed to be overhauled. He further compared airfields (Orly airfield near Paris) with the Gothic nave of Notre Dame, deeming the ferro-concrete airport hangar as the cathedral of twentieth-century progress. Le Corbusier understood that the technological transfer from aviation to the serialized urban building would ask for a new architectural

---

121 Koolhaas, S, M, L, XL, p 1252

122 Pearman, Airports: A Century of Architecture, p 54

123 Interview Norman Foster in IconEye:
http://www.iconeye.com/architecture/features/item/9300-interview-norman-foster

124 Le Corbusier, Aircraft, p 6: „L'avion accuse ..." (a speech from 1935), Le Corbusier plays here with "j'accuse", the title of Emile Zola's incendiary letter to the president of the French Republic in 1898, in defense of French officer Alfred Dreyfus who after lots of political turmoil was acquitted of his charge of collaboration with the German Empire. Zola's letter is a parable of fairness and accusation of political corruption and antisemitism.

aesthetic. The aerodynamics of aviation inspired Le Corbusier to the aesthetics of modernism.

Broadacre City was Frank Lloyd Wright's vision of an urban living idyll that had never been realized yet defined the design philosophy of its architect through idyllic, self-sufficient rural living with autonomous means of transportation. Le Corbusier's *Ville Contemporaine* was likewise an unrealized masterplan of urban design and theories. Like a decade earlier in Sant'Elia's *Città Nuova* vision, it consisted of a stretch of modernist skyscrapers, but in Le Corbusier's case they were aligned in a concentric pattern, slightly suspended from the ground so that the pedestrian walkways throughout greenery would indeed be reminiscent of Howard's Garden City. Both Sant'Elia and Le Corbusier put an emphasis on public transport, namely the railway station and motorways and topped off their models with an airport. "Means of transport are the basis of all modern activity" mentioned Le Corbusier.[125]

In his work *Vers une Architecture* (1923, translated as *Toward an Architecture*), Le Corbusier dedicates a whole chapter to the airplane. He writes that the technology transfer from the motorcar industry to the aviation industry requires a new design vocabulary and that means of transport build the basis of all modern activity.[126] [127]

The city center of Le Corbusier's *Ville Contemporaine* from 1922 for 3 million inhabitants is flanked by monolithic skyscrapers and also serves as an airport runway with a railway station beneath it, much like Sant'Elia's sketch of the Stazione Aeroplani for Milano (Figure 57).

This first rendering turned out to be spatially limiting and prevented expansion.

A decade on, in 1935, Le Corbusier presented the evolution of the *Ville Contemporaine*, the *Ville Radieuse* whose array of skyscrapers evoked stern, even totalitarian motifs.

This was a ubiquitous and expandable, linear and strictly symmetrical city with the airport situated on the outskirts: "Any concentrically designed city (all cities from the past) makes regular, organic development impossible: a biological defect."[128]

These city plans revolutionized mid-century high-density urban building and might have inspired Rem Koolhaas' generic city theories some fifty years later.

125 Le Corbusier, The City of Tomorrow and its Planning, p 84
    Nathalie Roseau, Aerocity: Quand l'avion fait la ville, p 36–37: Around the time of Sant'Elia and Le Corbusier, visionary French architect and urban planner Eugène Hénard was preoccupied with city-planning and had already partaken in various French exhibitions.
    Since the *Exposition Universelle* in 1889, Hénard had worked on roundabouts ("carrefours") and various modernizations in traffic, according to prolonged studies and plans of his. At the Town Planning Conference in London in 1910 he proposed his vision of Paris which had been conquered by air – that is aviation. His *Les Villes de l'Avenir* lecture showed sketches of individual and passenger planes circling the modernized city of Paris with now visible airports but the assumption that those flying machines could start and dock on newly envisioned high-rises. Such was the optimism at the beginning of the last century.

126 Le Corbusier, Toward an Architecture, p 159–161

127 Le Corbusier, The City of Tomorrow and its Planning, p 84

128 Pearman, Airports: A Century of Architecture, p 81

Figure 57: Ville Contemporaine, 1922, Le Corbusier, courtesy © FLC / 2019, ProLitteris, Zurich

Pre-fabricated apartments in the housing districts were predecessors of the "unités" of Le Corbusier's later realized Marseille housing project and the planned cities of Chandigarh by Le Corbusier himself and Brasilia by Oscar Niemeyer.[129]

The difference between Le Corbusier's urban theories *Ville Contemporaine* and *Radieuse* is that in the latter he abandoned the idea of the centrally situated airport in a modern city. On the contrary, by 1945, when he was president of the infrastructure section of the first congress of French aviation after the World War II, Le Corbusier proclaimed:

"Once on the ground, only one kind of architecture seems tolerable and perfectly admissible: that of the magnificent airplanes which have brought you or will take you away, and which in front of you occupy the visible space. Their biology is such, their form such an expression of harmony, that no architecture seems reasonable beside them, no other building possible. An airport then seems to have to be naked, entirely open to the sky, full in the center of the field, with the concrete runways. The beauty of an airport is in the splendor of wide open space."[130]

---

129 Gili Merin. "AD Classics: Ville Radieuse / Le Corbusier" 11 Aug 2013. ArchDaily. Accessed September 23, 2015. Between 1946 and 1952 Le Corbusier built the "Unités d'Habitation" in Marseille. Inspired by the unités of the Ville Radieuse this was a housing project with 337 apartments for low-income families (or those who lost their homes after the World War) with ideas of the communal living effect of the "vertical garden city", built in the rough cast concrete (beton brut) of the modernist movement – also the least costly in post-war Europe.

130 Le Corbusier, Oeuvre complète, vol. 4, p 199

In his new sketches of an airport structure, the terminal is positioned far away on the horizon whereas a single airplane, metaphorically monumental, stands in the middle of the airfield (tarmac) with all customs, functional, and utilitarian facilities banned below ground level and away from view. Nothing must compete with the machine and nothing must obstruct the view onto the machine. Architecture should be guided by the vastness of the landscape. The horizontal expansion of the runways set the benchmark for a building type where the division between structural and civil engineering became less important[131] (Figure 58).

"The beauty of an airport is in the splendor of wide open spaces!" Le Corbusier's sketch for a naked airport, 1946.

Figure 58: *Naked Airport* sketch, Le Corbusier, 1946, courtesy © FLC / 2019, ProLitteris, Zurich

This is the proverbial *naked airport* on which Norman Foster based his Stansted and subsequent airports with the easy accessible curbside and landside.

It is of utmost interest for this dissertation to understand the visions and thoughts of the contemporary architects at the time that aviation and airports started flourishing – how did they adopt this new architectural challenge? How did their work influence airport design?

4.4   Airports of the Jet Age

Two distinctive airport styles had evolved in the mid-century: The satellite type which consisted of the central terminal, surrounded with the individual terminals of airlines operating from there, often requiring the passengers to be transported to the terminals either via underground or on ground transportation. The second type was the finger terminal consisting of a central building and connecting to the air gates by fingerlike corridors. This was a necessity following the new "jet age" since the 1950s – airplanes with jet engines could not immediately dock at the terminal gates but were connected to them via jet bridges or so called "finger docks".

La Guardia Airport in New York (Queens), built in time for the world exhibition in 1939 by architects Delano and Aldrich as the self-realization of the mayor of New York City, Fiorello La Guardia, was the first airport to foresee a skywalk from both sides of the terminal to connect the travelers to the parked airplanes (Figures 59 & 60).

This skywalk, though open air, was the precursor to future airport concourses which led the passengers away from the main hall towards the airplane gates. Incepted as a city airport, that first terminal at La Guardia airport was a regress towards the early shed architecture of airports. Architecture critic Lewis Mumford criticized the unnecessary ornamentation of its façade and the steel eagle on its roof, which he deemed too defensive and totalitarian (which was the *zeitgeist* immediately before World War II). La Guardia Airport was understood as the gateway to the world exhibition in Flushing Meadows (New York) titled "The World of Tomorrow" with an emphasis on streamlined industrial design (with the participation of industrial designer Norman Bel Geddes) and future technologies, especially aviation.[132]

---

131 Marc Angélil, Terminal Space. Gedanken zur zeitgenössischen Architektur, p 8

132 Gordon, Naked Airport, p 107ff & Hugh Pearman, Airports: A Century of Architecture, p 134–140

Figure 59: La Guardia Airport, Aldrich & Delano 1939, infamous steel eagle on terminal roof, photograph courtesy of Historic American Engineering Record, Library of Congress

Figure 60: La Guardia Airport, Aldrich & Delano 1939, Skywalk, courtesy of the Library of Congress

The practice of building gateways for world exhibitions can be traced back to the Crystal Palace which was erected for the World Exhibition in London in 1851, the Eiffel Tower for the Exposition Universelle in Paris in 1889, the Gare d'Orsay for the Exposition in 1900, then to make a huge jump towards the Beijing Capital Airport by Norman Foster for the Olympic Games 2008.

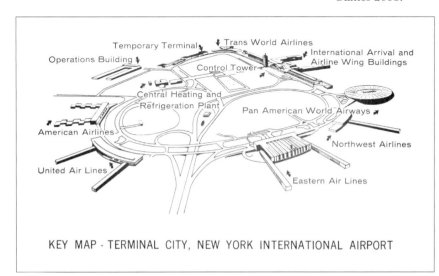

Figure 61: Terminal City Map, New York International Airport, courtesy of Morten S. Beyer Papers, Accession 2007-0060, National Air and Space Museum, Smithsonian Institution

New York's Idlewild Airport, since renamed into John F. Kennedy International Airport, was the first masterplanned "air terminal city", with both satellites and finger-type terminals developed for each operating airline around a vast airport plaza. In 1946, Wallace Harrison, one of Nelson Rockefeller's personal architects and co-designers of the Rockefeller Center, sketched the masterplan for an initial structure of the length of two miles and resembling an amoeba for Idlewild. Harrison had understood early on that retail was one of the most important economic factors of an airport and had incorporated abundant retail space into this project. Forbes Magazine had calculated that one third of airport revenue was garnered through retail.[133]

Harrison's amoeba model did not prove to be an economically successful undertaking and he came up with the idea of decentralized terminals around a semicircular roadway system including parking spaces in order to reduce the distance between car and plane. This Terminal City of the size of 655 acres provided a central public place with water fountains modelled after French gardens and fountains from the 1800s, called Liberty Plaza. It was the size of a theme park on the periphery of which were situated seven autonomous terminals, titled the Seven World Wonders (Figure 61).

The first one to open in 1957 was the International Arrivals Building by J. Walter Severinghaus & Skidmore, Owings & Merrill (SOM) which housed 14 different foreign airlines. This rather utilitarian terminal for the "foreign masses" was replaced in 2001 by SOM's Terminal 4. The large American airlines would each occupy their own iconic gateway-terminal surrounding Harrison's Terminal City plaza, creating a hodgepodge of contrasting styles. Two particular terminals stand out from these Seven World Wonders. Once again, Juan Trippe, the CEO of Pan Am, wanted

to excel himself and commissioned a terminal to show the people that Pan Am ruled the skies. Architect Walther Prokosch designed an elliptical structure with a four-acre roof that was engineered to act like a giant umbrella, supported by 32 concrete piers. Jet planes could park directly under the sheltering roof at the terminal. This terminal opened in 1960 but proved too impractical in the long term due to the noise of the jet engines being too close to the terminal hall.

The second terminal that stood at Idlewild was Eero Saarinen's TWA Flight Center which he finished designing in 1960.[134] This one became the icon of the jet age and set a paradigm for iconicity and aesthetics in airport design. Saarinen's expressive and romantic modernism was strongly based on Frank Lloyd Wright's organic architecture, but he also took inspiration from Erich Mendelsohn's expressionist curved designs and Alvar Aalto's phenomenological approach to building (Figure 62).

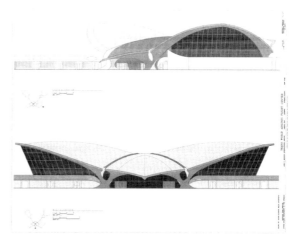

Figure 62: TWA Flight Center, Eero Saarinen, sketch, courtesy of Library of Congress, Prints & Photographs Division, NY-6371

---

133 Pearman, Airports: A Century of Architecture, p 140
134 Gordon, Naked Airport, p 188–196

Figure 63: Gateway Arch, St. Louis, Missouri; Eero Saarinen, photograph courtesy of Bev Sykes

JFK Airport still has the form of a horseshoe (the previous amoeba Wallace Harrison had planned) with 10 separate terminals surrounding the field. Gone are Liberty Plaza and its fountain; the center of Terminal City is made up of the interloping JFK Access Road which connects each terminal to the Van Wyck Expressway leading into Manhattan. Parking structures and airport maintenance, catering and facility buildings take up the rest of the space.

Eero Saarinen (1910–1961) designed three airports in his lifetime – the TWA Flight Center (1956–1962), the Dulles International Airport in Washington, D.C. (1958–1963; though technically that airport is situated in Chantilly, Virginia), and the Athens Airport (1960–1969).[135] Saarinen, who started his career in his father's architectural firm in Detroit, came to prominence when he won the competition for the United States Jefferson National Expansion Memorial in St. Louis, Missouri in 1947 with his proposal for a

futuristic looking giant Gateway Arch (Figure 63). This memorial site honors the Western expansion of the United States under President Jefferson and particularly the explorers Lewis and Clark when they had first crossed the Missouri River near St. Louis in 1804 (the Mississippi and Missouri Rivers merge north of St. Louis). Incidentally, Lewis and Clark were aided by a native Indian woman named Sacagawea who helped interpret. Sacagawea has become an esteemed female hero in American folklore. Many places of interest in the Midwestern United States carry the name "Lewis and Clark Landing" and many museums and cultural institutions praise Sacagawea as an indispensable companion of the expedition.

The Gateway Arch had taken over ten years to complete due to disputes over a railway line and was only completed in 1965. Unfortunately, Saarinen had died in 1961 of a brain tumor and did not live to see the inaugurations of his famous designs.[136]

It was Saarinen's first big commission and reflected his love of expressionist and organic architecture with curved concrete structures. For the TWA Flight Center, Saarinen drew inspiration from the Sydney Opera House (1957) by Danish architect Jørn Utzon (1918–2008). Saarinen sat on the jury selecting Utzon in 1956.

On his return flight from Australia to New York that year, Saarinen began his sketches for the TWA Flight Center, famously on the back of an airline menu. When he ate a grapefruit for breakfast a few days later he started experimenting with the peels, sculpting them into what would turn to be the outline of his terminal roof. Similar domed and curved airport architecture sitting on a plinth-like foundation by Minoru Yamasaki for Lambert St. Louis Airport (1955) provided further ideas to Saarinen.[137]

135 Susanna Santala, Catalogue Eero Saarinen: Shaping the Future, p 301
136 Hélène Lipstadt, Catalogue Eero Saarinen: Shaping the Future, p 157
137 Gordon, Naked Airport, p 198–199

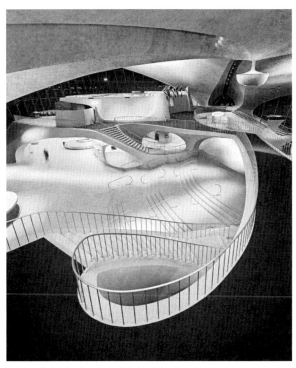

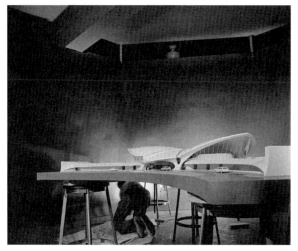

Figure 65: Eero Saarinen perfecting his model of the TWA Flight Center, photograph courtesy of Library of Congress, Prints & Photographs Division, Balthazar Korab Archive at the Library of Congress, LC-DIG-krb-00576

Figure 64: TWA Flight Center, Interior, 1964; photograph courtesy of Balthazar Korab, Library of Congress, Prints & Photographs Division, LC-DIG-krb-00604

The interior of the TWA Flight Center was designed to be a total environment with two different tiers flowing organically into each other. Everything inside was sculptural and aesthetic – even the air ducts (Figures 64 & 65).

The terminal has been immortalized in movies such as Steven Spielberg's *Catch me if you can*. Its four concrete curved domes evoke a sculptural aestheticism, reminiscing of a bird in flight and the wings of a plane set the paradigm for future iconicity airports. But it soon proved impractical for the jet age, for the arrivals and departures halls were within the same structure, much like a train station. Though the terminal connected to satellite concourses where the airplanes parked, it could not adjust to the expansion of air travel throughout the 1970s and onwards. When TWA was acquired by American Airlines in 2001, the terminal ceased its passenger operations.[138] It was later occupied by JetBlue Airlines, but since 2019 it operates as a stylized airport hotel, housing 512 rooms and celebrating its 1960s setting.[139]

Architectural Critic Vincent Scully initially called Saarinen's design exhibitionist and "curiously lunar and remote", which he later regretted and attributed to his (Scully's) being an evangelical modernist.[140]

---

138 Susanna Santala, Catalogue Eero Saarinen: Shaping the Future, p 302

139 https://www.twahotel.com/hotel

140 Vincent Scully, Catalogue Eero Saarinen: Shaping the Future, p 13

4.5   Rounding up

This chapter's aim was to show a chronological development of the architecture of travel until the first iconic terminal of the jet age, the TWA Flight Center. This is the moment where airport typology shifts, a paradigm shift in airport design which will be addressed separately in the following chapters, namely the beginning of iconicity airport building on a global level which is still ongoing. Airport architects and historians speak of the golden age of airports until the 1950s. These were the adventurous, fancy little Art Deco and Moorish Revival Style airports throughout the 1920s and 1930s in America, the elegant European modernist airports such as Speke, Tempelhof and Hamburg, but also the development from the shed to a representational main building. Further on, the importance and the genesis of Le Corbusier's formalism for later airport architects through his *naked airport* musings has been demonstrated.

Norman Foster's airports are notably based on Le Corbusier's characteristics of the *naked airport*, a concept Foster pioneered at Stansted Airport (1991) and a model since adopted by airport planners worldwide. It is characterized by a lightweight roof canopy, kept free of service installations; it relies on natural lighting; and it integrates beneath the main passenger concourse all the technical equipment for baggage handling, environmental services, and transportation. Foster's Hong Kong Chek Lap Kok Airport (1997) with its soaring spaces, bathed in daylight, picks up these same forms and is a spectacular gateway to the city. Whether arriving or departing, routes are easily navigable and orientation is simple: you are aware of the land on one side and the water on the other and you can see the aircraft. The vaulted roof provides a constant reference point as you move to or from your aircraft (Figure 66).

Departing passengers pass through the East Hall, the largest airport retail space in the world; if an airport on this scale can be thought of as a city in microcosm then this is its market square.[141]

The Terminal City at Idlewild set a precedent for future urban and aviation infrastructure of the jet age, such as *Aerotropolises* – actual urban city developments surging around airports.

American and European airports were the paramount example in airport architecture until the end of the twentieth century. Then the view shifted towards Asia, where aviation has been paramount to the regions' successes and a whole new infrastructural and mobility revolution has taken place.

From an architectural historian point of view, my intention was to trace where the origins of particular building ideas stem from. The role model function of train stations on airport terminals has been shown, as well as the multifunctionality they both share. The theme of viewing and spectatorship will be further discussed in the chapter about the performativity of airport architecture. The idea of dioramas and entertainment for travelers shall lead us on to the following chapter about the spatial and commercial aspects of airport design.

Figure 66: Hong Kong International Airport Chek Lap Kok, Norman Foster, Main Hall, photograph by Lilia Mironov

---

141 http://www.fosterandpartners.com/projects/chek-lap-kok-airport/

5   Tracing the Architecture of Leisure and Consumption in Airports

In this dissertation we are tracing spaces and places within airports, the aura, and the displacement or loss of belonging felt through globalization as caused by the hubris of an airport. Airports as well as train stations are the main places of transition that modernism has created. In the previous chapter we understood the beginnings of geographical mobility, which in a matter of a century has evolved into social mobility as well. Social mobility stands for the movement of individuals through a system of hierarchy and either gain or loss of class affiliation. It is the commute to work, the travel for business, the migration for better economic standing. Social mobility is also more metaphorical than local. Geographical mobility is moving by using means of transport.

The questions about *space* and the spatial in architecture have called into action not only architectural historians but geographers, philosophers, and anthropologists as well. Architects deal with the task of adapting human mobility of the nineteenth and twentieth century into the flow of urban infrastructure. We have seen the ideas of putting train stations and later on airports into the urban grids as envisioned by urbanists like Sant'Elia, Mendelsohn, and Le Corbusier. But philosophers and scholars see this mobility as an expression of upheaval and study the relationships between the inhabitants of the spaces and the spaces themselves.

Transitory spaces are a phenomenon not only of globalization, but of the advent of industrialism and modernism itself. They are places of movement, of industry, of self-determination, of superficiality – and of displacement, loss, homelessness. They are temporary as we only peruse them for certain actions, and make-

shift. They are inevitable for us as this is where we daily traverse from our private to our public lives through means of transport. They are arteries of liveliness and yet they are ephemeral. They encompass railroads, intersections, passageways, public places, and ultimately airports.

The present-day mix of identities and ethnicities makes it difficult to locate action and dwelling spaces of its inhabitants. To establish an academic discourse on the interpretation of our cultural use and identification through these spaces within the exceptional geography of an airport we need to go back in time to understand where the terms *home*, *private* and *public space*, *interior* and *exterior*, *transitory* and *hybrid* arise from, the places of dwelling and leisure and the so called *modern interior*.

The modern interior was formed in the second half of the nineteenth century in the new inside spaces of city arcades, commerce, culture, work, and public leisure.[142]

This chapter will introduce the theories and history of *space* and show how they have first shaped cities and how they correlate to airport design, especially how they have affected our consumption in places such as airports.

Space, which appears today to form the sum of our concerns, our theory and systems, is not an innovation, writes Michel Foucault; space has a history in Western experience, and it is not possible to disregard the fatal intersection of time and space. The space in which we live is where our time and history occur, we live inside a set of relations that delineate sites such as transportation, streets, trains, sites of temporary relaxation like

---

142 Penny Sparke, The Modern Interior, p 113

cafés and sites of rest like home. And there are spaces which are linked with all others, which, however, contradict all other sites – they are heterotopias and utopias.[143]

These questions about space and non-space have become more prevalent since the *spatial turn* which took place in the cultural sciences at the beginning of the 1990s – a time when sociologists and cultural theorists reconsidered the importance of space and its sciences for urban planning.[144]

We want to trace the *space*s of our existence, beginning with the spaces that we have lived, worked, and dwelled in since the industrialization.

5.1   Home

The dialectic between the outside and inside has been one of the driving discussions in the cultural sciences of the twentieth and twenty-first centuries. The French intellectual Gaston Bachelard (1884–1962) wrote in his *Poetics of Space* that a philosopher equals his thoughts on the inside and outside to that of being and not being. Openness and closeness are synonyms for the metaphysician who uses them to construct his thoughts. Concentrating on a phenomenological dissection of the house and its interior places such as the cellar, attic, drawers, wardrobes, corners, doors and their outdoor relations, Bachelard states that a house that has been lived in is not an inert box and inhabited space transcends geometrical space.[145]

Thus he concludes that in his example of Paris – and we will see further on in this work that Paris has been christened the Capital of the nineteenth century by German cultural critic Walter Benjamin (1892–1940) – there are no houses and its inhabitants live in superimposed boxes. Home has become a mere horizontality because we replaced stair climbing with elevators and the rooms pile up on top of the other in the multi-storied city buildings.

A house in a big city, according to him, lacks *cosmicity* and because it is no longer set in a natural surrounding its relationship with the space becomes artificial and mechanical. Such are Bachelard's thoughts on the complexity of the city house that he determines that really *any* inhabited space that has been appropriated by a human is *home*.[146]

This inhabited space is mainly a shell which takes over the imprints of its inhabitants, according to Benjamin:

143   Michel Foucault, Of other Spaces, p 317

144   Martina Löw, Raumsoziologie, p 9

145   Gaston Bachelard, The Poetics of Space, p 47

146   Ibid., The Poetics of Space, p 27

"The original form of all dwelling is existence not in the house but in the shell. The shell bears the impression of its occupant. [...]"[147]

Home is a big aspect in this dissertation as the longing for home or for a place that evokes the coziness, security, identification and feelings of being or belonging; home is the desire of many architectural endeavors, especially so in architecture of transitory spaces such as airports.

The importance of *home* as a safe haven has been a driving force in the movies of Steven Spielberg. In *E.T.* (1982), his little childlike alien phones home and wants to get home after a hapless stay on earth. And Spielberg's movie *The Terminal* (2004) tells the story of an Eastern European stranded in a New York airport terminal for months because a coup d'état in his home country rendered him stateless – a premise inspired by a real-life asylum seeker from Iran who spent years in the transit zone of a Paris airport.[148]

During the last decade and into the present, I have witnessed on select Swiss Air flights originating in Dar Es Salaam, Tanzania, UN-organized re-placements of refugees from Darfur via Zurich to their new home in detention centers in Chicago and Minnesota. Their journey is equally heartbreaking and alienating to witness. On the plane they are wearing yellow vests as a means of recognition and are subjected to the challenging obstacles of civilization such as flushable toilets and remote control video screens. In Zurich airport, during the hours-long transit they sit closely together in the "crisis heterotopia" that is the modern glass and steel terminal (2002, Marc Angélil architect). Three generations of refugees depicting the *biblical rest on the flight* into Chicago.

Tempelhof Airport was permanently closed for aviation in 2008, yet it is currently sheltering 2000 to 3000 refugees. The refugees are housed in tents within the old central terminal halls and on military beds. On the outside of the airside (towards the tarmac) 50 portable toilets have been set up for hygienic reasons. Somewhere in the terminal there is a makeshift playground for the youngest of them. How utterly alienating, that this place of progress, of repression and totalitarianism, of war and of hope (Rosinenbomber!) shall now house refugees as a safe haven. What is that place called like now? Is it a special zone? Keller Easterling depicts *ex-*

---

147 Walter Benjamin, The Arcades Project, p 221: "The original form of all dwelling is existence not in the house but in the shell. The shell bears the impression of its occupant. In the most extreme instance, the dwelling becomes a shell. The nineteenth century, like no other century, was addicted to dwelling. It conceived the residence as a receptacle for the person, and it encased him with all his appurtenances so deeply in the dwelling's interior that one might be reminded of the inside of a compass case, where the installment with all its accessories lies embedded in deep, usually violet folds of velvet. What didn't the nineteenth century invent some sort of casing for! Pocket watches, slippers, egg cups, thermometers, playing cards – and, in lieu of cases, there were jackets, carpets, wrappers, and covers. The twentieth century, with its porosity and transparency, its tendency toward the well-lit and airy, has put an end to dwelling in the old sense. Set off against the doll house in the residence of the master builder Solness are the 'homes for human beings'. Jugendstil unsettled the world of the shell in a radical way. Today this world has disappeared entirely, and dwelling has diminished: for the living, through hotel rooms; for the dead, through crematoriums."

Walter Benjamin's *Passagenwerk* (Passageways or Arcades Project), written between 1927 and 1940, is an epic kaleidoscope of reflections and discussions on societal changes examined through the setting in the mundane Paris arcades. It has become one of the defining cultural works of the twentieth century.

Tragically left unfinished due to his early passing (or murder or suicide), the Arcades Project was posthumously edited and released in Germany in 1982.

148 Paul Berczeller, The man who lost his past, The Guardian, 6 September 2004

trastatecraft as new constellations of infrastructure and governance through mobility and globalization:

"These special matrix spaces of infrastructure tutor and offer special techniques of formmaking and activism. Once relegated to the backstage, the *zone* has evolved from a fenced-off enclave for warehousing and manufacturing to a world-city template. For all its efforts to be apolitical, the zone is still a powerful political pawn, it is ripe for manipulation and its popularity makes it a multiplier of alternative technologies, urbanities, and politics."[149]

The *zone* is extrastatecraft, it is the appropriation of the original space. I also think that the refugee housing in Berlin Tempelhof Airport is extrastatecraft right here and now. It has been manipulated – or appropriated into this special zone by the politics of the migration crisis. Which again bridges to the 2016 Architecture Biennale of Venice which was dedicated to the infrastructure of the migration crisis.

How must the airport terminals in Tempelhof and Zurich feel like for these refugees, are they a temporary home, a symbol of freedom? Is the voyage, the airport, or the city the symbol of rescue, of home?

In the last two centuries, immigrants who sailed over the Atlantic towards the promised land *America* would first catch a glimpse of the Statue of Liberty on Ellis Island before entering Manhattan. Miss Liberty became a symbol of hope and arrival and ultimately home. Similarly, refugees from all over the world might get a first idea of salvation when passing through or arriving at an airport.

The symbolic and emotional relevance of an airport is tantamount to freedom and progress in society. The powerful emotions felt when arriving or departing since passenger flights were first invented have been described in literature and movies such as *Casablanca, A Foreign Affair, The Terminal* and many more where the symbolism of the airport is metonymic of a last goodbye and final escape into freedom.

Bachelard captures the sheltering feeling of home by stating that the house of the future is better built, is lighter and larger than all the houses of the past, so that the image of the dream house is opposed to that of the childhood home. He concludes that it is worthwhile to live in a state of impermanence with an image of a better home than in one of finality.[150]

We now have a distinct example of (temporary) *home* in an airport or the significance airports have for one's journey towards home.

The question arises here – away from the refugee sheltering aspect, which is indeed a special case and special *zone/extrastatecraft* – if an airport can separately perform as the house of the future or dream house, where one finds a temporary or surrogate *home* and flies away in an oneiric state of satisfaction.

The French philosopher Michel de Certeau wrote a book on peoples' rituals and actions in everyday life of mass culture and globalization, *The Practice of Everyday Life* (1980).[151] One of the most interesting chapters in this book is dedicated to spatial practices and aptly named "Walking in the City". In it, de Certeau discerns *space* from *place*. Basically, argues that our own

---

149 Keller Easterling, Extrastatecraft: The Power of Infrastructure, p 25–27
Easterling talks about the zones and free zones with their own special economics and custom-free wares in places such as China, Macao, Dubai, and South Korea. Easterling argues that contemporary infrastructure space is the secret weapon of the most powerful people in the world. Appropriation of places and spaces into special *zones* with new laws is what happens through globalization and politics.

150 Bachelard, The Poetics of Space, p 61

151 The French original title: L'invention du quotidien

identity which we carry to a physical place is created by the journey of traversing that space. This is a very personal journey for each of us and thus we bestow our identity onto the place – we imprint that connection onto the place with our journey through space – through our actions.[152]

De Certeau's spatial theories are in my opinion the most viable philosophical theories that can be transferred onto an airport terminal because, to say it bluntly, they make sense and they are directly transferable onto airports.

De Certeau gives the example of city maps, such as for New York, and how a tourist would choose certain attractions that he wants to visit:

He is probably connecting them via pen on this map. He has these still inert places in his mind and on the map and starts walking. Through this motion he begins a journey with experiences, no matter how minuscule or unimportant. Yet when he reaches each of the points of the map he has traversed a space which has become his personal experience of the city. Just as Bruce Chatwin described in his Songlines, it is the experience of the journey that creates space. It is this action of walking through the airport "shell" or "dwelling" which many airport architects have picked up as a means of experiencing the airport as a passenger.

When modern airports such as Incheon International Airport in Seoul, South Korea (2001), create a concourse with the specific intention of inviting the passenger to "experience" the culture and architecture by participating in cultural performances and craftworks in the art experience booths when they casually stroll by, then this is a direct translation of de Certeau's thesis on creating an own individual (journey-)space within a physical place (Figure 67).

Figure 67: Korea Traditional Cultural Experience Center in Incheon Airport, Seoul, 2001. Fentress Architects, Photograph by Lilia Mironov

This is an ephemeral experience of *home*, intended to pass the time in transit. But an experience upon which more and more importance is being laid as airport operators and retailers have understood the interconnection of "people experience" and consumption.

Similar reflections on the oneiric (dreamlike) effect of house and home come from Georges Teyssot's essay on the *Traumhaus: L'intérieur comme innervation du collectif* (2011) where we can read that the writer Charles Baudelaire thought of the city as an immense interior where at night you can close the curtains and light the candles.[153]

Teyssot sees Benjamin's *Arcades Project* (Passagenwerk), which he started in anthological form in 1928 and left unfinished until its publication in 1983, as an illustrious treatise of the oneiric and awakening world in the cityscape of Paris, as well as the thresholds of everyday life in Paris as experienced within its arcade architecture.

---

152 Michel de Certeau, Praktiken im Raum (The Practice of Everyday Life), p 345

153 Georges Teyssot, Traumhaus. L'intérieur comme innvervation du collectif, p 8

Coincidentally, in his *Arcades Project*, Walter Benjamin sought out to portray the dreamlike quality of the city of the nineteenth century and the thresholds of architecture that determine it by calling the interior an asylum of art. The collector is the true resident of the interior and creates his realm by accumulating commodities through which he can dream of a distant or bygone and certainly better world. To dwell means to leave traces and the traces of the inhabitant are imprinted in the interior.[154]

As such, Benjamin names arcades, winter gardens, panoramas, factories, wax museums, casinos, and railroad stations the "dreamhouses of the collective".[155] This again ties to the question if airports can be dreamhouses and offer a temporary home where passengers and workers leave traces and, if so, how this can be established. Given that we have seen that modern airport hubs take on the form of a city (Aerotropolis), the comparison of an airport with a city lies at hand.

5.2   The Interior and Exterior

By his expression of „sortilège des seuils", meaning *the spell of the thresholds*, Benjamin evokes the magic created by the passageways of Paris such as their porches, vestibules and beautiful entrances, bestowing upon them a dreamlike quality. This answers partly or at least superficially our question on the relation to airports. It is when airports recreate certain city and home motifs that travelers can experience in and identify with this place that is neither home nor work but aspires to be a little bit of all. Perhaps it is Benjamin himself who can give us the best answer when he states that the private

individual who works outside home in an office where he deals with reality, needs his domestic interior to sustain his illusions … and from this arise the phantasmagorias of the interior – this is where he brings theses commodities which he acquires outside, to recreate his dream world.[156]

In the previous chapter on the initial typology of airport terminals we saw early examples of American airports from the 1920s and 1930s modeled after French castles or Italian palazzi with porticos, columns, and vestibules. It is doubtful that their architects had intended to create an oneiric state of mind in the airport "dwellers" back then, rather than building them as a pioneering experimentation with a completely new building type which prevailed in the much liked historicism architecture found in America between the 1880s and 1940s.

No longer are such antiquated historical pastiches to be found in modern airport architecture, but the segregation within airport spaces above all is made of thresholds, such as entrances, check-in, control and security spaces, dwelling and consuming spaces, entertainment spaces.

As for the phantasmagorias of the interior of an airport, the Butterfly Garden, Kinetic Rain Sculpture, and an upscale shopping mall at Changi Airport in Singapore are only one of many examples for this. Its Terminal 3 (2007, SOM) is a steel-and-glass structure with four above-ground levels and a 9-acre roof that spans ticketing, departure and arrival areas. The overhead light modulation system consists of glass skylights and thousands of aluminum louvers. During the day, the sensor-driven louvers limit the amount of direct

---

154 Benjamin, The Arcades Project, p 9

155 Ibid., p 405

156 Ibid., p 405:
Phantasmagorias were a form of horror theater around the eighteenth and nineteenth century, often shown at fairs and exhibitions, with the use of magic lanterns and often with puppets or miniature figures. It was a cheap thrill that lasted a few seconds or minutes, as long as the projector rotated, involving fantastic stories. For Benjamin they were a materialistic expression, a commodity.

Figure 68: Kinetic Rain sculpture, Singapore Changi Airport, photograph courtesy of Choo Yut Shing

the traveler, such as various theme gardens (cactus, lily, orchid, butterfly, foliage) throughout its three terminals, as well as art installations.

The two *Kinetic Rain* sculptures in Terminal 1 are made of 1,216 bronze droplets and are the latest addition to Changi Airport's collection of art installations and displays (Figure 68). Kinetic Rain is the biggest and most complex kinetic sculpture of its kind in the world, located for the first time ever at Changi Airport.[158] Though an optical *spiel* and not a horror theater as was the original meaning of phantasmagoria, it is a magical illusion, which is what Benjamin's understanding ultimately was. It is supposed to add a contemplative element to the lively transit space of the departure hall[159] (Figures 68 & 69).

Figure 69: Singapore Changi Airport, Butterfly Garden, photograph courtesy of Dr. Raju Kasambe

sunlight that enters the space by filling it with diffused light. At night, artificial light reflects off the louvers to provide a uniform pattern of illumination. This is constructed primarily for aesthetic appeal, while the sophisticated technology helps minimize lighting and cooling costs.[157]

To tie onto Benjamin's excerpt on the place of dwelling that is opposed to the place of work and offers phantasmagorias of the interior, Changi Airport is the right example of a little city in itself, offering shopping, dining and entertainment venues (spa, movie theater) but above all an abundance of sensual experiences for

---

157 http://www.som.com/projects/changi_international_airport__terminal_3)

158 http://www.changiairport.com/en/airport-experience/attractions-and-services/kinetic-rain.html.

159 https://artcom.de/en/project/kinetic-rain/:
Measuring 9.8 meters by 4 meters, each sculpture can form 16 different shapes ranging from abstract art forms to recognizable patterns including an aeroplane, a hot air balloon, a kite and even a dragon. The design element in each shape shows the movement of flight through slow, fluid movements. Each droplet is connected to a motor which is housed in the ceiling of the Departure Hall.
The Kinetic Rain sculpture was created over a span of 20 months by the German design studio Art+Com which specializes in media installations and spaces in 2012. The collaboration of artists, programmers and technologists was tasked to develop an artwork that enhances the identity of Changi's new Terminal 1. Aptly themed "Tropical City", Changi's new Terminal 1 is synonymous with Singapore's garden city reputation where rain is a common feature in the tropical climate. With more than a thousand raindrops working together in harmony, the Kinetic Rain sculpture also symbolizes the coming together of the thousands in the airport community to provide a positively surprising Changi Experience for passengers and visitors. The visual experience of the complex computer-designed movement is completely different depending on the perspective.

Incheon Airport in Seoul, which is mentioned in this thesis a few times, offers many spaces for contemplation and recreation, such as Zen-Gardens and recreated Buddhist temples. It even offers scheduled classical concert performances throughout the day within the check-in terminal (Figures 70 & 71).

Referring to the sweeping gaze and perspectivism in connection with the first railway travel experience, mentioned in the first chapter, as well as to the empowered and self-determined viewer/traveler, we can see here that the play with perspective viewing and vistas within airport interiors is an ongoing theme. Contemplation and sublime seduction to linger create the foremost effect on the viewing traveler/spectator.

The spatial term *third place* was created by American sociologist Ray Oldenburg in his 1989 book *The Great Good Place*, depicting those places of modern civilization where people outside of home and work can thrive and exist.[160]

Figure 70: Seoul Incheon Airport, musical performance space, photograph by Lilia Mironov
Figure 71: Seoul Incheon Airport, Korean Garden, photograph by Lilia Mironov

160 Ray Oldenburg, The Great Good Place: Cafes, coffee shops, bookstores, bars, hair salons and other hangouts at the heart of the community

Here, the *third place* is a synonym for the sociable places that people frequent between the realms of home and work – and those include airports, where we can see the particular emphasis on this third place kind of setting. Anything outside of the workplace makes up an individual person's interior. For Benjamin, the advent of modernity coincided with the emergence of the private individual.[161]

Walter Benjamin defines the nineteenth century as the age of dwelling in a shell as opposed to a house. He deems the contents of the interior shell a decoration and imprint of the user, which then again reflect on the exterior found outside in the arcades. He suggests that the user of the arcades wants to recreate their splendor (phantasmagorias) in his empty shell-home. According to British academic Penny Sparke, the *modern interior* was incepted between the nineteenth and twentieth centuries and encompassed more inside spaces than those contained within the home.[162]

It was the women who were most responsible for this new awareness of interior decoration as they sought to replicate the interiors they saw outside of their home in the department stores, cafés and exhibition hall settings. Hence, this "interior movement" is defined by the everyday experiences, especially of women, during those years – they encompass the home, the office, the factory, the department store and the café. Sparke picks up on Benjamin's reciprocal relationship between the exterior of the arcades and the empty shell interior and the desire to decorate the latter with commodities from the arcades.[163]

The prevalent consumption of goods such as food, clothing, dwelling, and furniture at this particular period was the domain of the lady and the rest of the domestic establishment. Yet American economist Thorstein Veblen traces the specialized consumption of goods as an "evidence of pecuniary strength" back to predatory cultures of humanity, where the hunting and gathering of trophies was by far antedating the emergence of the lady.[164]

The interior is about our relationships and private affairs at home with regard to the outside city streets (which since the advent of industrialization had also been illuminated by gas and later electricity) and about the interior's role in defining modern identities – the exit from the home into the bustling streets, the construction of the modern "self" through this action of autonomy. There is a "constant tension" between our private interiors and public (as in work) identity. Sparke's *interiorization* effect describes the continuous expansion of interior spaces, which helped create and control social and cultural distinctions and hierarchies.[165]

---

161 Benjamin, The Arcades Project, p 8

162 Penny Sparke, The Modern Interior: a Euro-American paradigm, p 1. As a Professor of Design History at Kingston University, UK, Sparke specializes in The Interior as a defining philosophy in the field of architecture of modernism, globalization, glocalization (hybridity), and localization.

163 Ibid., p 8
In another essay for the magazine *Interiors*, Sparke corrects the use of *modern* when in context with interiors:
"Indeed, if the ideas of Walter Benjamin are to be embraced, the addition of the epithet 'modern' to the noun 'interior' is redundant as, for Benjamin, the (domestic) interior emerged as a defining feature of mid-nineteenth-century industrial modernity – manifested in the split between the private and the public spheres – and was, therefore, sine qua non, modern." (Penny Sparke, "The Modern Interior: A Space, a place or a Matter of Taste?", in: Interiors: Design/Architecture/Culture, Vol. 1, Issue 1, 2010. Ed. Anne Massey and John Turpin. p 9).

164 Thorstein Veblen, The Theory of the Leisure Class, p 43

165 Sparke, The Modern Interior., p 13

With that said, the domestic interior was defined by the outside world of mass consumption. Interiors in commercial spaces in which goods were displayed created the desire to purchase.[166] This "inside-out" effect has prevailed to present times, with seasonal window displays of upscale department stores on Fifth Avenue recreating nostalgic winter wonderlands and comfy and cozy interiors of homely quietude with the perfect family.

German philosopher Hannah Arendt's chapter "The Public and the Private Realm" in her book *The Human Condition* talks of the *vita activa*, as the human life which is actively engaged in doing something, and is always rooted in a world of men and man-made things which it never leaves or altogether transcends.[167]

For Arendt, the public realm is the essential human condition that creates remembrance and history – the human activity produces fabricated things and the environment of our world. Arendt's book even has a chapter titled "The Polis and the Household" which is devoted to the public versus private identities – the spheres of the polis and the spheres of the private household. She describes the distinctive trait of the household sphere as that of men (humans) living together driven by their wants and needs, where the driving force is life itself. She quotes this in relation to Plutarch, from a historical point of view on the ancient Greek democracy.[168] To leave the household in order to embark upon some adventure and later to devote to the affairs of the city, demanded courage, because only in the household was one primarily concerned with one's own private life and survival. The household was home and a safe haven.

The construction of the "self" as a conspicuous consumer was also apparent through the self-determined gazing view of the traveler or emancipated spectator. The traveling experience which emerged through the railways in the mid-nineteenth century and its panoramic effect on the viewer all led to new modes of perception which were tied to social mobility and consumption, with the Grand Tour leading the way. The architecture of consumption stems from all these interconnected ties between the modern interior, the gazing (panoramic) view, and the spectator traveling and seeking a third space in between it all.

Ultimately, Benjamin connects the newly emerged technologies in architecture, consumption, and art within the Jugendstil, on which he blames the shattering of the interior around the turn of the century. "Jugendstil transFigures the solitary soul and nurtures the individual". Van de Velde's house becomes an expression of personality (note from author: Henry van de Velde was the Belgian interior designer considered as the founder of *art nouveau*).

"Ornament becomes the signature of the house. Jugendstil evolved as an expression of the inwardness of the interior being besieged in its ivory tower by technology." The expression of the flower as a symbol of nature and nurturing was challenged by the new elements of iron and concrete construction and merged into Jugendstil.[169]

---

166 Ibid., p 55
167 Hannah Arendt, The Human Condition, p 22
168 Ibid., p 28
169 Benjamin, The Arcades Project, p 9

5.3   Glass and Iron

"The Glass House has no purpose other than to be beautiful. It is intended purely as a structure for exhibition and should be a beautiful source of ideas for "lasting" architecture but is not itself intended as such."[170]

Figure 72: Bruno Taut's Glass Pavilion, 1914

Bruno Taut's opening words in his contributing text for the Deutsche Werkbund Exhibition (The German Work Federation) 1914 in Cologne, for which he created his well-known glass pavilion, were quite subversive. According to Taut and his expressionist peers, glass and crystal were metaphors of an enlightened society, a symbolism inspired and nourished by the German enlightenment and the crystalline formality of gothic cathedrals. Taut devoted the pavilion to the German author Paul Scheerbart whose fantastic essays on glass architecture influenced him. One of Scheerbart's quotes picked up by Taut in his accompanying essay on glass architecture reads: „Der gotische Dom ist das Präludium der Glasarchitektur" – the gothic cathedral is the prelude to glass architecture.[171]

In 1913, Bruno Taut defined the symbolic architecture, which borrowed from the crystal, as *crystalline* (Figure 72). The crystalline as an object and classification has been discussed as a metaphorical device ever since the romanticists. The German novelist Novalis (who around 1800 had passed away in young age) was well versed in mineralogy and considered the crystal to be a topos of the whole. He connected the crystal to the innocence of a child, to potent romantic visions and utopias of peace, purity and artistry – metaphors picked up by the architects of expressionism and members of Taut's Crystal Chain like Hans Scharoun and Walter Gropius. Indeed, Taut conceived his paper *Alpine Architektur* (1917) as an anti-war manifesto. There was a reciprocity between literature and science in connection with the crystal.

Novalis would describe mineralogical peculiarities just like Johann Wolfgang Goethe did as inspector of mining engineering in Sachsen-Weimar-Eisenach. Along with the petrographic analysis of the crystal there was the symbolic perception which mainly addressed the aesthetic effect of the crystal and which opened the road for new architectural creations such as the Crystal Palace.

---

170 Bruno Taut, Glashaus, p 101, in German: „Das Glashaus hat keinen anderen Zweck, als schön zu sein [...]."

171 Ibid., p 287ff. Bruno Taut created a series of letters to his fellow expressionist artist friends which was aptly named the "Crystal Chain"; they imagined a world of artistry and visionary hope.

The romantic German philosopher Friedrich Schlegel is said to have compared the gothic cathedrals of Cologne and Strassburg to a forest from afar, with the little towers resembling soaring branches; but when approaching, those cathedrals alluded to a gigantic natural crystallization. The Gothic style with its harmonious perfection of composite work became a rather conservative topic during the Napoleonic occupation of Germany and paved the road to the reception of the crystalline as the most sought after and modern construction motif – the simultaneously emerging glass and iron construction.[172]

Thus, glass and iron ebbed the way to large, open, and transparent interior spaces. It proved a new architectural aesthetic to represent the modern age. It transformed public spaces and created new public interiors, emphasized the objects located in these interior places and connected to the outside visual spectacle of urban streets.[173]

Glass architecture captured a "light-space", with the "striving for lightness" being the main motivating force in the developmental history of interior space. It defined the transition between outside and inside that gives us our sense of interior space and the building its character.[174]

In his *Passageways*, Benjamin describes how the gaze of the allegorist (protagonist) falls on the city. This allegorist is the *flâneur* of the metropolis who represents the middle class. The crowd is the veil through which the familiar city beckons to the flâneur as a phantasmagoria – sometimes as a landscape, sometimes as a room. The flâneur (shopper) became a passive spectator. Both become elements of the department store which uses the flânerie to sell goods – the department store is the last promenade for the flâneur. The flâneur saunters, strolls around, reflects on the city.[175]

The emergence of the glass passages coincides with the boom in the textile trade, and as such "magasins de nouveautés" they became the forerunners of the de-

---

172 Bernd Nicolai, Kristallbau, p 43–46: In 1913 Bruno Taut declared the symbolic architecture which borrowed from the crystal a *Gesamtkunstwerk*. Based on the ideal of gothic architecture and its masons guilds, his vision inspired the later *Bauhaus-Manifesto* of Walter Gropius in 1919, wherein the Gesamtkunstwerk and the idea of the guild form a symbiosis of craftsmanship. The Bauhaus-philosophy is an appeal to architects and artists to work on future architecture as a collective.

173 Sparke, The Modern Interior, p 113

174 Schivelbusch, Geschichte der Eisenbahnreise: Zur Industrialisierung von Raum und Zeit im 19. Jahrhundert, p 46

175 Gerald Staib, Glass Construction Manual, p 10–13: "The word *glass* stems from the old Germanic term *glaza* for amber, but also depicts something shining or shimmering. The Latin *glaesum* is the denomination of amber. In French *vitre* and *verre* are the names for window and glass respectively. Glass has been used as a tool or ornament in its naturally occurring form as volcanic obsidian and other minerals since the Stone Age, but officially dated archeological evidence dates back to the fifth millennia before Christ, in ancient Syria and Mesopotamia. During the Middle Ages the technique was perfected north of the Alps. Glass factories ('Glashütten' in German) arose near forests where the wood was used for the heating process and along rivers, for the cooling needed by the water. Traditionally glass factories would go hand in hand with the production of churches and cathedrals.
In Venice, the glass tradition flourished between the fifteenth and seventeenth centuries, with the production of bowls, cups, drinking glasses and mirrors becoming characteristic of Venetian culture. To protect against incendiaries, the Venetian glass production was moved onto the islet of Murano where the glass artisanry bore the same name.
Yet glass has remained a very precious good throughout the centuries before mass production in the twentieth and twenty-first centuries. At the end of the eighteenth century, British coachmen would still remove the glass panels from their carriages at night in order to preserve them for the next day. In 1856, Friedrich Siemens took out a patent on a glass-melting oven. Meanwhile in England, the Brothers Chance succeeded in the production of cylinder blown sheet glass and in polishing it into a stable surface in 1839. This ebbed the way to the façade of the Crystal Palace for which they provided the glass sheets."

Figure 73: Shanghai Pudong International Airport, Paul Andreu, 1999

Figure 74: Seoul Incheon Airport, Fentress Architects, 2001 Glass and steel arcade architecture in the concourse and gate areas, different countries, different architects, same popular style. Photographs by Lilia Mironov

partment stores, a center of commerce in luxury items. Benjamin describes the arcades as a recent invention of industrialism and as glass-roofed, marble-paneled corridors extending through whole blocks of buildings, lined on both sides by the most elegant shops, so that there is a city, a world in miniature within them.[176]

Arcades and passageways define modern airport terminals:

The curved glass walls with steel framework and undulating roof of French architect Paul Andreu's Shang-

hai Pudong International Airport (1999) call to mind Walter Benjamin's famous passageways (Figure 73). Strikingly similar is Curtis Fentress' concourse for Seoul Incheon Airport, constructed only two years after Andreu's (Figure 74).

The societal need for a gathering place in the town or village center can be traced back to prehistoric times where a tribe or people would gather around a cult-like fireplace or temple. The *agora* of the ancient Greek was a forerunner to the inner city public places of modern times where outdoor markets (and in the nineteenth

---

176 Benjamin, The Arcades Project, Exposé of 1935, p 3

century glass arcades) would be erected. In the industrial age the individual would dwell in these public and semi-public places where he could dine, saunter and buy goods, thus create his own special sophisticated existence within these premises. City planners and architects would take on the task of creating such public gathering places in order to lure the people to consume within them.[177]

Benjamin's musings on the *Flâneur* are of utmost relevance to the humanities and the research on the *Interior* as through them we learn about the societal development and changes during and after the age of the industrial revolution, and the interconnectedness between the private and public interiors through consumer goods and architecture.

Benjamin states that the second condition of the emergence of arcades is the beginning of iron construction, in fact, "for the first time in the history of architecture, an artificial building material appears: iron."[178] This development was already visible from the 1820s onwards with the railway and locomotive and the first prefabricated iron components. Iron was not used in home construction but in buildings that served transitory purposes such as arcades, exhibition halls, and train stations.

When the wooden cupola of the Granary in Paris was destroyed by a fire in 1802, it was replaced by an iron and copper construction on which the architect Bellangé and the engineer Brunet collaborated. The new iron material substituted the ribs of the woodwork. Iron replaced previously solid stone walls into slender skeletons of columns and beams; interior spaces could thus be built on a grander scale and without intervening columns. Walls lost their loadbearing function and could be replaced by a transparent skin of glass to admit the light.[179]

It was the architect Jean-François Fontaine who first fused glass and iron architecture in his construction of the Galerie d'Orléans which belonged to the Palais Royal. Siegfried Giedion states that Fontaine, who with Percier founded the Empire style in his later years (1829–1831) used wrought iron to construct the glass roof of the Galerie d'Orléans.[180]

The glass-covered public shopping street flanked by shops was called an arcade and became a characteristic trait of nineteenth century architecture. From the 1820s the continuous pitched glass roof became a common feature, ensuring maximal daylight with minimum framing. Their glass panes were often imbricated and laid with a small clearance to allow hot air to escape.[181]

The now defunct Galerie d'Orléans distinguished itself from other such galleries like the Royal Opera Arcade in London, which has circular glass openings cut into the vaulting, allowing the light from the hidden

---

177 Benjamin, The Arcades Project: Paris, the Capital of the Nineteenth Century, Exposé of 1935, p 26

178 Ibid., p 4

179 Staib, Glass Construction Manual, p 17

180 Giedion, Space, Time and Architecture, p 136: Up until the 19th century, timber-frame constructions and vaults or domes made of stone were the methods of choice for erecting roofs over large interiors.
The passage of light through a dome was defined by the character of this construction and only possible through the apex like in the Pantheon or through smaller openings at the base of the dome as in the Hagia Sophia. But thanks to iron, vaults could now be broken down into immaterial supporting structures, replacing timber plank roofs with metal sheets and glass.
It was at the end of the eighteenth century that the technology became available to use iron as an independent material for construction when coke was determined as suitable for smelting iron ore. The steam engine and other technical improvements advanced the production of cast iron. Cast iron evolved into wrought iron with higher loading capacity and superior performance.

181 Staib, Glass Construction Manual, p 17

glass roof to pour into the building through these apertures. Fontaine's gallery, on the other hand, gave an impression of freedom and openness and the illusion of outdoorness. The glass-iron-vaulting of the Galerie d'Orléans was a complete novelty in architecture and the precursor of future grand galleries and arcades such as the Galleria Vittorio Emanuele II in Milano (1865–1867 by Giuseppe Mengoni) (Figures 75 & 76).

The Galerie d'Orléans was the gathering place of the elegant society, but was destroyed in 1935 when the Palais Royal was remodeled. In fact, the interplay between inside and outside which was facilitated by the glass and iron roofing in the Galerie d'Orléans set a precedent for the theme of this dissertation.

Figure 75: Galleria Vittorio Emmanuele II, Milan, drawing before 1891, courtesy of Immanuel Giel
Figure 76: Galleria Vittorio Emmanuele II, Milan, courtesy of José Luiz Bernardes Ribeiro

5.4   Crystal Palace

*"World exhibitions are places of pilgrimage to the commodity fetish.
World exhibitions propagate the universe of commodities."*

Walter Benjamin[182]

The first so called *event architecture* can be attributed to Joseph Paxton's Crystal Palace built for the first international exhibition – the *Great Exhibition of the Works of All Nations* – which was held in London's Hyde Park in 1851 in a gigantic greenhouse, named the *Crystal Palace*. Its interior spaces provided an encounter with modernity for one third of the British people.[183] During its five months of exhibition over six million visitors strolled through the galleries.

While industry was undergoing its greatest expansion in the second half of the nineteenth century, industrial exhibitions offered the opportunity for learning about creative architecture, new inventions, and merchandises. During that period new machines and processes were invented and the result of this work was demonstrated at early exhibitions about mines, mills, and machine shops. In 1798, the first industrial exhibition was held in Paris – that first exhibiting period ended in 1849. These exhibitions all had a national character and displayed national products.[184]

Joseph Paxton was primarily a gardening enthusiast and expert on greenhouses – he had specialized in creating those such as the Great Conservatory in Chatsworth in 1836, back then the largest glass and cast-iron building known. He had experimented with glasshouse construction, using prefabricated cast-iron, laminated wood and standard-sized glass sheets for his greenhouses before he was bestowed the task of constructing the Crystal Palace. Paxton's design was based on a 10 inch x 49 inch module, the size of the largest glass sheet available at the time. (Figures 77 & 79).[185]

The design was also influenced by Paxton's passion for biomimicry; he drew inspiration from the giant leaves of the Victoria Amazonica waterlily.

182 Benjamin, Arcades Project, p 7–8

183 Sparke, The Modern Interior, p 115

184 Giedion, Space, Time and Architecture, p 244: The first national industrial exhibition, the première exposition des produits de l'industrie française in Paris in 1798 was opened on the Champs-de-Mars grounds. There were only 110 exhibitors in this first exhibition, which had the character of a people's festival.

185 Chup Friemert, Die gläserne Arche: Kristallpalast London, p 7–11: Henry Cole, Digby Wyatt and the architect Owen Jones amongst others were members of the Society for the Encouragement of Arts, Manufacture and Commerce which was founded in 1754. From 1847 Prince Albert served as President. The abbreviated name is Royal Society of the Arts. https://www.thersa.org/about-us/archive-and-history/

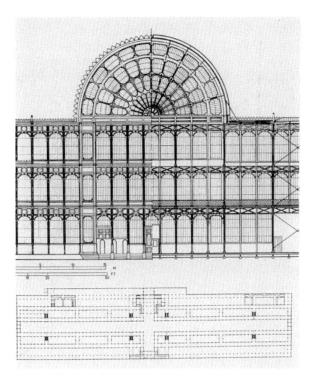

Figure 77: Crystal Palace, Joseph Paxton. Sketch from 1851

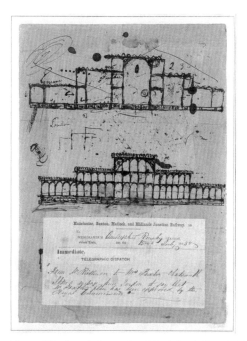

Figure 78: Joseph Paxton's original sketch from 1850, pen and ink on pink blotting paper, mounted on a sheet of woven paper with a telegram form. Courtesy of Victoria and Albert Museum

Figure 79: Crystal Palace, Joseph Paxton, photographic print ca. 1860. Courtesy of Library of Congress Prints and Photographs Division Washington

To counteract on the possibility of experiencing a feeling of being lost in this transcendental state (Philip Ursprung quotes Gottfried Semper speaking of a "vacuum" when describing the vast space), Paxton had the architect Owen Jones create a color schematic of red, yellow and blue for the metal parts of the interior in order to help structuralize the interior.[186]

With only eight months until the exhibition, 5000 laborers worked on the construction on site in Hyde Park, installing more than 1000 iron columns and 84,000 square meters of glass – all these parts were prefabricated and easy to erect, with every modular unit being self-supporting. The construction could be completed within five months. When the exhibition was closed six months later, the structure was disassembled and then reassembled in the south London suburb of Sydenham Hill. Unfortunately, that building was destroyed in a fire in 1936.[187]

On May 1, 1851 the exhibition was inaugurated by Queen Victoria. Hundreds of thousands of Britons lined the streets in celebration of the Royal Family. Albert, the Prince Consort, had proposed the four great divisions inside the building in 1849. They were: Raw Materials, Machinery, Manufactures, and Sculpture[188] (Figure 80).

Great Britain and its colonies (British Dependencies were approached through the Colonial Secretary to participate, whereas India was represented by the East India Company) supplied 7200 of the 17062 exhibitors in the premises. The rest of the world was represented by France, States of the German Empire, Austria, the United States, Belgium, Russia, Switzerland and many more in declining order according to their representation.[189]

Figure 80: Louis Haghe, color lithograph, 1851. Queen Victoria opens the Great Exhibition in the Crystal Palace in Hyde Park, London

186 Philip Ursprung, Phantomschmerzen der Architektur: Verschwindende Körper und Raumprothesen, p 22

187 Gili Merin, Archdaily.com

188 Hermione Hobhouse, The Crystal Palace and the Great Exhibition, p 40

189 Friemert, Die gläserne Arche: Kristallpalast London, p 44

The aesthetic effect of the Crystal Palace on its visitors was tremendous. It was the event of the decade for the Britons. In a letter to her father, dated May 30, 1851, the writer Charlotte Brontë tells of her experience visiting the Crystal Palace:

"[..] Yesterday we went to the Crystal Palace. The exterior has a strange and elegant but somewhat unsubstantial effect. The interior is like a Vanity Fair. The brightest colors blaze on all sides [...]"[190]

Charlotte Brontë's awe and emotional experience of the Crystal Palace were very telling of the psychological impact of the Crystal Palace, but also reveal the aforementioned synesthetic effect on the senses of vision and perception that were discussed in the earlier chapter about the synesthetic effects of railway travel. I am including Brontë's impressions because I love that author and like the book *A Room with a View*, both capture the sentiments of artworks on the flâneurs of their time.

The Crystal Palace was a bazaar of multitude indeed. The building became a sensation for its interior and a paradigm for consumerism and event architecture.

There is a duality within the Crystal Palace between the informality of its architecture and skin (in this case glass) and the prosthetic substitute of its abundant exhibitions on display. Never before had so much volume been encased by such a fragile mass.[191]

The blurred border between the interior and exterior seemed to dissolve and needed to be redefined by this novel construction style. The dissolution of established spatial categories and the perception shock of the membrane-like boundary let the architect Richard Lucae call it an "enchanted poetic air structure" and a piece of "cut-out atmosphere".[192]

Numerous notable European architects, such as Gottfried Semper or Richard Lucae offered views and thoughts on the building – Lucae considered the glass palace of Sydenham, where the Crystal Palace had been reassembled after the World Fair, as simply unique. He argued that unlike a train station, which is

---

190   Shorter Clement King, The Brontës: Life and Letters 512, p 212–217
      And in another letter dated June 7, 1851, Brontë writes: "[…] Yesterday I went for the second time to the Crystal Palace. We remained in it about three hours, and I must say I was more struck with it on this occasion than at my first visit. It is a wonderful place – vast, strange, new and impossible to describe. Its grandeur does not consist in one thing, but in the unique assemblage of all things. Whatever human industry has created you find there, from the great compartments filled with railway engines and boilers, with mill machinery in full work, with splendid carriages of all kinds, with harness of every description, to the glass-covered and velvet-spread stands loaded with the most gorgeous work of the goldsmith and silversmith, and the carefully guarded caskets full of real diamonds and pearls worth hundreds of thousands of pounds. It may be called a bazaar or a fair, but it is such a bazaar or fair as Eastern genii might have created. It seems as if only magic could have gathered this mass of wealth from all the ends of the earth – as if none but supernatural hands could have arranged it this, with such a blaze and contrast of colors and marvelous power of effect. The multitude filling the great aisles seems ruled and subdued by some invisible influence. Amongst the thirty thousand souls that peopled it the day I was there not one loud noise was to be heard, not one irregular movement seen; the living tide rolls on quietly, with a deep hum like the sea heard from the distance."

191   Ursprung, Phantomschmerzen der Architektur, p 21

192   Richard Lucae, Über die Macht des Raumes in der Baukunst, p 294–306

not a perfected and contained space per se, the Sydenham glass palace enchanted the visitors by its artificially created surroundings which ceased being contained by spatial boundaries.[193]

Philosopher-provocateur Peter Sloterdijk muses that with its crystalline construction, the principle of the interior overstepped a critical boundary: it began to reconfigure the outside world as a whole with a magical immanence transfigured by luxury and cosmopolitanism. "Converted into a large hothouse and an imperial culture museum, it revealed the timely tendency to make both nature and culture indoor affairs. Further, it anticipated the era of stadium pop with classical schedules presented to huge audiences."[194]

Only through the genius loci – the exhibition space contained within glass walls – being illuminated by natural lighting and yet detached from the outside world and offering whole new little worlds on display did the Crystal Palace approach the Phantasmogara that Benjamin later mentioned in his Passagenwerk.

German intellectuals speak of the "Wahrnehmungsschock" – the aesthetic perception shock so to say, when talking about the building's effect on the spectators.[195]

A lot has been attributed to the effect of the Crystal Palace – being the aesthetic origin of modernism as well as creating a new spatial perception by the use of glass which dissolves the interior and exterior threshold. It was also a precursor to globalization – a World Exposition displaying arts and crafts from different parts of the world under the same roof, yet for each spectator a different phenomenological experience.

The dissolution of boundaries and spatial expansion within the premises stole the limelight from the actual wares and arts on display.

Monika Wagner mentions perception problems ever since the exhibition opened.

Citing the London Times coverage of the event (May 23, 1851), she writes that when one first visited the exhibition one was not really aware of the spectacular displays as the senses were fully immersed into grasping the vast architectural and crystalline openness of the building. It was the sublime overall impression of the building as an aesthetic experience that struck the visitors most.[196] Alas, that kind of overall impression had to be a confusing one on the spectator. What we nowadays call the Guggenheim or Bilbao effect – how an aesthetically created museum can turn a city or region into a cultural hub and its architecture overshadow the exhibitions within – firstly occurred with the Crystal Palace.

Peter Sloterdijk, not unaccustomed to philosophical provocations, speaks of the "establishment and arrangement of the capitalist world interior" in regard to the Crystal Palace and cites the Russian writer Fyodor Dostoyevsky's novel *Notes from the Underground* (1864) as a metaphor for the large-scale enclosure of the Great Exhibition of 1851 in London. He describes how Dostoyevsky believed that the Crystal Palace held the essence of Western civilization. The Russian writer deemed it to be a man-eating structure, a "cult container in which humans pay homage to the demons

---

193 Ursprung, Phantomschmerzen, p 21: Ursprung mentions the difference between the nave and transept of the Sydenham palace which was mainly built in order to preserve three old elms when originally standing in Hyde Park. This gave the transept more of a greenhouse effect.

194 Peter Sloterdijk, In the World Interior of Capital, p 170

195 Monika Wagner, Die erste Londoner Weltausstellung als Wahrnehmungsphänomen, p 31

196 Ibid., p 32

of the West: the power of money and pure movement, along with voluptuous and intoxicating pleasures."[197]

The construction of the Crystal Palace was followed by the "crystallization" – the "intention to generalize boredom normatively and prevent the re-irruption of history into the post-historical world."[198] Here Sloterdijk obviously draws parallels to our current capitalist society with the concept of human rights being inseparable from the self-fulfillment of the consumer. Sloterdijk compares both Dostoyevsky's interpretation of the Crystal Palace as well as Benjamin's of the Parisian arcades. In both cases an architectural form was declared as the key to understanding modern capitalism and consumer society.

Although deeming Benjamin's eponymous oeuvre on as an anachronistic phenomenon by remaining fixated on an architecturally, economically and aesthetically obsolete type of building which "carried the burden of a hermeneutics of capital", and calling Benjamin's pretensions in searching the timeless within the outdated as "unclear", Sloterdijk does grant Benjamin the observation that the arabesques of arcade architecture reveal a Marxist observation that the shiny surfaces of the commodity world conceal the less pleasant and bleak working world.[199]

When the Great Exhibition was over, the Hyde Park site had to return to its previous green state. Paxton set up a company to arrange for a new home for the Crystal Palace, despite it initially being intended as a temporary structure. The Crystal Palace was dismantled, shipped, and re-erected in Sydenham on the outskirts of London, its second and last site. The rebuilt building used twice the glass it had at Hyde Park to accommodate an increase in size and the addition of a barrel-vault transept at each of the two ends of the nave. For over eighty years it had functioned there as one of London's major venues for events and exhibitions until it was destroyed in a fire in 1936. A loss which, by the way, was mourned even by Le Corbusier.

What perseveres at Sydenham are the Grade II listed remains of the garden terraces, and the vaulted subway that once connected the Crystal Palace to the Crystal Palace (High Level) station, now demolished. The Chinese Zhong Rong Group announced in October 2013 that it intended to rebuild the Crystal Palace as part of a £500 million project.[200]

The paradigm that was set by the Crystal Palace – the growing dissolution of the solid cube-like building – was later reinterpreted by Frank Lloyd Wright through his "destruction of the box". The load bearing walls that would clearly limit the inside and outside of a building were being broken up. Columns, walls, glazing and large overhanging eaves detached themselves from the closed configuration of the cube and became elements of their own – their separating attributes were transformed into flowing and open space.[201]

As a matter of fact, Giedion stated about J.M.W. Turner's painting *Simplon Pass* (1840) which was exhibited there that it uses a "humid atmosphere to dematerialize landscape and dissolve it into infinity. The Crystal Palace realizes the same intention through the agency of transparent glass surfaces and iron structural members. In the Turner picture the means employed are less abstract, but an equivalent insubstantial and

197 Sloterdijk, In the World Interior of Capital, p 169
198 Ibid., p 171
199 Ibid., p 172–174
200 Wilson Yau, British Architectural Library, RIBA, 2014
201 Staib, Glass Construction Manual, p 22

hovering effect is produced. [...] a dream landscape seen in the clear light of midday."[202]

This "dissolving" was picked up by certain artistic and architectural movements at the beginning of the twentieth century – expressionism, cubism, Russian constructivism and futurism. The constructivists and suprematism artists eliminated all content from the surface and reduced pictorial elements to a minimum.[203]

One such movement was De Stijl (Dutch for The Style). It was founded in Amsterdam in 1917 by all-round artist (writer, critic, designer, painter) Theo van Doesburg and was based on a publication of the same name for which van Doesburg engaged such artists and architects as J.J.P. Oud, Jan Wils, Piet Mondrian and others. De Stijl was understood as a movement towards a new formalism in architecture and consisted of the reduction of surface decoration and elements to pure geometric forms and primary colors. It simultaneously emerged as the Bauhaus and new formalism (Neue Sachlichkeit) movements, yet primarily defined the Dutch building of that time. One of its characteristics was the openness of the buildings created by large frame-worked window fronts and an emphasis on the horizontal. Van Doesburg and his peers had further created a manifesto in which they explained the characteristics of their style.[204]

Parallels between De Stijl and Mies van der Rohe's International Style as well as Frank Lloyd Wright's Prairie Architecture consist because of their new perception of modernism in terms of openness, space, and use of light (windows) – very much the destruction of the box.

Frank Lloyd Wright's houses blend into the landscape and break the object down into individual elements, greatly influenced by the traditional Japanese house which has one big living space that can be individually separated by moveable sliding doors and folding screens. Lloyd Wright's houses were anchored around the big masonry hearth at the center with the space around it to be formed and organized freely. Freestanding brick and stone walls and lavish window fronts extended into horizontal and vertical planes and were adorned with wide cantilevered roofs, all this to form a synergy and integration with nature and earth, thus called *prairie style*.[205]

By the end of the nineteenth century, ferro-vitreous architecture became expendable due to the inexpensive artificial electric light. There was of course still a need for large structures for the display and storage as well as merchandising of commodities, but the dependence on natural light disappeared. The ferrous mode of construction remained necessary for the stability of large rooms and buildings but detached itself from the vitreous aspect and took the form of steel skeletons for edifices constructed in traditional massive materials.[206]

Airport architecture has evolved from the ferroconcrete big shed architecture, such as Saarinen's TWA Flight Center to a reinvented steel-and-glass framework design borrowing from the arcade architecture and Crystal Palace.

---

202 Giedion, Space, Time & Architecture, p 254–255

203 Staib, Glass Construction Manual, p 22

204 Theo van Doesburg, Der Wille zum Stil, p 63

205 Staib, Glass Construction Manual, p 22–23: Fallingwater, built in 1935 in Pennsylvania (also called Kaufmann weekend house at Bear Run) is one of Frank Lloyd Wright's most famous creations, a private estate hovering above the rocks of a waterfall, built with natural materials which make the house blend with nature itself. Reinforced concrete, steel, wood and huge amounts of sedimentary rock for the walls and floors in the living area.

206 Schivelbusch, Geschichte der Eisenbahnreise: Zur Industrialisierung von Raum und Zeit im 19. Jahrhundert, p 49

5.5   Crystal Palaces of Aviation

The motif of the arcade architecture made its transition into airport architecture with Renzo Piano's Kansai International Airport in Osaka in 1994 (Figure 81). Piano's terminal was constructed on a manmade island in the bay off Osaka, Japan with according infrastructure and a railway system. Its principal design idea of a long slim terminal with a glass fronted landside and airside is based on Le Corbusier's Naked Airport theory. The terminal at that time was the longest ever constructed airport terminal, stretching over 1.7 kilometer. A large, clear-span, steel-trussed and undulating roof was designed to span over the terminal and concourse, interpreting the curve of a toroid (Figure 82 & 83).

Figure 82: Kansai International Airport, Osaka, Renzo Piano. Photograph courtesy of © RPBW – Renzo Piano Building Workshop Architects© Fondazione Renzo Piano (Via P. P. Rubens 30A, 16158 Genova, Italy) © KIAC© Kawatetsu

In diametrical view, this alluded to the form of a wave or a glider seen in plan, the main body of the airport forming its fuselage – a connotation to its surrounding topography and purpose. From an economic aspect, the shape and interiority of the terminal and roof were constructed to promote air circulation, forcing the air to circulate against the curvature of the building. 42 gates are housed under this roof.[207]

Figure 81: Kansai International Airport, Osaka, Renzo Piano. Photograph courtesy of Terence Ong

---

207 Simone Korein, "Toroid und Welle. Renzo Piano: Kansai International Airport, Osaka 1988–94", in: Archithese, p 42–45 & Kansai International Airport, Renzo Piano Building Workshop, hrsg. von Noriake Okabe, Tokyo 1994

Figure 83: Kansai International Airport, Osaka, Renzo Piano. Photograph courtesy of Shinkenchiku-sha Co., Ltd © RPBW – Renzo Piano Building Workshop Architects© Fondazione Renzo Piano (Via P. P. Rubens 30A, 16158 Genova, Italy)

But from an aesthetic point of view this terminal concourse is a gigantic passageway – a steel trussed arcade with a glass front alongside which the gates with their seating arrangements were situated and various dining and retail opportunities were located.

I first visited Kansai Airport and Osaka in the autumn of 1999. I was beyond awe of the fact that this was the first airport created on an artificial island. Renzo Piano had won the competition for the airport by proposing a manmade island and infrastructure in harmony with nature and topology. The latter meaning the philosophical origin, the anthropological place – after all, the ancient empire residences of Nara and Kyoto are all within a one-hour drive away. Renzo Piano wanted to emphasize this sense of place.[208]

The English philosopher Francis Bacon wrote his fable *The New Atlantis* in 1617, a story about European adventurers who stumble onto an exotic island in the South Seas (possibly near Japan) called Bensalem. Its inhabitants live in harmony in a sophisticated and technologically far advanced society and devote themselves to the sciences and studies of the sky and stars. There's quite some symbolism in this Bensalem utopia and Kansai Airport. Both are technically far advanced islands with stunning architecture and both welcome travelers from the far side of the earth to dwell and enjoy on their premises.[209]

The wavelike terminal roof might be interpreted as an homage to the sea that swallowed Atlantis but was

208 Teiji Matsumasa, Kansai International Airport passenger terminal building, Renzo Piano Building Workshop, Process: Architecture, 1994, p 24

209 Thomas Fischer, Kansai International Airport passenger terminal building, Renzo Piano Building Workshop, Process: Architecture, 1994, p 30–31

resurrected by Bacon by means of technical progress and prosperity.

Like other big Asian airports, it is located quite far away from its city – some 25 miles from Osaka. Japan has 47 prefectures, each of them governed locally, with their own train stations, universities. Osaka Kansai International Airport serves the Osaka, Wakayama, Nara, Kyoto, and Hyogo prefectures and is the third busiest Japanese airport. In 2003, a second terminal has been erected on a parallel manmade island despite a well-known sinking problem of 20 inches in the first year and down to three inches in 2003 due to porous sediment, called the Holocene Layer.[210]

Kansai Airport is admirably Japanese in its efficiency, transparency, and texture. The pear-skin finish of the roof neither reflects the gleam of light nor interferes with the control tower or airplanes. The interior is Japanese understatement: light, clean, quiet and of minimal aestheticism which fascinates the Western traveler.

Figures 84 & 85: Bangkok Suvarnabhumi Airport, photograph by Lilia Mironov

210 Kansai International Airport Land Company, LTD: http://www.kiac.co.jp/en/tech/sink/sink3/index.html

A similar, yet different kind of steel and glass passageway can be found at Suvarnabhumi Airport in Bangkok, constructed in 2006 by architect Helmut Jahn and engineer Werner Sobek. That terminal excels through its sense-of-place design and Buddhist ornamentation, but to me is reminiscent of the arcade architecture of the Galleria Vittorio Emmanuele.

It is indeed the roof structure and steel framework that most impresses the traveler within this airport. The temple-like roof and tubular concourses are unique in aviation design. The building consists of long span, lightweight steel support structures, with exposed precast concrete elements and a translucent membrane covering the roof elements. The concourses were designed for future expansion; in fact, right now there is expansion work taking place for a new concourse. The roof is reduced of mechanical loads, creating an aesthetic, airy and light atmosphere within the terminal and concourses. Landscaped courtyards on the outside and inside and abundant motifs of Thai Buddhist architecture emphasize the cultural traditions of Thailand. Much like the Crystal Palace, the inside is a curious smorgasbord of retail and Thai temples and sculptures.

In my opinion, Bangkok Suvarnabhumi Airport (Suvarnabhumi meaning *golden land* in Sanskrit), is the airport with the most sense-of-place design philosophy. While Kansai Airport's interiors follow the Japanese aestheticism of understatement and clean design, Suvarnabhumi's interiors are a realm of colorful and gilded ornaments and decorations (Figures 84 to 87).

Figure 86: Bangkok Suvarnabhumi Airport, photograph by Lilia Mironov

Figure 87: Bangkok Suvarnabhumi Airport, photograph by Lilia Mironov

You feel submerged in Thai culture the moment you set foot inside the terminal.

The Chicago based architectural firm of Murphy/Jahn, now called Jahn Architects (with principal Helmut Jahn at the steers) had already designed the United Airlines Terminal and underground concourse of Chicago O'Hare Airport. Building in a tropical clime such as Bangkok was a big challenge which they accepted, given their specialty of *archi-engineering*. This interdisciplinary collaboration of architect and engineer created a low-energy-need building with cutting edge technology, reducing the cost of air conditioning by 50% through its elaborate structural engineering.[211]

Juxtapositions of luxury brands and gilded sculptures of Thai culture alternate with specialty shops of local cuisine and artifacts in the terminal. The Figures 88 to 90 depict the Hindu legend of *Samudra Manthan* – the Churning of the Milk Ocean.[212] This sculpture greets the passengers right after the security check in the main terminal hall. I appreciate Suvarnabhumi Airport for all the sensations of the exotic and cultural, further on paired with the extraordinary "archi-engineering" design of Helmut Jahn and Werner Sobek.

Yet, I am aware that it is a kind of Potemkin Village on our way to our plane. A feeling I am beset with in many airports. Nowhere is the clash between culture, identity and conspicuous consumption as big as in this airport. This celebrated monument of the Hindu fable being flanked by Chanel and Gucci stores remind me of the alienation I felt at the Pyramids of Gizeh and the Pizza Hut close to them.

211 Helmut Jahn, Suvarnabhumi airport: Bangkok, Thailand, 2007

212 A plaque for this sculpture reads: "This scene depicts the Vishnu Kurmavatara and the churning of the Milk Ocean. The naga (the king of serpents), Vasaki, is curled around the mountain Mandara. Vishnu, incarnated in the form of a great turtle, supports the mountains on his back. Devas (demigod) and Asuras (demons) pull on the naga's body to churn the water of the ocean for thousands of years in order to produce the nectar of immortality, Amrita. From the churning, numerous opulent items are produced, including Dhanvantari carrying the pot of Amrita. In the end, the cooperation between Devas and Asuras is shattered. The Devas fulfill their plan of acquiring all Amrita, disperse the Asuras out of Heaven to the Underworld."

Figures 88, 89 & 90: Bangkok Suvarnabhumi Airport, "Scene of the Churning of the Milk Ocean", photographs by Lilia Mironov

5.6   Places of Consumption

"There are relations between department store and museum, and here the bazaar provides a link. The amassing of artworks in the museum brings them into communication with commodities, where they offer themselves en masse to the passerby – awake in him the notion that some part of this should fall to him as well."[213]

The first department store to have a complete iron frame was the Magasin Bon Marché, built in 1876 by Louis-Auguste Boileau and Gustave Eiffel (Figure 91).[214]

The name "store" rather than "shop" denominates its original purpose of storage place. The early stores in Paris around the 1860s were known as *docks à bon marché*, literally meaning cheap storage spaces. Though the department store originated in Europe as just described, so called commercial buildings were erected in business centers in Boston, St. Louis, and New York in the 1840s. The Washington Stores in New York City (1845) were a row of stores all under one roof and arranged thus that several units could be put together to house a single establishment. The individual stores were rented to both retail and wholesale dealers. The origin for theses American department store forerunners was the ready-made clothing trade. And the big difference between both continents' stores was that the American stores dealt in cheap ready-made clothing, whereas the European department stores specialized in dry goods.

Figure 91: Le Bon Marché à Paris, photograph ca. 1900, courtesy of Archives Moisant-Savey

---

213 Benjamin, The Arcades Project, p 415

214 Staib, Glass Construction Manual, p 17. This building was still faced with stonework and not completely created with iron.

The American department store building derives from the big seven- or eight story warehouses which were common during the second half of the nineteenth century.

The Magasin au Bon Marché in Paris posed a complete contrast to the warehouse type with superimposed, artificially lighted stories. Built by engineer Gustave Eiffel and the architect Boileau, who deemed thick walls as unsuitable and instead worked with pillars of small diameter, the building was covered by large reinforced glass surfaces like an arcade. In a way, one could say it was a self-contained arcade within a building, its corner even built to resemble a pavilion (a motif that certainly inspired Louis Sullivan's Carson, Pirie and Scott store in Chicago, which was built around 1900) (Figure 92).[215]

Figure 92: Carson Pirie Scott Building, Chicago, Illinois. Ca. 1900. Louis Sullivan, architect. Present day photograph by Chris Smith

Making a huge jump forward by a hundred years, we find ourselves in the age of megalomania and megastructures. The biggest, the newest, the highest, the most spectacular.

The West Edmonton Mall gained an entry into the Guinness Book of Records as the world's largest shopping mall when it opened in 1982 in Edmonton, a city some 200 miles north of Calgary in Western Canada. It was not just the world's largest mall. It also offered the world's largest indoor amusement park, the world's largest indoor water park, and the world's largest parking lot. Beside more than 800 shops, 11 department stores and 110 restaurants there was a full-size skating rink and a 360-room hotel on site as well as an artificial lake, chapel, movie theaters, and nightclubs. The shopper could walk down recreated nineteenth-century Parisian boulevards or New Orleans' Bourbon Street[216] (Figure 93).

Figure 93: West Edmonton Mall, "Europa Boulevard", Edmonton, Canada, photograph courtesy of Dylan Kereluk

215 Giedion, Space, Time and Architecture, p 235–239
The sophistication of the European department store in comparison to the American warehouse type was culminated in this particular building type – whereas in the New World one unbroken floor area was built on top of another, in France the light court and perforated interior space let in natural light and allowed for a *flâneur*-like experience as in the city arcades outside.

216 Margaret Crawford, The World in a Shopping Mall, p 3

The mall represented dizzying attractions and diversions for the visitor to soar into a spending rapture. Fake waves on a fake lake with a fake Santa Maria replica of Columbus' fleet recreated a phantasmagoria of experiences that were intended to recreate the world in a shopping mall – a utopia – or rather dystopia of consumption.

At the mall's opening one of its developers, Nader Ghermezian, claimed that no one would have to go to Paris or Disneyland anymore, as they had put it all there, in Edmonton.

Such were the developers' intentions (or delusions?) that they claimed that the goods on display and for sale in the mall offered the abundance of the world in its variety.

Alas, the mall was made up of the usual ubiquitous American-Canadian clothing chains and fast food outlets and thus only offered the typical American version of mid- to late- century visions and consumer goods. Yet it dominated the local economy and brought in visitors from over 70 countries.[217] The mall turned into a 24-hour factory with over fifteen thousand employees and with intentions to repeat the success in the suburbs of Minneapolis with the Mall of America opening in 1992, run by the same developers as in Canada.

Urban historian Margaret Crawford suggests that Fourier's Phalanstery, the utopian Kibbuz-like microsociety, merged the arcade and the palace into a prefigurative mall form with glass-roofed corridors that would encourage social intercourse and communal emotions rather than stimulate consumption.[218] This might be the distinctive social change of ways the arcade has gone through in the last two centuries. From the intended sense of place within the city center to a designated place of consumption.

American Cultural Historian William Leach states that in the decades following the Civil War, American capitalism began to produce a distinct culture which was disconnected from the traditional community and family values. This was the secular and business-market culture and at its foundation it was constituted by the exchange and circulation of money and goods. According to Leach, the acquisition and consumption of goods as the means of achieving happiness are the cardinal features of this culture.[219]

It was by World War I that Americans were being enticed into consumer pleasure and indulgence rather than diligence and work as the means of achieving happiness. No matter the stern Protestant values of the settlers, the American myth of the land of the plenty was transformed into an urbanized and commercialized one with new pleasure palaces like department stores, theaters, hotels, restaurants, dance halls, and amusement halls. A cult of the *new* had emerged as means of a stark contrast to the *old* (Europe); it culminated as *desire*. It came in parallel with the democratization of the United States.

Accelerated by the rapid industrialization of the country and paired with ideas of democracy, a *culture of desire* emerged that followed where the money and the goods were – the big cities. It also created a codependency of the working-class or rural demography to supply to the "owners of the capital" in return for salaries and desires.

Gradually from the 1880s onwards (before that America was largely an economy of farmers), Americans owned less and less land and flocked into the cities in search of steady work within its capitalistic mills. While in the past people made their own goods within their communities or settlements, these new city dwellers became dependent on salaries within its factories as

---

217 Crawford, The World in a Shopping Mall, p 4

218 Ibid., p 6

219 Archibald Leach, Land of Desire: Merchants, Power, and the Rise of a New American Culture, p 3

well as on goods made by others, creating a perpetual motion machine of consumption. The visual materials of the desire of consumption were color, glass, and light.[220] These same materials were part of the phantasmagorias in Benjamin's Parisian arcades and the Crystal Palace.

Billboards advertised the American way of life with typical American products from chewing gum, Coca Cola, and Gillette razors. The electrical sign advertising evolved after 1900 and re-invented the American city-scapes. Broadway and Times Square became the most famous centers of electrical advertising.

Window display arrangements became a new work of art, if not exhibition venue, borrowing from the theatrical stage. Nothing captured the consumer's imagination as ardently as show windows. They belonged to a constantly expanding landscape of glass, according to Leach, which might have been the most graphic indication of a new economy and culture of desire.[221] The window displays were department store dioramas, which Leach calls the culture of desire, with nothing else than the presentation of phantasmagorias, commodities of longing and dreaming, behind glass encasings.

A new class culture emerged – uptown shopping like in New York City became metonymic with glass and affluence, whereas downtown shopping with its stalls and open-air markets was intended for the lower social classes and immigrants.

Social economist Thorstein Veblen (1857–1929) coined the term of *The Leisure Class* around 1899 in the US. His treatise is a social critique of consumerism and traces its origins in the higher stages of the Barbarian culture – feudal Europe or feudal Japan and Brahmin India, which he considers as the development of the institution of a leisure class, as in such communities the distinction between the classes is rigorously observed.

The leisure class comprises the noble and priestly classes, and is exempted from manual labor.[222]

Originally the leisure class would demonstrate its wealth by not pursuing labor or work, but as industrial society evolved, *conspicuous consumption* became the demonstration of wealth. The consumption of luxuries is directed to the comfort of the consumer himself and is therefore a mark of the master, the luxury brand being his signature and identification.[223]

Conspicuous Consumption (retail) had been recognized as one of the thriving economic factors in air-

---

220 Leach, Land of Desire: Merchants, Power, and the Rise of a New American Culture, p 4–8:
A whole new advertising industry had sprung up, with "advertising cards" in the 1880s and 1890s being distributed by circuses, theaters and department stores. These brightly colored advertising cards depicted various activities of the places they were advertising. But also mail-order catalogues by department store chains Sears, Roebuck and Company and many more came into play, reaching around six million Americans throughout the continent with their promises of desire and improved living. Inside those catalogues drawings, artwork and photographs would entice the readers into consumerism, to buy what they could not see themselves in person in the city stores and to thus feel worldlier.
From this arose the American Advertising Industry. Between 1890 and 1915, posters, signboards, billboards, and electrical images sprung up in American cities. Colored posters, particularly designed for theaters and city centers, were hung up at subways and major people intersections were largely inspired by French poster artists such as Jules Cheret and Eugene Grasset, who thus projected joy and abundance into the acquisition of commodities.

221 Ibid., p 44–55

222 Veblen, The Theory of the Leisure Class, p 1–3: The upper classes were excluded from industrial occupations and reserved for employments which have a degree of honor, with warfare and priestly service considered among the most honorable tasks, but also government work and even sports. Their superior rank is also an economic expression.

223 Ibid., p 47–50

ports as far back as in the late 1940s when Wallace Harrison was working on the masterplan for Idlewild Airport (JFK International Airport) in New York. He had provided around 30% of interior space in his sketches for retail alone.

Nowadays, Dubai Duty Free has been named the world's largest single airport retailer in 2013, with sales Figures around USD 1.8 billion. Global duty free and travel retail sales were estimated at USD 60 billion in 2013, a 7.5% increase since the previous year. Dubai's duty free incentives include, next to the tax free aspect, lucky drawings to win luxury cars and other consumer goods, much like at a fair. Its retail slogan, printed on the retail bags, is captured in the slogan "Fly – buy – Dubai".[224]

Coincidentally, many duty free retail stores look like bazars or stalls within an arcade or department store, as can be seen in the example of Los Angeles International Airport (Figure 94).

Figure 94: Conspicuous consumption in the Great Hall of Los Angeles International Airport, photograph by Lilia Mironov

5.7 From Non-Places into Places of Enjoyment

French philosopher Henri Lefebvre criticizes in his works the alienation of our everyday life by our consumer culture. He notes that the spaces of enjoyment cannot consist of a building, of rooms and places determined by their functions, nor can they be found in dance halls or entertainment venues, because these places are restricted by a multiplicity of codes and encodings and programmed behaviors. Rather, the space of enjoyment shall be sought in the countryside or landscape, in friendships and festivals, it shall be a genuine space of moments and encounters, places and instants of moments.[225]

Lefebvre's thoughts in "Toward an Architecture of Enjoyment" (Vers une architecture de la jouissance) from 1973 on the relationship between bodily pleasure, space, and architecture reflect the pinnacle of the spatial theories and their definition of societal space and its meaning for the individual.

Lefebvre delivers an analysis of the principles of classification (taken from fields such as philosophy, anthropology, history, and architecture) for architectural works that is related to enjoyment and the virtual space of enjoyment. He understands architecture not as "the prestigious art or erecting monuments" but the production of space at a specific level, ranging from furniture to gardens and parks and extending to landscape, though he excludes urban planning from that meaning. Lefebvre attributes this attitude to the beginning of the twentieth century when architects began to design furniture and express their views and projects on "the environment". Much like Verblen's theories on conspicuous consumption, Lefebvre states that the bourgeois apartment of which the user believes to be his own private realm is in fact appropriated by capitalism – by the consumerist need to live in a certain

---

224 http://gulfbusiness.com/dubai-duty-free-named-worlds-largest-airport-retailer/#.VI6bK9KUe-4

225 Henri Lefebvre, Toward an architecture of enjoyment, p 152

way and identify with advertising rhetoric and products of brands associated with luxury. The opposite of this would be the proletarian housing which is reduced to a minimum and lacks luxury, therefore depends on social space. There is no connection with enjoyment other than in and through external space, which remains one of social appropriation.[226]

To Lefebvre, various monuments which we revere, such as the pyramids, Taj Mahal, the Castel Sant'Angelo and many more bear witness to the architecture of death which is not enjoyable due to the negative connotations. This also affects the architecture of social rites such as funeral ceremonies and processes.[227] Lefebvre understands the "architecture of death" or devoted to death as one dictated by constricting social rites, such as religion. Like Foucault, Lefebvre discerns a ritualistic use in social places. How do we find enjoyment in works devoted to death and its rites? Is there a counterpart, an architecture devoted to life, to happiness, joy and enjoyment? He gives a hesitant affirmative answer, as many palaces and castles provide wealth and power and a materialistic objective enjoyment – they provide the superficial enjoyment of conspicuous consumption.

We witness around us habitats full of monotony, boredom, and repetitive elements whose variations call to mind some fundamental identity. This is where Lefebvre reduces architecture to mere construction.[228]

The architecture of enjoyment which Henri Lefebvre searches for is also the quest for the anthropological place in Marc Augés *Non-Places*.

Sense of place is a combination of the characteristics that make a space unique. It involves the human experience within a landscape that consists of not only the land mass but the interplay of the people and their culture. In search of uniqueness and identity and their own values and principles, architects and (architectural-)historians have started to re-examine their own traditions and rediscover indigenous roots of architecture in their countries, and as such, in the wake of postmodernism the term *critical regionalism* was defined in the 1980s.[229]

Architects and cultural critics distance themselves from the former term *regionalism* which stems from the romantic era and was used by the National Socialists where regionalism meant a backward-looking folkloristic and propagandistic national architecture. Thus, architectural theorists Alexander Tzonis and Liane Lefaivre coined the term *critical regionalism* in 1981 to discern the diverse architectural variants in a world of globalization. [230]

The *International Style* has been subjected to harsh criticism over the last few decades, due to its contribution to globalization and ubiquitous architecture – the habitats of monotony which Lefebvre mentions. The fundamental principles of modernity included architecture as volume with the proper surfacing material, regularity, and avoidance of all decoration. The international style offered opposition to the architecture of the Beaux-Arts with its historicism and decorations. When in 1932 the newly formed Museum of Modern Art in New York exhibited the architectural creations of Walter Gropius and the Bauhaus, its curators Henry-Russell Hitchcock and Philip Johnson provided a manifesto for the new style and dismissed the architecture of historicism. Rooted in German modernism of the Bauhaus in Weimar, the international style sought

---

226 Lefebvre, Toward an architecture of enjoyment, p 3–5

227 Ibid, p 6

228 Ibid., p 17

229 Stephanus Schmitz, Identity in Architecture – A Construction? p 22

230 Alexander Tzonis, Introducing an Architecture of the Present. Critical Regionalism and the Design of Identity, p 18

to break with the past and get rid of any references to classicism.[231]

Postmodernism changed the work of architects from rational problem-solvers into a more autobiographical dimension. As a consequence, personal preferences, hobbies, and opinions became relevant for their work. Architecture turned into a form of artistic self-expression in which designs and buildings present reflections of personal associations and world-views. [232]

It is the era of the star architects who also create a lifestyle, a brand, through their architectural expressions and who are very preoccupied with merchandising this feeling. Deconstructivist, sculpture-like museums such as Frank Gehry's in Bilbao (1997) and Seattle (2002), Mario Botta's Museum of Modern Art in San Francisco (1995), Renzo Piano's Zentrum Paul Klee in Bern (2005) and many more naturally provide more than a museal experience but a whole leisure effect within the urban landscape; additionally, they are monuments to their architectural creators.

This architectural self-expression of architects of postmodernism is a self-reflection which draws parallels to Michel Foucault's thoughts on mirrors in his essay about heterotopias and the difference between unrealized ideas (utopias) and places outside of places (heterotopias).[233]

The way postmodernism fits in the architecture of enjoyment is through its self-expression; when everything becomes possible, architecture gets to leave its original building task and becomes playful – joyful.

It is the decorated duck versus shed topos of Robert Venturi and Denise Scott Brown. Ducks are the buildings that represent their function through their form and shape, whereas the decorated sheds are buildings which have applied décor and added ornamentations to distinguish their purpose. Favoring the decorated shed over the programmatic duck architecture, Venturi and Scott Brown seek to evolve from the dry, empty, and "boring" expressions of modernism and the International Style.

"The duck is the special building that is a symbol; the decorated shed is the conventional shelter that applies symbols. ... We think that the duck is seldom relevant today although it pervades modern architecture." [234]

While this distinction came up during Venturi's and Scott Brown's study of Las Vegas architecture in the

1970s, which was mainly derided as kitsch back then, it set a paradigm for postmodern architecture as more

---

231 Philip Johnson, Henry-Russell Hitchcock, The International Style, p 18–19

232 Hans Ibelings, Supermodernism: Architecture in the Age of Globalization, p 27–28

233 Foucault, Of Other Spaces: Utopias and Heterotopias, p 330–336:
Foucault portrays spaces as sets of relational configurations, of mental space and concrete experience and writes of the mirror as a utopia, since it is a placeless place. The mirror functions as a heterotopia in this respect: it makes the place we occupy at the moment when we look at ourselves in the glass at once absolutely real, connected with all the space that surrounds it, and absolutely unreal, since in order to be perceived it has to pass through this virtual point which is over there.

234 Robert Venturi, Denise Scott Brown, Learning from Las Vegas, p 88–89
The "decorated duck" was a real life fast food outlet in New Jersey in the form of a giant sitting duck, called the "Long Island Duckling".

than pseudo-historical décor. In my opinion, this discussion paved the way to an architecture of symbolism and enjoyment at the time of capitalism and globalization as a reaction to the purity of modernism.

After all, modernism had an opponent of everything decorative and beautifying in Adolf Loos, the Viennese architect who abhorred decoration in architecture in favor of clean and clear forms and rejected the Vienna Secession and subsequent Jugendstil, calling his infamous manifesto *Ornament and Crime*. Loos considered ornament as planned obsolescence.

But the creative self-expression of postmodern architecture some 70 years after Loos also opened a Pandora's box of kitsch and Disneyfication, which in turn is closely tied to the capitalistic event-space of theme parks – that is the pitfall of postmodernism.

Hans Ibelings, the architectural historian and author of *Supermodernism: Architecture in the Age of Globalization*, states that from the postmodernist perspective, sensitivity to context – contextualism – and the assimilation of elements from its surroundings – genius loci – are what give a building its right to exist. He calls *references* – to architecture or art history or context – a typical 1980s word, typical of the heyday of postmodernism.[235] Those references are the beautifications of that particular architecture. One could call it post-/neo-historicism, as postmodernist architecture refers to the locus or history by projecting images and appliqués into this architecture which in their essence linger on the superficial.

Lefebvre continues in his search for enjoyment and nearly finds it – in the Alhambra in Grenada which in our imagination is covered with rugs and couches and is perfumed and populated with birds and fountains and the beauties from One Thousand and One

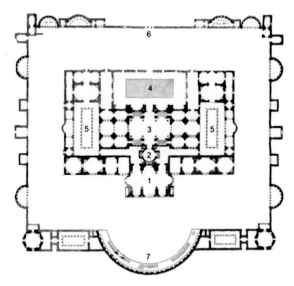

Figure 95: Floorplan of the Baths of Diocletian, Rome. Drawing by Rodolfo Lanciani between 1893–1901

Nights. But the Alhambra does not exist in its original state. The architecture of leisure so far is a simulation of enjoyment.[236] We finally learn what Lefebvre deems the successful architecture of enjoyment. Namely that the most important pleasures of any society are experienced within a *social framework*, that is, before the private and public were separated (nowadays in our society the social and socialization are met with disapproval as there is an emphasis on the individual).

This was the case in ancient Rome, where the most pleasurable activity might have been to visit one of the many baths, such as the Baths of Diocletian (Figure 95).

The baths, built AD 306 during the reign of Emperor Diocletian, encompassed an enormous space that covered the acreage of a small city within the city of Rome.

---

235 Ibelings, Supermodernism: Architecture in the Age of Globalization, p 18

236 Lefebvre, Toward an architecture of enjoyment, p 21–100: What is enjoyment in the philosophical sense? The term refers to the relationship of need and even desire to the object, emphasizing the act rather than the result. Today we find this term in everyday use though with egocentric connotations such as to obtain pleasure and satisfaction.

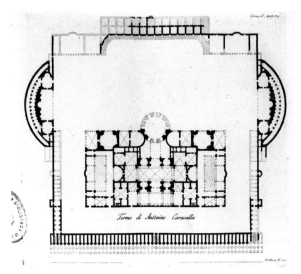

Figure 96: Terme di Antonino Caracalla, Rome, drawing by Ridolfino Venuti (1705–1763) courtesy of the Biblioteca General Antonio Machado, Sevilla

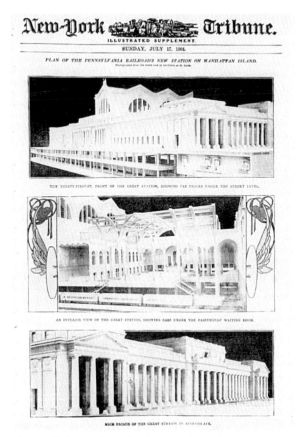

Figure 97: Pennsylvania Station, print in the New York Tribune, 1904, courtesy of the Library of Congress

Intended to cultivate body and mind, the Roman baths are one of the most original architectural creations in history. A succession of rooms and halls followed by a long axis led to a gigantic open-air pool. Many spaces and pools followed, gyms, massage rooms, and a variety of sporting facilities. The pool was a marble lake surrounded by colonnades. There was also a park for visitors to meet and talk and even a public library. No one in Rome was excluded from partaking in this luxury with different days assigned to women, from slaves to the emperor himself. The baths were a space of enjoyment and, according to Lefebvre, the most successful of architectural spaces. They were also a place where the body and mind prepared for sensuality. The whole surroundings – the statues, the beauty prepared for a sensual approach to eroticism. Thus, these baths remain a firm example of multifunctional architecture – "polymorphous and polyvalent".[237]

Thermal baths have some pull on architects: The Swiss architect Peter Zumthor built the remote mineral baths *Therme Vals* (1996) in the Swiss Alps with local granite as a phenomenological and sensual experience, so much focused on the sensory that no mobile devices are allowed inside and quietness is closely observed by the guards/employees.

---

237 Lefebvre, Toward an architecture of enjoyment, p 137–138

Figure 98: Istanbul New Airport; Nordic, Grimshaw and Haptic Architects, 2016, photograph courtesy of Nordic / Grimshaw / Haptic_Produced by MIR

This connects to Pennsylvania Station which was mentioned earlier in this work.

Pennsylvania Station's original outline was created to resemble the Caracalla Terme in Rome, built AD 212 during the reign of Antoninus Caracalla (Figures 96 & 97).

This is an elegant rounding up of Lefebvre's theories on leisure and enjoyment and their relation to airport architecture. Lefebvre sees the multifunctional architecture of the Diocletian baths as the most successful space of enjoyment. This multifunctionality is also a theme in Foucault's heterotopias which presuppose a system of openings and closings that both isolates them and makes them penetrable, but not freely accessible like a public place. Either the entry is compulsory, as in the case of entering a barracks or a prison, or else the

individual has to submit to rites and purification (note from this author: the Diocletian Baths).[238]

This *spiel* of inclusion and exclusion to exclusive places of leisure is a recurrent theme in airport architecture. It is one of the traits of heterotopias that they have a function in relation to all the space that remains. They create a space that is other, perfect, and well arranged. This is the heterotopia of compensation – and not of illusion – and this compensation heterotopia exists in places of colonization where human perfection wants to be achieved or recreated.

I believe that in relation to airport architecture with its recreation of spaces of enjoyment, spaces of identity and multifunctional use (not unlike the Diocletian Baths – after all there are spas and massage parlors in every modern airport terminal) we are dealing with

---

238 Foucault, Of Other Spaces: Utopias and Heterotopias, p 330–336

the heterotopia of compensation. We want to fill these voids, these shells of living which Benjamin's flâneur would have filled with the goods he encountered in the passageways of Paris. We want to fill them with recreations of our life's experiences of enjoyment and identity.

The bath symbolism of the architecture of enjoyment translates into airport terminals, not least because most of them offer spa services to some extent. The Istanbul New Airport was completed in 2016, a joint design of the architectural firms Grisham, Haptic and Nordic. It is currently the biggest airport in the world measured by square feet – roughly 15 million.[239] Istanbul's byzantine history is reflected inside this terminal in the vaulted ceilings pierced with skylights and the numerous giant columns, giving it an aura of the Blue Mosque and a hamam – the Turkish Bath (Figure 98).

The motif of enjoyment continues: While we wait and saunter in an airport like Incheon, we can enjoy one of the many daily dance and concert performances in the airport. We can partake in the dance or enjoy the professional dancers performing, we can listen to live classical concerts, and we can participate in Korean handicrafts in the Korea Traditional Cultural Experience center (Figure 99).

Figure 99: Snapshot of dancing couple, Incheon Airport, Seoul. Photograph by Lilia Mironov

239 https://hapticarchitects.com/work/istanbul-airport-istanbul-turkey/

6 Architecture of the Senses – Experiencing the Airport

6.1 A Phenomenological Introduction of the Sensorial and Auratic in Airport Design

"To build, to plant, whatever you intend, to rear the column, or arch the bend, to swell the terrace, or sink the grot; In all, let Nature never be forgot. [...] Consult the genius of the place in all ..." [240]

Alexander Pope (1688–1744)

The *genius loci* in Latin means spirit of the place. Its essence is as ancient as mankind, with past civilizations believing in a deity guarding the region or place. In Alexander Pope's verse it is the call to mind not to forget your origins when seeking to build or expand.

The Norwegian architectural historian Christian Norberg-Schulz investigated the genius loci in the human environment as a holistic phenomenon: topography, cosmology, cultural landscape and buildings – with dwelling being a romantic-poetic connection between people and their environment. "Phenomenology was conceived as a return to things", he writes, as opposed to abstractions and mental constructions in architecture. [241]

If there is a genius loci in our current city architecture, then it is the microcosm of the people that dwell poetically in this place and know of its history. This is a very similar approach to Augé's thesis of the anthropological place that needs to be sought in non-place architecture.

Phenomenology as a science was established by German philosopher Edmund Husserl around the turn of the twentieth Century. Husserl's motivation was to understand the essence of consciousness through the subjective experience of phenomena – conscious experiences. The perception of architecture (as well as art, music and travel) on the senses had already been brought up by the philosophers of romanticism such as Immanuel Kant and Georg Wilhelm Friedrich Hegel who were writing about their attempts to capture the effects of the sublime (art, architecture, music ...) and its emotions on the intellect, with the experience raising an awareness and conscious self.

A sense of place experience inside the airport terminal can elevate the general state of mind of the traveler. There is a relationship between sense of place, the haptic, the sensorial, natural light and creating an uplifting environment that can help reduce the anxiety associated with every aspect of air travel. Ideally, it shall decelerate the hassle without delaying the trip. The non-

---

240 Alexander Pope, Epistles to Several Persons: Epistle IV, 2007 (original source: 1744), verses 47–57

241 Christian Norberg-Schulz, Genius Loci: Towards a Phenomenology of Architecture, p 8

place becomes a space with a cultural meaning, a sense of place and an identification with its local culture.

We have so far discussed that modern airport design strives to create airports as gateways to cities, regions, and countries and offers a unique arrival or departure experience that connects the airport to its local community. Where some airports have sought to recreate features of the local landscape or vernacular architecture in their terminal, others have tried the use of local materials, colors or visual forms, and art with a cultural resonance.

Genius loci (tongue in cheek) in Mongolia to me is the aptly named Chinggis Khan International Airport, southwest of Ulaanbataar (Figures 100 & 101). I took the two pictures from the cockpit of a Swiss Airbus 340. How original that the Mongolians named their gateway airport after the warrior and founder of their ancient Empire, Chinggis (Genghis) Khan.

Sense of place is about feelings and orientation, but especially about identity. Sense of place also encourages dwelling and strolling. Lucius Burckhardt created his concept of strollology (Sparziergangswissenschaft) in 1977, when taking the ur-stroll in Riede, Germany. It was the mindfulness and awareness of the aesthetic aspects of the environment, which until then had not been deemed important enough in social studies, that had driven him to dedicate himself to this topic around the same time as Norberg-Schulz took up the investigation of the genius loci.

Burckhardt had taken many more strolls, which were rather research trips through European landscapes and cityscapes. In a way, this reminds me of Bruce Chatwin's book about the Songlines, mentioned earlier in this thesis. Both men strolled through the countryside in research of the past and identity. In Burckhardt's case, the strollological served to experience the way or route or building in its original form, the sequences in which a person perceives things, because in our generation (of building) the place itself must explain its aesthetic intent; it is no longer intuitively known by us.[242]

The philosophers Maurice Merleau-Ponty, Edmund Husserl and Ernst Cassirer established a discourse on phenomenology that transcends into architecture, and as such provide a philosophical and aesthetical experience thereof. Phenomenology is the study of essences, perception and consciousness, the visual and the tactile. For Cassirer, space has a mythical quality of human actions.[243]

Sensation is part of perception; it is to be understood as the experiencing of a state of oneself. *Gestalt theory* informs us that a Figure on a background is the simplest sense-given available to us, which leaves an impression on us. This is the definition of perception. The pure impression is thus imperceptible and inconceivable as an instant of perception.

Merleau-Ponty attributes colors and lights to seeing, sounds to hearing, and defines the *sense* as to have *qualities*. To know what sense-experience is, then, is the combination of our senses and their qualities.[244]

The bodily stimuli here are part of the physical experience of architectural space. For Finnish architect and phenomenologist Juhani Pallasmaa, phenomenology is his understanding of "multi-sensory architecture".

---

242 Lucius Burckhardt, Landschaftstheoretische Aquarelle und Spaziergangswissenschaft, p 45–49

243 Ernst Cassirer, Mythischer, ästhetischer und theoretischer Raum, in: Dünne/Günzel: Raumtheorie, Grundlagentexte aus Philosophie und Kulturwissenschaften, p 495

244 Maurice Merleau-Ponty, Phenomenology of Perception, p 5–39
   Various senses interact in perception as the two eyes collaborate in vision. Vision is defined in the empiricist way as the possession of a quality impressed upon the body by the stimulus; perception becomes the interpretation of the signs that our senses provide in accordance with bodily stimuli.

Figures 100 & 101: Chinggis Khan International Airport and Ulaanbataar, Mongolia, photographs by Lilia Mironov

In *The Eyes of the Skin*, he expresses the significance of the tactile sense for our sensual experience and understanding of the world, as the very essence of the lived experience is molded by hapticity and peripheral unfocused vision. All the senses, including vision, are extensions of the tactile sense.[245]

In Western culture, sight has been historically regarded as the noblest of senses, with Plato regarding vision as humanity's greatest gift. The invention of perspectival representation turned the eye into the center point of the perceptual world as well as of the concept of the self. Architecture is our primary instrument relating us with space and time and gives these dimensions a human measure. Pallasmaa believes that many aspects of the pathology of everyday architecture today can likewise be understood through an analysis of the epistemology of the senses and a critique of the ocular bias of our culture in general, and of architecture in particular. As such, the inhumanity (non-place) of con-

temporary architecture and cities can be understood as the consequence of negligence of the body and the senses and an imbalance of our sensory system. Pallasmaa speaks here of a sensory imbalance and estrangement which is often evoked by the technologically most advanced settings, whereas Augé recognizes the lack of anthropological connection to the non-place.[246]

Pallasmaa advocates a turn toward haptic experience, which is grounded in a gradual and slow comprehension of architecture because it affects all the senses and the body as a whole. Sensory experiences are experiences of touch – with our eyes, ears, nose, as well as the skin. Hence his book is named *The Eyes of the Skin*.

All real experiences of architecture are embodied and multi-sensory.[247] In many modern airports there are spaces for haptic interaction, such as the Cultural Experience Center located in Incheon Airport where passengers can pass their waiting time experimenting in Korean handcraft and such as the sensorial installa-

245 Juhani Pallasmaa, The Eyes of the Skin, p 10

246 Pallasmaa, The Eyes of the Skin, p 15–19

247 Pallasmaa, "Dwelling in Light: Tactile, Emotive and Life-Enhancing Light", in: Daylight & Architecture Magazine, issue 26, 2016

tion Kinetic Rain in Singapore Changi Airport as well as many other art and mood installations to entertain the traveler.

Nihilistic and non-place architecture makes the world become a hedonistic and meaningless visual journey lacking sensuality and identification. As a consequence of the current deluge of images, architecture of our time often appears as a mere retinal art of the eye; the loss of tactility causes architectural structures to become flat, immaterial and devoid of authenticity.[248]

The sense of *aura*, the authority of presence, which Walter Benjamin regards as a necessary quality for an authentic piece of art, is lost.

In his *The Work of Art in the Age of Mechanical Reproduction* Walter Benjamin discusses the shift in perception through the new media film and photography in the twentieth century. The sensory changes are immense, the way we view the visual work of art changes drastically through reproduction.

The work of art has always been reproducible, as man-made objects could always be copied by humans. Replicas have long been made by pupils as a way of practice and learning and by their masters; during the Renaissance, *scuole* (schools) of pupils were practicing and painting in the style of their respective masters. Graphic art was first made technologically reproducible by the woodcut, long before written language became reproducible by movable type.

The technology of reproduction was enabled by lithography which was soon surpassed by photography. Technological reproduction had achieved a standard that permitted it to reproduce all known works of art around 1900, thoroughly modifying their effects.[249]

What withers at the age of the technological reproducibility of a work of art is the latter's *aura*. The au-thenticity of a thing is the quintessence of all, but the technology of reproduction detaches the reproduced object from the realm of tradition. By replicating the work many times, it substitutes a mass experience for a unique existence. It loses its aura.

"What, then, is the aura?" asks Benjamin, "By reproducing the uniqueness of viewing the original, by enabling present-day masses to get closer to the work of art and by assimilating it as a reproduction (in print, photography, distribution), the object loses its uniqueness. The uniqueness of the work of art is identical to its embeddedness in the context of tradition, that uniqueness is its aura."[250]

In the context of this thesis, the loss of aura is very close to the loss of identity as described by Augé: Modernism is accompanied by loss and destruction of place. His realization is that supermodernism creates non-places which as spaces are not anthropological places. Non-places have lost contact with history and therefore do not generate place-related identities. Augé also writes that supermodernism turns history into a spectacle of its own, as happens with all exotic and local peculiarities. Thus, he mentions tourism as an example of the construction of such localism. The marketing of the local and the celebration and construction of cultural differences compensate for the facelessness of cities and cultural emptiness.

The observer or tourist or passenger thus recognizes his own identity only by looking at his reflection in the mirror. "This also stands for the premise by which cultural identity, as a likeness of the self, forms and constructs itself by distancing itself from the self. This distance serves the construction of the own identity through the image as seen by the other or, more pre-

---

248 Ibid.

249 Benjamin, The Work of Art in the Age of Mechanical Reproduction, Cambridge, 2008, p 21

250 Ibid., p 23

Figure 102: LAX Los Angeles International Airport, Theme Building, photograph by Lilia Mironov

cisely, by the foreigner and results in the construction of a myth of the place as non-locatable".[251]

As per Benjamin, through the loss (death) of the aura the cult of genius has to be moved into a mythological space, the genius loci. This is where our own myths and experiences will make the aura live on in our own mythological space, the *auratic*.

The aura of Los Angeles is strongly tied to its film-making business. LAX International Airport received its theme building in 1961 from renowned Los

---

251 Stephanus Schmitz, "Identity in Architecture – A Construction?", in: Constructing Identity in Contemporary Architecture. Case Studies from the South, p 18

Angeles architect William Pereira. The theme building underwent a thorough renovation and modernization from 2007 until 2013 when its restaurant *Encounter* (which used to be revolving) definitely closed.

This mid-century modern style landmark is the gateway to Los Angeles. Pereira's brother worked as an art director in Hollywood and co-designed the tripods for H.G. Wells' 1953 film *War of the Worlds*. The stilt-like legs of these extraterrestrials are said to have inspired William Pereira for his iconic building which can be seen from the Los Angeles area highways from miles afar.[252]

In search for the auratic, uniqueness and identity, and regionally symbolic, contemporary architecture plays an important role in countries experiencing rapid economic changes and increasing pressure from global value systems.

Christian Norberg-Schulz used the term *Genius Loci* in his 1982 book, whereas Critical Regionalism was defined by Alexander Tzonis, Liane Lefaivre, and Kenneth Frampton in the 1980s. When discussing a connection to place it was one of the first attempts within modernism to emphasize the connection of architecture to place and culture on an abstract level. For Tzonis, Lefaivre and Frampton the connection of the building as an individual object to its location is the primary element of this concept.

Frampton argues that in postmodernism there is the danger of a universal system with a media presence that has lost its capacity for self-criticism and self-reflection. He also references Hannah Arendt who considered images in today's society degraded to an empty message carrier. Postmodernism does not only deal with symbols, it also deals with the their own symbols. Frampton also criticizes the global spread of functional separation that comes with urban planning. The car-centric city structure and high-rises accelerate the loss of public space and can only be reestablished by thorough urban and cultural densification. [253]

Essentially, Frampton proposes the opposite of Rem Koolhaas' generic city that has no recognizable connection to its own history and identity.

Even Frampton, Lefaivre and Tzonis have their critics: Professor Barbara L. Allen speaks of "social blindness in architecture" when discussing their thoughts on critical regionalism. She reproaches their use of examples of buildings devoid of people. She appeals for more tools to understand the interactions of cultural practices and regional places. Under culture, she understands the totality of behaviors, beliefs, customs, habits, and knowledge. She interprets this meaning of culture as identity. Thus, regionalism in architecture should be based on the spaces of people's practices and normative behaviors, what people actually do in that region that marks them of that place.

She defines the region, which is a socially constructed concept, as a collection of shared geographically located identities.[254]

---

252 Pearman, Airports: A Century of Architecture, p 126

253 Schmitz, "Identity in Architecture – A Construction?", in: Constructing Identity in Contemporary Architecture. Case Studies from the South, p 20

254 Barbara L. Allen, "On Performative Regionalism", in: Architectural Regionalism: Collected Writings on Place, Identity, Modernity, and Tradition, p 421–422: Examples are: Chinatown and Little Italy, regions in New York which have context for cultural practices and offer meaning and identity via those activities.

Figure 103: Oriental Pearl Tower and postmodern office building; Shanghai World Financial Center, Jin-Mao Tower and Shanghai Tower, photograph by Lilia Mironov

Critical Regionalism necessarily involves a more directly dialectical relation with nature than the more abstract, formal traditions of modern avant-garde architecture allow. Frampton calls the tendency which modernization favors a *tabula rasa* method, favoring economic factors in the realization of construction. It is this fundamental opposition between universal civilization and autochthonous culture. The bulldozing of an irregular topography into a flat site is clearly a technocratic gesture which aspires to a condition of absolute *placelessness,* whereas the terracing of the same site to receive the stepped form of a building is an engagement in the act of "cultivating" the site.[255]

Present-day Shanghai is a juxtaposition of eclecticist postmodern architecture with futuristic skyscrapers and new office buildings sporting historicist applications such as Corinthian columns. These buildings are ten to twenty years old, at most, the Shanghai Tower being the youngest addition, completed in 2015. The Jin-Mao Tower stems from 1999 and its unique form draws from the tiered Chinese pagoda architecture (Figure 103).

Along Shanghai's river promenade, The Bund, dozens of buildings from the nineteenth Century in the Beaux-Arts and Art Deco styles still bear witness to its colonial past, with a still existing preserved quarter named The French Concession, stemming from the mid-nineteenth Century. The place where most of the modern high-rises are situated, across the river from The Bund, is called Pudong. A little more than twenty years ago, Pudong was just some farmland on the outskirts of the city. Now it has become a special zone of finance and power, bearing most of Shanghai's landmarks on its premises.

Shanghai is a prime example of the generic city that becomes liberated from its (ancient) city center, its former "straitjacket of identity". It is now the city without history: when it gets old, it self-destructs and renews itself. "It is the post-city prepared on the site of the ex-city."[256]

Koolhaas, a bit like Sloterdijk, is an agitator in architectural theory. As Philip Ursprung once said in a lecture, Koolhaas mimics the tech tycoon.[257] His outstanding rejection of the historic city centers is puzzling. It may make sense as a whole to explain how urban architecture has evolved. But I tend to think that not all of the generic architecture and generic cities consciously intended to abolish the history of their place. Rather, it all arose from a necessity and the historic city center got neglected.

We see here that in the phenomenological discourse on the sensorial experience of architecture, perception, and aura as well as the multisensory are of utmost importance. But the location, the region, and the sense-of-place are all part of the tactile and tectonic perception.

All these different theories by the philosophers presented, from Benjamin, Foucault, Lefebvre, de Certeau, Pallasmaa, Augé, Frampton – are they not all describing the same basic notions of sense, location, aura and perception?

---

255 Kenneth Frampton, Towards a Critical Regionalism. Six Points for an Architecture of Resistance, p 16–30
   Frampton favors the tactile as the ability to read the environment. Just as the multisensory touch Pallasmaa deems important, Frampton argues that our whole range of sensory perceptions are all an important perception in the built form. In this way, critical regionalism seeks to complement our normative visual experience by readdressing the tactile range of human perceptions. In attempting to counter this loss, the tactile opposes itself to the scenographic and has capacity to arouse the impulse to touch the architect to the poetics of construction and to the creation of works in which the tectonic value of each component depends upon the density of its objecthood. The tactile and the tectonic jointly have the capacity to transcend the mere appearance of the technical in much the same way as the place-form has the potential to withstand the relentless onslaught of global modernization.

256 Koolhaas, S, M, L, XL, p 1250

257 Philip Ursprung, lecture at the conference Hybrid Spaces, Bern, November 8, 2014

6.2 Airport Empire – Crisis Heterotopia and Panopticon

Michel Foucault calls society's isolation of those individuals who are going through a socially aggravating experience or a personal change (adolescence, sickness) a *crisis heterotopia*. Those individuals are going through their personal turmoil in a "nowhere/elsewhere place". They are being replaced more and more by the heterotopia of deviation. This is where they are placed if their behavior deviates from the norm – hospitals, care homes, prisons, etc.[258] More and more so I believe that the airport terminal is a crisis heterotopia. It is this nowhere land where all our emotions pass through.

In Michel Foucault's essay *Discipline and Punish* he considers the panopticon as Enlightenment's disciplinary model par excellence: it is where he evokes the theatrical machinations of spatial authority. In *Discipline and Punish*, Foucault builds on Jeremy Bentham's (1748–1839) conceptualization of the panopticon (a circular building with an observation tower in the center, designed as an institutional building or prison in the eighteenth century) as he elaborates upon the function of disciplinary mechanisms in such a prison and illustrates the function of discipline as an apparatus of power (Figures 104 & 105).

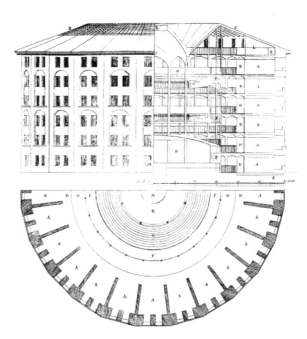

Figure 104: Panopticon, 1843, Jeremy Bentham sketch courtesy of The Works of Jeremy Bentham

Figure 105: Postcard of Interior view of Illinois State Penitentiary, Stateville, Joliet. 1923

---

258 Foucault, Of Other Spaces, p 330–336

Figures 106 & 107: Newark Airport, Star Alliance Lounge. Privileged view onto the Central Terminal Hall below. Photographs by Lilia Mironov

Foucault describes the spatial partitioning of the panopticon, where each street is placed under the authority of a syndic (guard) who keeps it under surveillance and inspects every movement with a gaze that is everywhere. This surveillance is based on a system of permanent registration from the intendants or magistrates who have complete control over this enclosed, segmented space where power is exercised without division by hierarchical figures. Constant surveillance is exercised over the individual.[259]

This summary of Foucault's view on panopticism describes modern airport terminals. Ever since 9/11 the atmosphere within airports has changed dramatically, with attempts to conceal it by making it more agreeable to the traveler through all kinds of psychological devices like entertainment and dwelling spaces. But ultimately, airport terminals are huge panopticons and the authority ruling in there is border control, customs,

TSA (USA), and the police. Figures 106 to 108 demonstrate the panopticism in Newark and Denver airports.

Foucault declares our society one of surveillance rather than spectacle, and both the amphitheater (place of surveillance) and the stage (space of spectacle) are constituent of the panoptic machine manufacturing social control.[260] By combining the spectacle of the festival with the idea of surveillance, the diverse nature of the crowd is disciplined into a collection of separated individuals. Panopticism is the theory of social control. The Panopticon is a form of behavior control.[261]

Airport or cruise ship, golf resort, special zone for agriculture and logistics/infrastructure with their own special laws outside of local laws are denominated by Keller Easterling as *outlaw spatial products* which aspire to establish worlds or global regimes with non-national sovereignty. Of cruise ships, Easterling says that they

259 Foucault, Discipline and Punish: The Birth of the Prison, p 196–199

260 Doritah Hannah, Event-Space: Theater Architecture & the Historical Avant-Garde, p 106

261 Foucault, Discipline and Punish: The Birth of the Prison, p 201

Figure 108: Denver International Airport, Great Hall from upper lever. Fentress Architects, 1995. Photograph by Lilia Mironov

are serving an "elastic assemblage of programs and services which are styled and accessorized with the signatures of a tourist brand".[262] The ship is the het-erotopia par excellence, according to Foucault. In civilizations without boats, dreams dry up, espionage takes the place of adventure, and the police take the place of pirates.[263]

In our context, the metaphor of the ship is the airplane. The (regional) brand is the identity of most airports which are deterritorializing spatial products.

Exile, diaspora, statelessness, and migration in the twentieth century are all associated with airports (and with seaports and infrastructure nodes) one way or another. These keywords all describe the uprooting from our original places through wars, globalization, and sociocultural changes in our society.

The British-Indian scholar Homi Bhabha speaks of empiricism, idealism, mimeticism, monoculturalism, and dislocation as the attributes of postcolonialism.[264]

When describing the arrest and deportation of populations during the Iraq war, Judith Butler distinguishes the imposed and enforced sense of placelessness which, she claims, is an extreme form of dispossession and the barriers of the extra-territorial prison. This placelessness, which is acting outside of the territorial domain of state power, materializes sovereignty as *Empire*.[265]

Empire – synonymous of the global economy – is also depicted as the enemy in Hardt and Negri's book of the same title. According to them, Empire has no fixed boundaries or barriers. It is a decentered and deterritorializing apparatus of rule that progressively incorporates the entire global realm within its open, expanding frontiers. Deterritorialization is the loss of the relations between culture and the geographic location, national

262 Keller Easterling, Enduring Innocence, p 24

263 Foucault, Of Other Spaces: Utopias and Heterotopias, p 330–336

264 Homi Bhabha, "Signs Taken for Wonders: Questions of Ambivalence and Authority under a Tree outside Delhi, May 1819." In The Location of Culture, London, 1994, p 111

265 Butler/Chakravorty Spivak, "Who sings the Nation-State", p 9–19. Displacement and statelessness are key elements in the formative experience of the German intellectual and cultural theorist Hannah Arendt who lived the unsteady existence of a stateless person for 18 years until she became a naturalized US citizen in 1951. Arendt's experience led her to critically research the fate of stateless people during the mid-twentieth century and the relationship between statelessness and the modern nation-state. She warns that the sovereign power of the modern state can lead to the formation of superfluous human beings.

identity. *"Empire* manages hybrid identities and plural exchanges through modulating networks of command."[266]

Hybridity is the new form of multiculturalism in the postcolonial discourse. *"Colonial mimicry* is the colonist's desire for a reformed, subjugated, recognizable Other", as Bhabha writes, "almost the same, but not quite". The Third Space is the ambiguous area that develops when two or more individuals/cultures interact, the colonizer and the other.

There is a distribution of power between the industrialized countries and developing countries as former colonies. Regional architecture is confronted with the decline of local traditions for architecture design. Architecture that is considered to be regional is often influenced by external ideas of cultural identity. [267]

I dare say that colonial mimicry can be discerned in Middle Eastern and Far Eastern *iconicity* airports. This is not a reproach, but a mere statement, given that Edward Said's *Orientalism* deals with Europe's conscious *Exoticism* of the East. Exoticism belittles and glorifies at the same time. This may attribute to an auratic effect of the mythical in non-western airports.

The HSBC Headquarters in Hong Kong, a skyscraper erected by Norman Foster in 1986, is considered to be a display of *Empire* and finance in what was one of the last colonies of our modern times, Hong Kong. After all, the Hong Kong and Shanghai Bank was established by the British Empire after the opium wars in China to further the colony.

This landmark of Hong Kong has integrated Chinese geomancy and feng shui principles within its aluminum cladding system and floors suspended from the trusses – the appropriate architecture for "financial and diplomatic warfare".[268]

I have seen its ground level, which is an open-air atrium, being re-appropriated on Sundays as a picnic- and meeting place by the Filipina nannies of its wealthy expatriate employers. It is one of the social phenomena in Hong Kong. Sunday is the day off for the (mostly Filipina) maids and nannies of Hong Kong, and there are hundreds of thousands of them. They picnic in groups of dozens to hundreds in the island's public places. It is their re-appropriation as a democratic place of their employer's *Empire*.

I cheer for the nannies of Hong Kong; after all, they peacefully occupy the places of imperialist entitlement. It is modern day slavery in one of the world's biggest financial centers, the same kind of exploitation that construction- and migrant workers experience in any of the uprising metropoles of the empires of oil.

Indian architectural critic Krishna Menon states that the consciously external view of the vernacular architecture heavily influences the design of the work of a local architect. In this process, an ethnic identity is constructed which does not always correspond to real-

---

266 Hardt/Negri, Empire, p 45

267 Bhabha, "Signs Taken for Wonders: Questions of Ambivalence and Authority under a Tree outside Delhi, May 1819." In The Location of Culture, p 85–92
     The colonial subject is located in a place of hybridity, its identity formed in a space of iteration and translation by the colonizer. Like mimicry, hybridity is a metonymy of presence. Hybridity opens up a space, figuratively speaking, where the construction of a political object that is new, neither the colonizer nor the Other, properly defies our political expectations. However, like Bhabha's concept of mimicry, hybridity is the image of being in at least two places at once. This turn in the effect of hybridity makes the presence of colonist authority no longer immediately visible.

268 Oliver Wainwright, Norman Foster's Hong Kong HSBC headquarters tore up the rule book – a history of cities in 50 buildings, day 45, The Guardian

Figures 109 & 110: HSBC (Hong Kong and Shanghai Bank) Headquarters, Hong Kong Island, 1986 Norman Foster, architect. Photographs by Lilia Mironov

ity, but it serves the interest of an external, non-ethnic, global market.

The actual problem is that the creation of identity in these places does not really take place through local crafts but through the projections of the imaginations of external (foreign) architects. It is very much what can be considered post-colonial.[269]

Homi Bhabha does not denounce colonial mimicry as a narcissistic self-expression (of architects, writers – Bhabha is an English scholar and his research is literature-based), but rather as an ambivalent feeling between colonizer and colonized. It has more to do with metonymy, such as the difference between being English and being Anglicized. Mimicry appropriates the Other and visualizes power.[270]

Colonial power establishes control and dominance, as we have seen throughout literature in works such as Robinson Crusoe and Heart of Darkness. But the appropriation of the Other by foreign architects often resulted in cultural hybridity, such as the style of Orientalism which emerged in the nineteenth century. British architects in India merged local and vernacular architecture with their own scholarly historicism and created landmarks like the Victoria Terminus in Bombay, which can now be interpreted as colonial hybridity in architecture.

269   Schmitz, "Identity in Architecture – A Construction?", in: Constructing Identity in Contemporary Architecture. Case Studies from the South, p 32

270   Bhabha, "Signs Taken for Wonders: Questions of Ambivalence and Authority under a Tree outside Delhi, May 1819." In The Location of Culture, p 85–92

An example of an airport that is full of colonial mimicry and regional iconography is Bangkok Suvarnabhumi Airport which was presented earlier in this thesis.

I like Suvarnabhumi Airport very much, for it appeals to my idea of the oriental and exotic and is a masterpiece of engineering. I never considered it from the critical viewpoint of post- or neocolonialism (neocolonialism is used in newer times for developing countries which are subjected to globalization and capitalistic exploitation). Alas, the fact is that its inception came up from a Western architectural conglomerate and their view of the exotic in Thai Culture. Projections of ideas and dreams about far away, exotic airports are also of an auratic, phenomenological nature. They appeal to our senses despite the post-colonial aftertaste.

One of the most striking airport projects ever is the Hajj Terminal of King Abdul Aziz International Airport in Jeddah, Saudi Arabia. It was completed in 1981 by Skidmore, Owings and Merrill (SOM), the Chicago Architecture firm which also built Shanghai's Jin Mao Tower, Singapore Changi Airport, Mumbai's Chhatrapathi Shivaji Airport, San Francisco Airport and many more. Founded in 1936 by Louis Skidmore and Nathaniel Owings, they merged in 1939 with John Merrill and later specialized in skyscrapers of the International Style like the John Hancock Center in Chicago. Their style is based on "Miesian" principles – large, sleek steel frameworks with glass panels, especially glass curtain walls. SOM are renowned for their "corporate signature urban buildings".[271]

The American structural engineer and architect Fazlur Khan, whose roots originated in present-day Bangladesh, was SOM's main man when it came to complex tubular designs and high-rises and he stands behind such buildings as the Sears (Willis) and Hancock Towers and the Hajj Terminal. In a way, Khan was an external architect but with inherited knowledge of the internal vernacular culture of the Orient.

The Hajj Terminal in Jeddah looks like a free-standing tent city on stilts (Figure 111).

It is in operation only for six weeks per year for the Holy Month of Hajj, which is the pilgrimage to Mecca. During that special time of the year the structure houses dozens of Jumbo Jets at its gates and offers camping and cooking facilities within its premises to hundreds of thousands of pilgrims. The Hajj Terminal is located next to the King Abdul Aziz International Airport of Jeddah.

It was the world's largest cable-stayed, fabric-roofed structure. The facility has two identical roofed halves — each 1,050 feet by 2,250 feet — separated by a landscaped central mall. The Teflon-coated fiberglass roof structure consists of 210 semi-conical fabric roof units. Each module is supported by 45-meter-tall steel pylons and further supported with steel cables along the rooftop. At the top of the pylons are openings, so that the air can circulate and smoke from fires can easily escape. This roof structure is reminiscent of the Bedouin culture of the region, mimicking their tents.

It offers space to 80,000 pilgrims at any day during its operation, allowing them to cultivate their traditions, to camp on the premises and light fires. These pilgrims spend between eight and 36 hours on the premises before or after their arrival. Some of them have been on a voyage or a plane for the first time in their lives. Some of them travel in groups of (only male) family or congregation members and they appropriate the space for their religious rites. That is the purpose of this special place (Figure 112).

271 Anne-Catrin Schultz, Skidmore, Owings & Merrill, International Terminal, San Francisco International Airport, p 7

Figure 111: Hajj Terminal at King Abdulaziz International Airport, Jeddah, Saudi Arabia; Photograph by Yousef Madari

Figure 112: Hajj Terminal at King Abdulaziz International Airport, Jeddah, Saudi Arabia. Interior view. Photograph by Sasikan

The fiberglass of the roof was made of Beta yarn which is finer than silk but has the strength of steel. The Teflon coating deflects the heat of the sunlight. As a result, the billowy structure allows light to pass through to the floor below but can withstand temperatures of up to 1,500 degree. Arriving passengers pass through the first half of the terminal which contains air-conditioned buildings where health and immigration facilities, baggage claim, and customs are housed. The second half is a vast, open-sided temperate waiting- and support area where travelers are given rest, water, shade, and food.[272]

This is an exceptional airport in the sense that for around 46 weeks per year it is not in use and remains empty. When in use, during the Hajj pilgrimage, it performs as a multifunctional cultural site, a temporary religious infrastructure. The abundance of columns and the airy site confer references to Lefebvre's architecture of enjoyment within the Roman thermal baths.

There are certain parallels to Norman Foster's Droneport project which he presented at the Architectural Biennale in Venice in 2016. The ephemeral and social use of aviation infrastructure in a desert climate is indeed unique and turns this into an event architecture.

The famous Teflon fabric roof was developed by Khan together with engineer Horst Berger who got his inspiration from Frei Otto's pioneering tensile structures.[273] The latter had been influenced by Pier Luigi Nervi's large-span structures such as the Palazzetto dello Sport

(1960) which in itself is a form of biomimicry – the conscious emulation of nature's genius.[274]

Biomimicry is a term which first appeared in 1962 amongst material scientists. Biomimicry depicts the use of nature for beneficial purposes in scientific materials. As for architects who seek out forms and symbols used by nature, biomimicry has produced some famous examples already mentioned in this thesis: Eero Saarinen's TWA Terminal with its biomorphic forms which depict movement in flight, possibly a dove. Frank Lloyd Wright and Le Corbusier adhered to biomimicry in their designs, with allusions to natural forms and their symbolism.

So far, biomimicry has been applied in architectural design in a limited way, rather through industrial design and computer based technology; however, it is considered to be the future of efficient building.[275]

The Italian engineer and architect Pier Luigi Nervi (1891–1979) based the structure of his Palazzetto dello Sport in Rome on the Amazon water lily. Both used the principle of ribs to give effective structural depth to a thin planar surface with a dome / shell form.

Nervi also invented the ferro-cimento (ferro-concrete) with which he could create his structures.[276]

Further above, we learned that Paxton, too, was inspired by the Victoria Amazonica water lily for its rib structure for his design of the Crystal Palace. Biomimicry has thus prevailed in architecture throughout centuries.

---

272 Simone Korein, Landen unter Zelten. Skidmore, Owings & Merrill, Haj Terminal, Jeddah, Archithese, p 36

273 Horst Berger, Light Structures – Structures of Light, p 79–101

274 Michael Pawlyn, Biomimicry in Architecture, p 2 & 14
     Italian structural engineer Pier Luigi Nervi (1891–1979) was famed for his large-span structures of ferro-cimento. He studied biological forms such as the giant Amazon water lily which has leaves of up to three metres in diameter with smooth top surfaces whose underside is strengthened by branches of radial ribs. This is incorporated in his ferro-cimento moulds to reinforce his vault-like structures.

275 Ibid., p 2

276 Ibid., p 14

Figure 113: Olympiastadion München, Frei Otto, architect. 1972. Photograph by Fritz Geller-Grimm

German engineer Frei Otto (1925–2015) pioneered tensile structures and cable-net buildings. His Olympiastadium in Munich, which was completed for the 1972 Olympic Games, serves as a prototype in tensile structures (Figure 113).

The tensile Teflon roof of the Hajj terminal was recreated by Horst Berger and architect Curtis Fentress for the Denver International Airport in 1995. The form evokes the majestic snow-capped peaks of the Rocky Mountains, Colorado's international signature. Sustainably, the fabric roof provides considerable daylighting, and low heat absorption reduces build-up due to sunlight radiation (Figures 114 & 115).

In this case, the allusions are neither Orientalism nor Exoticism. Curtis Fentress always spoke of the allusion to the snow peaks of the Rocky Mountains reflected within the Teflon roof of his airport. The symbolism of the tensile roof can also be adhered to the local indigenous Native American tribes who dwelled in tipi tents. This is all part of the airport aura, a curtsy to the history of the region.[277]

---

277 Curtis Fentress, in his personal interviews with me

Figure 114: Denver International Airport study, photograph taken by Lilia Mironov during visit of the headquarters of Fentress Architects in Denver.

Figure 115: Denver International Airport, photograph by Lilia Mironov

6.3   Event-architecture in Airports

In the cultural sciences, events are considered a form of social function and interaction. Their frequently temporary character of community building and their setting within places of publicness has become a subject of sociological investigation as they are steadily influenced by current social influences. Whereas in the social sciences events are considered as characteristic phenomena of the current society, in the anthropological and ethnological context they stand for social interaction, staging and performative production.

Thus, events are understood under the veil of sociology as forms and expressions of social life in society, whereas cultural anthropology sees them as spatial manifestations and their interaction within the landscape or immediate surroundings.[278]

Events have the connotation of offering easy entertainment and commercial mass consumption, such as fairs, carnivals, and even the Street Parade in Zurich or

278 Birgit Kröniger, Der Freiraum als Bühne, p 13

open air festivals. Events are the characteristic form of festival culture. Public spectacles are not just a form of leisure and pleasure; rather, they define the appearance of public and open spaces. This kind of spectacle has a centuries-old tradition and was part of the history of European cities. Processions, religious ceremonies, parades, demonstrations – they are all events. A new trend came into being since the 1990s – landscape architecture has turned to presenting itself as an event. Partly due to marketing strategies, this form of mixing nature and landscape with pleasurable activities and events has merged with other forms of temporary exhibitions, such as art and gardening installations. This temporary landscape-event-form includes Lucius Burckhardt's strollology.

Burckhardt's approach to cityscape and architecture by walking and strolling through it in order for the individual to have his own experience and opinion of that space is remarkably similar to Walter Benjamin's *flâneur* and Michel de Certeau's space vs place theories in his *Practice of Everyday Life*, where the emancipated pedestrian creates his own event-space by connecting different places.

The conjunction of festival events and gardens was an important motif in French palace gardens during the Baroque period. These festivities had a representative character and a show-like impact. By contrast, English gardens used to serve for contemplation and quietude and were never used for mass celebrations.[279]

This analogy can be found in various modern airport terminals. The Zen-Garden in Incheon Terminal and the various gardens in Singapore's Changi Terminal all serve as a place of contemplation and peace for the transiting passengers. As a matter of fact, architect Moshe Safdie is building a whole new such garden and event-space for Singapore Changi Airport:

The Jewel, scheduled to be inaugurated in 2019, is a development that shall transform the city-state's main airport into a public gathering space replete with gardens, retail outlets, and entertainment facilities. Moshe Safdie calls it a Paradisal Oasis (Figure 116).

This project has been conceived as a destination in its own right, boosting Singapore's appeal as a welcoming stopover location. *The Jewel* will be connected to Changi's Terminal 1 through its expanded arrival hall and linked to terminals 2 and 3 via pedestrian bridges. But it will also be open to visitors from Singapore who are expected to make up to 60% of the visitors. Moshe Safdie wanted to offer more than a Disney-like attraction, making *The Jewel* attractive for return visitors and open 24 hours a day, offering a lush urban oasis.

Beneath a soaring glass dome, a 40 meter-tall waterfall will cascade from a central oculus positioned at the top of the vaulted roof canopy. This feature, named the rain vortex, is surrounded by an indoor landscape of vegetation, with walking trails – referred to as the forest valley – traversing the site. Recalling the tradition of metropolitan centers with great parks, the vegetation associated with Safdie's design is continued externally, with the approach to the airport lined with large canopy trees and lush greenery.[280]

The Jewel culminates in the evolution of the Crystal Palace and the Parisian passageways. It is not only a garden experience, but a whole event in itself.

Event-space as a term emerged in the 1990s and in the context of this thesis is understood as a means of articulating how space performs through time and movement and how performance is spatialized through the event, especially so in theater architecture.[281]

As new forms of publicness and performance have been discussed during the last few decades, the term

---

279 Ibid., p 10

280 https://www.safdiearchitects.com/posts/inside-safdie-architects-13-billion-jewel-changi-airport-complex

281 Dorita Hannah, Event-Space: Theater Architecture & the Historical Avant-Garde, p 2

Figure 116: Singapore Changi Airport, *The Jewel* HSBC Rain Vortex, Moshe Safdie Architects, 2019, photograph courtesy of Matteo Morando

Figure 117: Seoul Incheon Airport, The Walk of the Royal Family, photograph by Lilia Mironov

new institutionalism was established around 2003 as a relatively young endeavor in curatorial practices and art exhibitions, a term which covers the *creation of new active spaces* for art and performances outside of the hierarchic formulaism of the traditional exhibiting institutions, such as theater or museum. This *new genre public art* allows for immediate participation by the viewers.

Curator and art professor Nina Möntmann appeals for the need of new interpretations of curating and exhibiting as well as using the public space as an opposition to the codifications of globalization and capitalism – creating an active space that is part community center, part laboratory, and part academy.[282]

This enables art performances in public spaces to become new forms of institutions by providing a social and sociological aspect to the venue. It enables emancipated spectatorship and ownership of non-places, thus contributing to giving them identity and meaning.

At Incheon Airport, as part of the Korea Cultural Heritage Foundation which also provided the Korea Traditional Cultural Experience Centers within the terminal premises, there is a celebratory performance of Korea's ancient royal heritage. The Walk of the Royal Family takes place twice daily with actors and actresses recreating the lives of the Joseon Dynasty which ended in 1897. It is all part of the performatory effect of the airport.

In the *Manhattan Transcripts*, postmodern architect Bernard Tschumi explains how the relationship between three levels of event, space, and movement makes for the architectural experience. Tschumi puts emphasis on movement and performance space as the complete synesthesia of the body. Space is created by an event taking place; the activity taking place inside of architecture defines that architectural space. Hence, architecture shall give space to event-space. [283]

6.4   Performative Architecture

Architects and architectural critics view buildings either as objects that result from design and construction techniques or as objects that represent various practices and ideas.

In performative architecture, a building is a technical and aesthetic work but is especially known for its actions and performances. Through the action of the people using these buildings, the character of the building shows itself.[284]

The term *performative* was coined by John L. Austin during his Harvard Lecture "How to do things with words" in 1955 (in previous works Austin would speak of *performatory* but decided on the shorter and more traditionally concepted *performative*). He meant to describe linguistic, oral sentences and performances as social actions. So-called speech acts expand beyond language into action itself. This roots from strong theatrical connotations which projected onto society and

---

282 Nina Möntmann, lecture "Kollektive Handlungsräume: Ein Blick auf die politischen Perspektiven neuer Gemeinschaften" (December 4, 2013, Bern):
The term new genre public art refers to public art, often activist in nature, that was created outside institutional structures in order to engage directly with an audience. The term was coined by the American artist, writer and educator Suzanne Lacy in 1991 to define a type of American public art that was not a sculpture situated in a park or a square.

283 Bernard Tschumi, Manhattan Transcripts, p 277

284 David Leatherbarrow, "Architecture's unscripted performance", in: Performative Architecture: Beyond Instrumentality, p 7

culture. At around this time Erika Fischer-Lichte discerns the performative turn in the arts.[285]

Performance has become popular in the last two decades throughout the arts and literature sciences. The manifestations of performance and performance art are manifold. Noted theatre historian Marvin Carlson calls performance art both historically and theoretically an American phenomenon, though it has an international diffusion.[286]

An action on stage that is identical to one in real life is considered "performed" on stage and "done" off stage. Performance can move from the stage and ritual or defined cultural situations into everyday life.[287]

Everyone, to a certain extent, plays a role socially. Carlson recognizes that our lives are structured around repeated modes of behavior and all human activity could potentially be considered as performance. The difference between doing and performing would thus be that we do the former actions unthinkingly, as a coded pattern of behavior (ritual), but as soon as we think about an action and introduce a consciousness to it, we give it a quality of performance.

Even the architecture of (critical) regionalism is understood as the relationship between people and their place of performance. This performativity is defined by iterative acts, verbal and physical that instill norms yet conceal the conventions of Foucauldian power force behind the acts.[288]

The ritualistic and the conscious are consequently denominators of performance.

The ritualistic has already been mentioned in this thesis in Michel Foucault's description of heterotopias as heterotopias which always presuppose a system of opening and closing that both isolates them and makes them penetrable, where the individual has to submit to rites and purifications. Social rites, as defined by Lefebvre, also make way for the architecture of enjoyment.

Surveillance and control rites are undertaken within the panopticon of the modern airport terminal. The check-in and screening processes, the endless queuing lines contribute to the dehumanization since every passenger is a potential terrorist. It is a performance of the extrastatecraft power of the operating system *airport*.

The main question of architectural performance is in which ways a building acts, how the architectural work actually expresses itself. The building "acts" to house activities and experiences such as places for catering and consuming and places for gathering, dwelling, and working.

Aldo Rossi's critique of functionalism explains how the use of a building often changes throughout its life

---

285 Erika Fischer-Lichte, Ästhetik des Performativen, p 31:
Cultural studies were mainly literature studies. Yet in the 1990s, in the wake of postmodernism, performative aspects of the arts and culture were understood as cultural actions. In 1988 Judith Butler introduced the term performative in her essay "Performative Acts and Gender Constitution: An Essay in Phenomenology and Feminist Theory" in which she explained that gender is an identity instituted through a "stylized repetition of acts". Butler calls this action "performative" which also carries the meaning of dramatic and non-referential. Thus, performative actions (as bodily actions) are non-referential, as they do not refer to given situations. In this case, expression is a diametral opposite to performativity because the physical actions which are considered performative do not derive from given identities or previously experienced actions but are only now defined with their own identity – through this performative action.

286 Marvin Carlson, "What is Performance?", in: The Performance Studies Reader, p 70–71: Carlson gives the example of how prestigious publications such as the New York Times and the Village Voice include the special category of "performance" separately from theater, dance or film. Tautologically we recognize any specific theatre event as a performance.

287 Ibid., p 72

288 Barbara L. Allen, "On Performative Regionalism", in: Architectural Regionalism: Collected Writings on Place, Identity, Modernity, and Tradition, p 422

by its different tenants –private houses become clinics, theaters turn into apartment blocks and so on. Function is not being discussed for typology. For urban buildings the function changes with time and its typology may become different.

Rossi concludes that functional use cannot define the building itself but the criterion instead is the type.[289]

In this case, the airport is defined by the type of building which is logically the airport terminal. This becomes complicated when airports no longer look like airports but urban event areas, as seen in the examples of the Far Eastern Airports presented in this work. Architectural performance in that sense aims to improve the quality of life within the built environment by using high-performance materials and technology.

The famous buildings of our time no longer insert art into functional solutions, but they use it to drape or cover them – here it transpires that sculptural form is essentially a compensation for the inadequacy of functionalist solutions.

To underline this, architectural theorist David Leatherbarrow talks of two paradigms for understanding architecture's performances: The device paradigm and the topographical paradigm. The device paradigm claims that the building has moving or movable parts which are manual and mechanical. This is the action part of architecture, manifested by our movements – stops, levels, intervals triggered by apertures, screens, furnishings.

This sort of design is called the device paradigm.[290] The architectural drama comes alive by the building's performance. It is aided by those parts of the building that give it its static equilibrium, such as thermal, material and structural stability through columns and beams and roofing systems. Examples of this device paradigm can be found in any modular and movable

architecture, such as Annette Spillmann and Harald Echsle's Freitag Tower (2006) in Zurich West which is constructed out of 17 stacked used shipping containers. The tower has become one of Zurich's landmarks with the containers stacked and mounted from elements used in the shipping industry. Large window openings provide the showrooms with natural light and allow views in both directions: from the inside out and vice versa. Customers are led past the range of products, consisting of over 1500 bags, to an observation platform approximately 25 meters above ground. The platform offers extraordinary views over the city of Zurich, the traffic, the lake, and the mountains[291] (Figure 118).

Spillmann and Echsle's other famous project was the House of Switzerland at the Sochi Winter Olympic Games in 2004 (Figure 119). This building, too, is a mobile structure, intended to represent Switzerland abroad. Manufactured industrially from prefabricated wooden elements with a reusable, flexible structure, its interior structure is installed in a "plug + play" way to ensure a short assembly phase. The house has since gone "on tour" to different athletic and culinary venues within Europe.

Of major interest to our thesis are Norman Foster's droneports. His *Droneport Project* is a device paradigm in performance as well – modular airport architecture and an evolution of Foster + Partners' previous experience in building airports, as well as earlier lunar building studies conducted in association with the European Space Agency. Additionally, it provides social space and space for cultural actions: The framework of performative architecture.

---

289 Leatherbarrow, Architecture's unscripted performance, p 7

290 Ibid., p 9–12

291 http://www.spillmannechsle.ch/wp/?p=140

Figure 118: Freitag Flagship Store, Zurich, 2006 Annette Spillmann & Harald Echsle

Figure 119: House of Switzerland, Sochi Winter Olympics 2014, Annette Spillmann & Harald Echsle, Photographs courtesy of Spillmann Echsle Architekten

Figure 120: Construction Drawing of Droneports, courtesy of Foster+Partners © and the Norman Foster Foundation

Figure 121: Visualization of Droneports, courtesy of Foster+Partners © and the Norman Foster Foundation

Figure 122: Visualization of Droneport Interior, courtesy of Foster+Partners © and the Norman Foster Foundation

The droneport uses local material and labor along with light formwork to create the emblematic forms that would eventually become a recognizable part of the African landscape. Firstly developed in 2015 with the intention to revolutionize the subcontinent within the next years, this is primarily a philanthropic project and infrastructural experiment which came to prominence during its exhibition at the Biennale Architettura 2016.

The droneport project explores the potential of an infrastructural leap using cutting edge technology to surmount the challenges of the future. Drones can be of help wherever there is a lack of roads. They can transcend geographical barriers such as mountains, lakes, and unnavigable rivers without the need for large-scale physical infrastructure. The proposal for droneports in Africa seeks to support a network of drone routes capable of delivering urgent and precious supplies, particularly blood, to remote areas on a massive scale (Figures 120 to 122). The vaulted brick structure has a minimal ground footprint and can be constructed by the local communities. It allows for flexible spaces, as multiple vaults can be linked together. On the ground, the droneport project offers a new typology for a building of ubiquitous presence, much like petrol stations have become dispersed infrastructure for road traffic. The droneport will have a strong civic presence, based on sharing and multiple uses. It allows for safe landing of quiet drones in a densely packed area, and includes a health clinic, a digital fabrication shop, a post and courier room, and an e-commerce trading hub, allowing it to become part of local community life.

The droneports will also be manufacturing centers for drones, generating employment opportunities for the local population. By giving the local people the construction knowledge, the project seeks to leave a legacy that will initiate a change that is bigger than the building itself.[292] These droneports are thus a moveable, modular multipurpose airport architecture with a humanitarian aspect to it.

The topographical paradigm is less obvious and focuses on the parts of the building that are static, like in material stability. This encompasses the reciprocal relationship of the building and its ambient conditions, weather and other forms of wear and tear, much of which will be seen in the façade of the building. These traces of life sedimented on the building are considered an enrichment for architect Peter Zumthor who puts great emphasis on a phenomenological architecture in his buildings, such as the thermal baths in Vals.[293]

Because this kind of movement on the buildings cannot be precisely predicted, it is considered an unscripted architectural performance. Such an example would be the topography of Herzog & de Meuron's De Young Museum in San Francisco's Golden Gate Park (2005), which works with the surrounding nature, allowing for the copper facade to slowly become green due to oxidation and therefore fade into its natural surroundings. The facade is also textured to represent light filtering through a tree. Herzog & de Meuron thought of a kind of organism with several limbs or extensions and arranged the building in three parallel bands in order for the park to fill the places in between. Nature, trees, plants, and water, in various forms, are an integral part of the building.[294] (Figure 123)

Topographies and facades tend to be viewed as sense of place designs as they enter a relationship with their

292 http://www.fosterandpartners.com/projects/droneport/

293 Leatherbarrow, Architecture's unscripted performance, p 14

294 https://www.herzogdemeuron.com/index/projects/complete-works/151-175/173-de-young-museum.html Jacques Herzog & Pierre de Meuron on the De Young Museum

Figure 123: De Young Museum, San Francisco, 2005 Herzog & de Meuron, photograph by Lilia Mironov

surroundings. This is the haptic, multisensual architecture Juhani Pallasmaa appeals to.

To show the interconnection between topographies and airports – back in 1966, landscape artist Robert

Smithson was one of the first artists to collaborate in the design of an airport. His sketches of what was later called *land-art* for the masterplan of the Dallas Fort Worth Airport were eventually dismissed. But his collaboration on this big scale project inspired him to his *nonsites* and *earthworks* creations, the most famous of which was the Spiral Jetty on the shores of the Great Salt Lake in Utah[295] (Figure 124).

Smithson's most remembered work was the Spiral Jetty (1970) in the Great Salt Lake. An earthwork sculpture created out of rocks and salt crystals, it represented a counterclock spiral one third of a mile long and jutting from the shore into the lake. Visitors could walk on this man-made natural formation, depending on the water level of the lake. Malcontent from the inert art presentation in museums, Smithson envisioned his land-art to be site-specific and in relationship with nature, much of which Leatherbarrow explains in this topographical device. The jetty resembles a galaxy in its shape. However, the flâneur walks around it in an anti-clockwise direction, and is thereby prompted not only to consider cosmology but also to move backwards through geological time. Smithson voiced an institutional critique of the cultural limitations and neutral spaces of art museums and emphasized that his *site* was a place in the world where art is inseparable from its context. His sites included locations in the American West as well as Mexico.[296]

The Spiral Jetty is evocative of Lloyd Wright's entry for the Lehigh Airport Competition in 1929. They are both organic and topographic structures. And both

295 Catherine Caesar, Long Read: The Cultural Politics of Air Travel: Art at Dallas Fort Worth Airport, Then and Now, http://www. fluentcollab.org/mbg/index.php/interview/index/181/116:
Historically, building an airport between Dallas and Fort Worth was a challenge. Since 1927, these rivaling cities, separated by only 30 miles, fought all propositions for a consolidated airport. Dallas and Fort Worth each had their own airport and could never agree on plans. It was only in the mid-1960s that the concept was accepted by both cities, in part because of Dallas's desire to disassociate itself with its main (and still extant) airport of Love Field and the charge of right-wing extremism in the days and months following JFK's assassination on November 22, 1963. DFW airport was meant not only to serve as a novel and distinct entrance to the area, but was also part of a city-wide initiative of progress and commercial growth to counter its critics.

296 Eugenie Tsai, Robert Smithson, Exhibition Museum of Contemporary Art, p 11

Figure 124: Spiral Jetty, Great Salt Lake. Robert Smithson. Photograph courtesy of Ian Longton

were not turned into airports, but belong to the airport aura of this thesis.

In July 1966 Smithson was hired as an "artist-consultant" by the engineering and architecture firm Tippetts-Abbett-McCarthy-Stratton (TAMS) to work with them on design proposals for the Dallas-Fort Worth Regional Airport. Smithson's interest in crystalline structures seemed to please TAMS's conception of the DFW terminals as modular units. He experimented with placing large structures on the fringes of the airfield and invited his friends Andre, LeWitt and Morris to submit proposals. The idea was that passengers taking off and landing would be able to view these "earthworks" or grid type frameworks. Smithson cre-

ated various sketches for his *Aerial Map-Proposal for Dallas-Fort Worth Regional Airport*. Anticipating his *nonsites*, Smithson also proposed for the terminal complex to include a gallery (aerial museum) that would provide visual information about where these aerial sites were situated.[297]

Nonsites is the oeuvre Smithson had begun in 1968 that encompasses geologically and geographically based works. He created hybrids made of minerals, metal containers, photographs, maps and other documents which were based on the natural materials of their geographical source and their relocation in a museum or gallery, which Smithson named the non-site.[298]

---

297 Eugenie Tsai, Robert Smithson, Exhibition Museum of Contemporary Art, Los Angeles, 2004, p 24

298 Robert Smithson, Selected Writings by Robert Smithson, *A provisional Theory of Non-Sites*, https://www.robertsmithson.com/essays/provisional.htm: "By drawing a diagram, a ground plan of a house, a street plan to the location of a site, or a topographic map, one draws a logical two dimensional picture. […] *The non-site* is a three dimensional logical picture that is *abstract*, yet it *represents* an actual site in N.J. (The Pine Barrens Plains). It is by this dimensional metaphor that one site can represent another site which does not resemble it – this *The non-site*. Between the *actual site* in the Pine Barrens and *The non-site* itself exists a space of metaphoric significance. It could be that 'travel' in this space is a vast metaphor. Everything between the two sites could become physical metaphorical material devoid of natural meanings and realistic assumptions. Let us say that one goes on a fictitious trip if one decides to go to the site of the *non-site*. The 'trip' becomes invented, devised, artificial; therefore, one might call it a non-trip to a site from a Non-site. Once one arrives at the 'airfield', one discovers that it is man-made in the shape of a hexagon, and that I mapped this site in terms of aesthetic boundaries rather than political or economic boundaries."

Figures 125 & 126: Spaceport America, New Mexico, Norman Foster, 2014, courtesy of Nigel Young, Foster + Partners

Ultimately, neither the TAMS design nor any of Smithson's proposed artworks were ever constructed. Although never realized, Smithson's designs mark a turning point in his career. The DFW project is the origin of two key concepts in his oeuvre: *Nonsites* and *earthworks*, and the TAMS commission definitely put him on the landscape.

Smithson rang in a new era in airport design: That of the collaboration with artists and artworks.

Another airport which heavily underscores the topography is Norman Foster's Spacesport for Virgin Galactic in the desert of New Mexico.

This is one of the most futuristic airports ever realized. It won the international competition for the first private spaceport in 2006 and was completed in 2014 in the desert of New Mexico. The building of Spaceport America emerges from the landscape like an elevation or little hill. The roof's texture merges with the local topography – the desert prairie. Taking on some of the organic forms of Saarinen's TWA terminal, the Spaceport was designed by Norman Foster so that it

"captures the drama and mystery of flight itself", with a sleek modern interior and minimal impact on the environment[299] (Figures 125 & 126). This spaceport literally performs as a science fiction vehicle.

For those who will not be able to buy a ticket on Virgin Galactic – which might cost anything upwards of USD 100,000 – there is a visitor's center on the premises so that this curious, Star Trek worthy architecture is not wasted on the select few.

Spaceport America may be the most extraterrestrially fantastic airport of our century, but in 1974 the first futurist airport was completed: The young Paul Andreu, who led the conglomerate of Aéroports de Paris, conceptualized Terminal 1 of Paris' Charles de Gaulle Airport as a giant circular organism with an open skylight. It was beyond avant-garde design on ten floors in a circular building which was surrounded by satellite buildings. Like an octopus, that main building housed all of the relevant functions of a terminal, with tubular glass walled escalators within its body (to protect from the weather) connecting the different floors.[300]

299 https://www.fosterandpartners.com/projects/spaceport-america/

300 Paul Andreu, Fifty Airport Terminals, p 44

Figures 127 & 128: Terminal 1, Aéroport Charles de Gaulle, Paris. Paul Andreu architect, 1974. Photographs by Lilia Mironov

Terminal 1 was developed around the same time as Renzo Piano and Richard Rogers' Centre George Pompidou in Paris, which was then spectacularly demonstrating the inside-out architecture with its mechanics and structural system, as well as escalators exposed and attached on the outside of the building. These buildings performed on many levels and were precedent-setting to the postmodernist and high-tech architecture.

6.5   Art in Airports

Art Commission Programs have been implemented in many airports in different countries. Some airports have opened museums and curate alternating exhibits. Others proudly display works by Urs Fischer, Robert Rauschenberg, Frank Stella, and Roy Lichtenstein. Atlanta's new international terminal spent USD 5 million on art. San Francisco International, considered a leader in airport art, has spent more than USD 15 million since the 1970s.

The Rijksmuseum Amsterdam has an annex at the airport. London Heathrow recently unveiled a permanent installation at Terminal 2. Slipstream is Europe's largest privately funded sculpture and one of the longest artworks in Europe at 70 meters. Created in 2014 by British sculptor Richard Wilson, its purpose is to make the passengers stop in their tracks and marvel

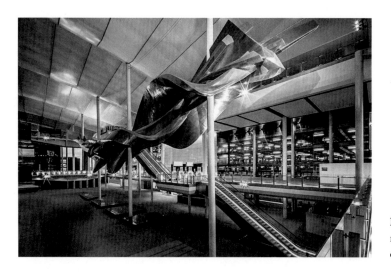

Figure 129: *Slipstream* by Richard Wilson, Heathrow International Airport Terminal 2, photograph courtesy of Richard Wilson

at its depiction of a twisting stunt plane maneuvering through the volume of the new terminal, frozen in time and space[301] (Figure 129).

The American Association of Airport Executives has held an annual meeting of airport art program officials ever since 9/11, as airports were desperate to make the experience calmer and more humanizing for passengers. New security requirements create a panopticon of surveillance and suspicion for the traveler and art can de-stress and classy up the airport experience.[302]

Denver International Airport was the first airport created with an integrated art program, with 30 permanent art exhibits on display and varying exhibitions. In 1988, seven years before its completion, Mayor Federico Peña established the "... policies and procedures for the funding and implementation of a public art program for the City and County of Denver." The purpose of this new Public Art Program was to "... expand the opportunities for Denver residents to experience art in public places, thereby creating more visually pleasing and human environments." Denver International Airport even has its own website presenting the artworks and announcing exhibitions and a Public Art Policy of 39 pages depicting the requirements and regulations of art in Denver Airport.

Denver International Airport's Art and Culture Program administers the City and County of Denver's *one percent for art* ordinance which enhances public places and features nearly 40 site-specific works including sculptures, murals and other installations. The pieces are displayed in outdoor landscapes, inside Jeppesen Terminal and on airport concourses, as well as in the train tunnels and on the train itself. In addition to its permanent art collection, the airport curates temporary exhibitions, collaborating with museums, cultural institutions, and arts organizations to present the highest quality two- and three-dimensional work.[303]

The aim is to create a cultural experience that engages passengers and presents the cultural legacy of the region.

301   Richard Wilson, http://richardwilsonsculptor.com/sculpture/slipstream-2014.html

302   http://www.nationalartsprogram.org/news/airports-art-lovers

303   https://www.flydenver.com/about/art_culture/program

When arriving at Denver International Airport from the highway, one is greeted by a giant blue Mustang. It is the airport's landmark sculpture. A 32-foot (9.75 m) tall fiberglass sculpture with the characteristics of the Mexican muralists, it bestows honor to the sense of place – the Southwestern prairies and their wild horses. It was conceptualized by Luis Jimenez back in 1993 for the newly established Denver Airport "public art program", but was erected only in 2008 at the crossroads of Peña Boulevard at the entrance to the airport[304] (Figure 130). To add to the (macabre) legend, Luis Jiménez died in 2006 in his studio in New Mexico where he was finishing work on Mustang and a large section fell off and struck him.[305]

Airport art programs have emerged all over the world – at Miami Airport, Dallas Fort Worth, San Francisco, Philadelphia, Los Angeles Airports, Doha and Mumbai airports …

Many airports have long housed iconic works, such as the Alexander Calder sculpture "Flight" at New York's Kennedy International Airport and Michael Hayden's 1987 neon light show set to music in an underground walkway between the United Airlines concourses at Chicago O'Hare International Airport.

Unlike the terminals of the past, new airports typically boast large, open spaces and atriums that create unique opportunities for large-scale sculptures.

Amsterdam's Schiphol Airport has a large collection of contemporary sculpture. But the airport also has a collection of Dutch masterpieces from the Rijksmuseum on rotating display. The airport takes extra precautions for its expensive paintings. Its museum is in one of the most secure places in the airport, after passport control. The paintings are secured behind glass in a climate-controlled environment.[306]

Figure 130: *Mustang*, by Luis Jiménez, in the background Denver International Airport, Jeppesen Terminal, photograph by Lilia Mironov

304 https://www.flydenver.com/about/art_culture/mustang

305 David A. Belcher, Luis Jimenez, Sculptor, Dies in an Accident at 65, The New York Times, 15 June 2006

306 Scott MacCartney, Airports for Art Lovers, The Wall Street Journal

Figure 131: Hamad International Airport, Doha, with Lamp Bear by Urs Fischer. HOK Architects, 2014, photograph Tim Griffith/ Courtesy of HOK

While exhibiting artworks in the context of the airport's location/culture is an altruistic intention, what we are witnessing, especially in airports of Middle Eastern countries which can afford that kind of luxury, is the acquisition of Western trophy artworks which seems totally random and oftentimes an effort of vanity to adorn oneself with the most expensive of the current artworks. These airports are not museums and not the white cube kind of gallery interiors. They are a new hybrid exhibition place that might revolutionize the world of curating, exhibiting art and even auctioning art.

The giant Urs Fischer teddy bear sculpture "Lamp Bear", which weighs 35,000 pounds and stands 23 feet tall, was previously displayed in front of the Seagram Building on New York's Park Avenue (Figure 131).

The teddy bear was auctioned off at Christie's New York for just over USD 6.8 million in 2012 to a member of Qatar's royal family. The Qatar Museum Authority (QMA) oversees public art installations by local and international artists in its continued commitment to the development of its Public Art program which also covers the airport.[307]

307 Salma Awad, Delayed Doha airport gets USD 6.8m giant teddy bear, Arabian Business, 16 Dec 2013

Figure 132: Chhatrapati Shivaji International Airport, Delhi, SOM. Waiting area in concourse level with traditional jali window screens. Photograph by Lilia Mironov

Chhatrapati Shivaji International Airport (SOM) opened its new Terminal 2 in Mumbai in early 2014 to present the world's most art-filled airport. This terminal is at the peak of the current airport-museum hybrid trend. Measuring 4.4 million square feet, the elegant Chhatrapati Shivaji International Airport Terminal 2 shall serve 40 million travelers per year, nearly twice as many as the building it replaces. The new terminal combines international and domestic passenger services under one roof, optimizing terminal operations and reducing passenger walking distances. Inside the building, walls of lights inspired by temple oil lamps, discreetly light the passageways and concourses.

Inspired by the form of traditional Indian pavilions, the new four-story terminal stacks a grand central processing podium on top of highly adaptable and modular concourses below. All concourses radiate outwards from a central processing core permitting them to swing between domestic and international service. The terminal is adorned with references to the local setting, history, and culture. Regional patterns and textures are subtly integrated into the terminal's architecture at all scales and intricate jali window screens filter dappled light into the concourses[308] (Figure 132).

The Times of India boasted that the potential audience for this art is beyond that of any world museum

308 http://www.som.com/projects/chhatrapati_shivaji_international_airport__terminal_2

and that this is to be the most visited museum in the world. They are confident that with a capacity to handle 40 million passengers annually, the airport's *Jaye He Museum* could comfortably surpass Paris' Louvre, currently the most visited art museum in the world with nine million annual visitors. The Jaye He Museum plans to exhibit around 7000 artworks and artifacts. The collections form part of six thematic compositions that employ collaborative works by about 100 artists to depict India's many facets with mediums like wood, glass, canvas, fiber glass, ceramics, papier-mache, terracotta, metal, stone and cloth (Figures 133 to 135). Many objects, like the nineteenth-century artifacts and totems needed restoration. They have been catalogued, their provenance established and registered with the Archaeological Survey of India, just like in a proper

Figures 133, 134, 135: Art Installations in Mumbai Chhatrapati Shivaji International Airport, photographs by Lilia Mironov

Figures 136 & 137: Mudras in Arrivals Hall at Indira Gandhi International Airport, Delhi. Photographs by Lilia Mironov

museum.[309] This airport has its own art curator, Rajeev Sethi, who believes that India is so rich in historic art and living artists that "the whole country is a living museum"; hence he envisages Terminal 2 as a new kind of public museum and art forum.[310]

And yet the biggest critical blow of this hybrid art space/airport terminal comes from the British The Guardian: "This terminal shows what's going wrong with Mumbai", writes its art critic Naresh Fernandes. He accuses the Indian middle class of being brainwashed after two decades of economic liberalization and of believing that privatization is the solution for all their problems; and that they have forgotten what public actually means. As art historian Rahul D'Souza points out: "Richer residents are quite willing to accept the idea that an art exhibition can be public, even if it

can be accessed only by people who have bought an international air ticket." This aspiration for exclusivity by the middle-class will have a profound effect on Mumbai's politics in the near future.[311]

When arriving at Delhi's International Airport named after Indira Gandhi and constructed in 2010 by HOK, one is greeted by a sculptural wall extending all along the terminal, complete with nine giant *mudras*. These friendly hand gestures stem from ancient Hinduist and Buddhist rituals. They were created by designer Ayush Kasliwal with Indian design firm Icubis Consultants. Their intention was to stand out from other airports and incorporate the classic gestures used in Indian dance forms and rituals, as the Indian culture is very vivid. Yet, as to not insult international travelers, the chosen mudras are not expressively religious, but rather friendly and welcoming. One of the mudras is

---

309 Manju V, Mumbai airport's T2 to double as largest museum, The Times of India, 5 Jan 2014

310 Louise Nicholson, Art in the Airport: Terminal 2 Mumbai, Apollo Magazine, February 15, 2014
In Mumbai, nativists have ensured that almost every new building is named after the seventeenth-century warrior-king Shivaji, with Victoria Terminus already renamed to him.

311 Naresh Fernandes, Cities in motion: Why Mumbai's new air terminal has gone off the rails, in The Guardian, 20 Feb 2014

the *abhaya mudra* – the fearless gesture (an open hand with the fingers slightly bent)[312] (Figures 136 & 137).

That to me is one of the most unique and beautiful airport art installations and an honorable reminder of the sense of place, without any notes of kitsch or post-colonialism.

Hanging pictures in a museum is an art on its own. J.M.W. Turner was famous for his hanging requests which he even stipulated in his will. There is an original sketch of his in the Tate Gallery, "Hanging Plan for an Exhibition in Turner's Gallery", dated to ca. 1812.[313] His sketch depicts a corridor-like hanging area on both sides. The art displayed in the 200 m long, dimly lit arrival corridor in Mumbai's Terminal 2 is neatly arranged behind glass walls along a curved stone wall. It does resemble Turner's idea of arranging artworks.

There are many reasons why people go to galleries. People go in search of visual wonders centered on the aesthetic masterpiece, some want to be emotionally moved. Visiting a gallery can be part of the visitor's quest for a sense of identity, even validation, through the self-absorbed, lingering gaze in the museum. Seeing and being seen mobilize desires and the senses. Here again, we have a sensual experience which is auratic or phenomenological.

The notion that not all visitors at the gallery/museum are there to look at the pictures goes back in time. In the early nineteenth century, curators at the National Gallery complained that mothers came there solely to teach their children to walk.[314] Here, the lingering gaze, the flâneur and the emancipated spectator all merge together.

The conduct and behavior in museums were indirectly steered by the design and layout of the rooms. Museum historian Charlotte Klonk addresses the color schemes of the background walls, the lighting, the height and abundance of artworks displayed, furnishings (or lack thereof), dimensions and configuration of rooms, and the flow of visitors which were thoroughly orchestrated by the curators who were in control of the experience people should gain in the galleries.[315] These color schemes and interior design are equally important in airport terminals, "curated" and controlled by architects and interior designers. Interior airport design either substitutes or enhances art in airports.

In Beijing Capital Airport (2008, Foster and Partners), the sense of place approach of design expresses itself through the traditional colors of China and Feng Shui, red and yellow, that prevail in the terminal, as well as through the motif of the dragon scales which are re-interpreted in the structure of the roof – a mythical animal of positive and protective connotation in Chinese culture[316] (Figures 138 & 139).

Another airport which heavily relies on the sense of place design is Dane County Regional Airport in Madison, Wisconsin (1998, Alliiance Architects), shortly presented earlier in this thesis in the chapter on railway stations.

---

312 Tripti Lahiri, Delhi Airport's Hands Sculpture, The Wall Street Journal, 28 July 2010

313 http://www.tate.org.uk/art/research-publications/jmw-turner/joseph-mallord-william-turner-hanging-plan-for-an-exhibition-in-turners-gallery-r1146843

314 Charlotte Klonk, Spaces of Experience, p 1

315 Charlotte Klonk, The white cube and beyond, Tate etc., issue 21: Spring 2011

316 David Jenkins, Foster40/Norman Foster, p 296

Figure 138: Beijing Capital Airport, interior color schemes, photograph courtesy of Absorbb

Figure 139: Beijing Capital Airport, interior, photograph courtesy of Pascal Sun

Alliiance Architects translated Frank Lloyd Wright's prairie style architecture, which was predominant from the 1890s to the 1920s, into the terminal. The prairie school stood for an architecture that connected to the earth and the prairie. Horizontal lines and flat roofs with large interior spaces, with earthen colors like

brown dominating. Only regional materials were used for the airport interiors, and red and brownish colors prevail throughout the terminal and in the mosaics of the flooring. Art-deco style lamps enhance the vernacular and sense of place.[317]

Museums are on the border between the public and the private and the contemplation of art is supposed to be a rather intimate and personal act and museum institutions have a public responsibility. Predominantly frequented by women in the nineteenth century, this is similar to the interiorization effect we read about earlier on. It was women who left their domestic space to seek out merchandises and have a social life in the public spaces, while the men worked in factories or city offices. Art galleries started opening late only after the general introduction of electric light around 1900.[318] To experience a museum is more than an intellectual activity, it is about feeling and perceiving as well, taking on parts of strollology and phenomenology.

As we have seen through Charlotte Klonk's research, the genesis of the art museum is strongly tied to enlightenment, and also the self-awareness of the women who were the first to appropriate that semi-public place. Appropriation of public places which give them a completely new social meaning is ongoing. The current refugee housing in Berlin's Tempelhof Airport is one such example, the nannies squatting in the spaces of power and finance in Hong Kong is another one.

My critique of the aspirations of Chhatrapati Shivaji Airport's Jaye He integrated art museum are the exclusivity access only for the flying elite. After all, Spaceport America offers a visitor center with tours of the terminal for those who cannot afford to fly into space. Providing a museal experience to airport passengers is a tricky endeavor. Many of them do not acknowledge

---

317 Steve Thomas-Emberson, Airport Interiors, p 58–60
318 Charlotte Klonk, Spaces of Experience, p 3–9

the art on display. Just as many pilots I know do not care about airport design. It is in the nature of us all to be unappreciative. I appreciate the artworks, but my background is art history.

In his essay "The Exhibitionary Complex" (1988), Tony Bennett argues that the Crystal Palace was the inverted mirror image of the panopticon with reversed mechanisms, while still doing some of the same disciplinary and disciplining work. Whereas in Foucault's model seeing without being seen provided the mechanism of the panopticon and the organizing metaphor of the modern carceral complex, Bennett's theories explain that in the Crystal Palace the emphasis was reversed and the order of power and knowledge were exposed to the public view – the institutions involved in the "exhibitionary complex" were also involved in the transfer of objects and bodies from the enclosed and private domains in which they had previously been displayed into more open and public places.[319]

We have seen in this work that the Crystal Palace smoothed the way to airport architecture, not at least because it was an exhibition venue like the Jaye He art museum. The order and power of the patrons of the Jaye He museum are exhibited by their mere presence there. It is a semi-private museum for the affluent.

It is a problematic critique, though, as we are all well aware that airports will always be secluded from outside masses and only those who pass through surveillance and have an airplane ticket will be able to experience it. What I hope to see is art installations predominantly in the public spaces of airports, made democratically available to everyone; but that, too, proves logistically impossible. What remains of Mumbai's Jaye He airport museum is the dreamlike world of the flâneur with an airline ticket. The phantasmagoria may be the airport experience which is in fact a commodity. And it is a form of experience that, despite promising cultural fulfilment, remains essentially ephemeral.

6.6 The Airport is a Stage

"All the world's a stage" from the monologue in William Shakespeare's *As You Like It* (1599) is ever so present and relevant in the realm of the airport terminal. The social organization and performance rituals of space inside an airport play out like a theater performance. Airport terminals heavily borrow on elements from theatre and opera architecture of past times.

The emphasis here lies not on the architecture itself, but on how the architecture performs within the interior space to create social codes and rites for its users.

Charles Garnier's Opéra de Paris (1861) set a paradigm for performing architecture that has conveyed into designing modern public places and modern terminal interiors.

Both airport architect and theatre director set up the stage of the performance that unfolds as a voyage for the spectators and performers in this theater of social life[320] (Figure 140).

The term *Theater* can mean the dramatic practice of performance as well as the building (architecture) housing that performance. Walter Gropius' *Totaltheater* design involved the dissolution of the limitations of the stage, mixing the threshold between spectator-actor by activating the spectator as a participant.[321] The 1875 Opéra de Paris by Charles Garnier was the utmost architectural model for the fusion of performer and spectator. The vista and promenade through urban space towards the opera were of great importance to the de-

---

319 Tony Bennett, The Exhibitionary Complex, in: New Formations, p 78

320 Gray Read, Introduction: The Play's the Thing, Architecture as a Performing Art, p 1

321 Hannah, Event-Space: Theater as a Performing Art, p 3

Figure 140: Grand Opéra Paris, Charles Garnier. Photograph courtesy of Benh Lieu Song

sign of the total theater experience, and as such, the Avenue de l'Opera and the opera house at the end of its axis were linked projects. Garnier himself created a design principles manifesto for his opera house where he stated "to see and to make oneself be seen, to understand and to make oneself be understood."[322]

A hierarchical layering of space distributes theatergoers according to economic class and gender. Although arriving by separate prescribed access points, all entered the cubic space of the grand stair only to split again according to class – the majority at the parterre level, while the privileged took their places in private, tiered loges where they were identified by the all-too-visible onlookers.

Garnier recognized the importance of the social theater that played out in the pre-performance space on the grand stair. This juxtaposition between performer and spectator and the paradigm of non-participating spectators increasingly irritated critics.[323] In the *Society of the Spectacle* Guy Debord further critiqued a society of passive spectatorship, consumption and mediated experience. This critique continues today in the form

322 Karsten Harries, "Theatricality and Re-Presentation", in Perspecta: Theater, Theatricality and Architecture, 26, p 23

323 Beth Weinstein, "Turned Tables: The Public as Performers in Jean Nouvel's Pre-Performance Spaces", in: Architecture as Performing Art, p 164

of debates around participation and performativity in theater and other spatial and cultural disciplines.[324] Rancière endorsed a conscious viewing as a spectator as opposed to the spectator who uses viewing instead of knowing. For Rancière, spectators had been incapable so far to understand the power of knowing and the power of acting. He appealed to the conscious much in a Cartesian sense.[325]

The passive spectatorship that Guy Debord mentions and that goes hand in hand with consumerism might be the most fitting description of airport travelers. Unlike Debord or Garnier who emphasized the participatory and consciousness of social theater, my observation is that airport interiors invite the passenger/dweller/flâneur to indulge in consumption through the form of passive spectatorship and participation.

The baroque or neoclassical theater auditorium tended to be a U-shaped configuration of shallow tiered balconics and boxes that encircled a flat central area called the pit, parterre, orchestra, or stalls. The royal box remained as the psychological, social, and pivotal center of the auditorium, something that has been copied in public theaters to suggest aristocratic elegance without the patronage of a royalty.[326] This enabled the spectators to see the stage as well as other spectators. This spectatorial surveillance is a way of self-reflection of the spectator and the comparisons between theater boxes and airport lounges with their privileged view from the top onto "the masses" lie on hand. The Star Alliance Lounge in the Tom Bradley International Terminal in Los Angeles (2013, Fentress Architects) offers very theatrical characteristics. There are no boxes but vast balconies from atop which offer a generous view onto the spacious terminal hall and onto other passengers (Figures 141 & 142).

Figures 141 & 142: Great Hall, Los Angeles International Terminal, Fentress Architects 2013, view from the mezzanine Star Alliance Lounge, photographs by Lilia Mironov

324 Ibid., p 165
325 Jacques Rancière, The Emancipated Spectator, p 2
326 Marvin Carlson, Places of Performance, p 172

One observes and one is being observed. This is all part of the human spectacle.

This again has a very panoptical connotation; to Foucault, our society is more one of surveillance than spectacle, and again this culminates in social control. Airport interiors with their compartmentalization of lounges for the more privileged and displays of phantasmagoria are consequently exhibiting social control on the travelers. The travelers are not as emancipated as they might think to be, as they are actors in a machinery of consumption, hierarchy, and patronization. Sitting in a lounge which is reserved to the more affluent and worldly is a message of power but also a surrendering of one's own identity by being pushed into a role of passivity and conspicuous consumption – that of exclusivity.

7 Airport Aura

The semiotics of an airport is generally understood on every continent and still the ubiquity of that transitory space renders us indifferent. It is through the phenomenological perception of this non-space and our re-created emotions within it that architects try to guide us through this sense of place Potemkin Village.

While Benjamin mourns the loss of the aura through mass reproduction techniques of the early twentieth century, such as postcards, Martino Stierli says of the postcard that it stands for a cultural condition in which images and their circulation are more important than their referents; not so much the real New York is deduced in these postcards but the images and imitations circulating about it. These postcards are a repository of "Manhattanism", a realm of ideas about the city.[327]

The auratic that perseverates does so through the image. Images and feelings are part of the auratic apprehension of the architectural work. The image as criterion of postmodernism does not limit our view on airport aura as to excluding airports from earlier than postmodernism, but it enhances our notion of so called *iconic* airports.

"If postmodernism can be characterized by one single criterion, it may be the concept of the image. This is because images have always been visually present and a return to the original is no longer desirable because it never existed in the first place. What is essential for the postmodern aesthetics of production is montage – the particular way that fragments are arranged and re-composed into a new visual entity, the constructedness of the postmodern object."[328]

Robert Venturi recognized signs and symbols as place-makers in our head, as the architecture of communication. His postmodern way of communicating to our senses with architecture is through "cultural iconography". Venturi is not a phenomenologist but he apprehends that seeing – sight – is one of our most important senses. And he understands the power of the image. Venturi sees more importance in the signage of architecture than in the emphasis on space. Venturi and his wife and collaborator, Denise Scott Brown, argue that architecture should no longer deal in abstract expressionism but use iconography. This is the kind of iconography that Venturi mentions in his famous duck vs decorated shed quote. It is when the building becomes a sculpture and discerns itself from the decorated shed. And it is surprisingly mostly found in the megastructure airports accompanying generic or globalized cities.

Seoul Incheon Airport by Fentress Architects (2001) was constructed on a man-made island in the Yellow Sea. It does not feature Byzantine mosaics (as per Venturi's iconography) but a very rich architectural iconography of Korean Buddhism and architecture. This is why it has been awarded numerous times the world's "best airport" by trade publications (Figure 143).

---

327 Martino Stierli, "The Architect as Ghost-Writer: Rem Koolhaas and image-based urbanism", in Postmodernism: Style and Subversion, 1970–1990, p 137–139

328 Ibid., p 137

Figure 143: Seoul Incheon Airport, Fentress Architects 2001. Zen, contemplation, culture, steel and prosperity. Photograph by Lilia Mironov

Vertically straight and horizontally curving elements recall traditional Korean architecture. Landscaping included the planting of forty thousand trees native to Korea plus six hundred thousand flowering plants. The unique roof structure incorporates local materials, namely steel – the Korean steel industry is the largest and most sophisticated in the world. Curtis Fentress approached this airport with the belief that it should serve as a regional signature, as a branding device.

The most prominent structural motif is the catenary curve, the natural arc formed by a chain suspended between two points. The catenary defined the rooflines of countless structures in Korea and has been employed in Korean architecture for centuries. In the abstracted version in Incheon, the arc is braced by cables span-

ning the roof with a skin of aluminum stretched between structural beams. The effect is weightlessness and tension. As in every Fentress terminal the Great Hall features ample natural lighting and in this case soaring trees native to the Korean peninsula.[329]

Seoul Incheon Airport is the duck, the sculpture, not the decorated shed. It is also not colonial mimicry but it does reflect its region's history and culture. The multi-sensory effect which Pallasmaa appeals to is translated into the *Cultural Performance* and *Experience* which are given their own spaces within this airport. The Incheon International Airport Traditional Culture Workshops and Cultural Performance Centers situated within the terminal (behind security and customs) are exhibition areas where traditional Korean culture

---

329 Catalogue Now Boarding: Fentress Airports and the Architecture of Flight, ed. Christoph Heinrich and Curtis W. Fentress, Denver 2012, p 68

experiential programs are being offered for passengers awaiting departing international or connecting flights. Participants can learn how to make jewelry boxes out of hanji (traditional Korean paper) or make cell phone straps using traditional sewing techniques that were used to make clothing and accessories.

The aptly named Korean Cultural Street (located in the central area of the 4th floor Passenger Terminal) is lined with Korean traditional architecture including Giwa (tiled roof) houses, Jeongja (pavilion), and the afore mentioned catenary line motifs of Korean architecture, allowing visitors to uniquely enjoy Korean architectural traditions in Incheon Airport. Traditional Events, such as Korean classical chamber concerts as well as the Royal Family's procession are regularly held at the Cultural Street.[330] The idea here is to enhance the passenger experience of the sense of place by pulling Benjamin's *flâneur* and present-day passenger into an activity of leisure and culture, to help de-stress the traveler and ultimately and most probably, make him consume more within the airport retail shops.

Airport architects and authorities like the term "humanizing"; I use the term auratic to describe this sensation.

Which other airports do I consider to be auratic – mythical, dreamlike and sensual (appealing to the senses)? In architectural writings, the term iconic or iconicity architecture are attributed quite liberally to a lot of postmodern megastructure starchitect buildings.

The truly first iconic terminal was Eero Sarinen's TWA terminal in John F. Kennedy Airport, New York. Here too, the iconography is eye-catching, evoking biomorphic forms from nature or even the wings of a bird in flight. This iconic terminal design became the branding device for its in-house airline, TWA. In this age of the corporate showpiece movement, whose architects are SOM and Mies van der Rohe with their monolithic corporate skyscrapers in the international style, Saarinen's masterpiece stands out against the formalism of the mid-century. It is of organic quality, a sculpture, much of what is to be expected in current postmodernist architecture such as Frank Gehry's deconstructivist buildings. Saarinen was fond of expressionist forms, such as his Gateway Arch for St. Louis a decade earlier. His organic architectural approach followed Frank Lloyd Wright's earthy style.[331] The sensuality of this terminal is not only the visual, but also the haptic and tectonic architecture – flat stairways and rounded vaults make for a cave-like feeling, appealing to our homely instincts.

As to the difference in the auratic effect of the airport between the traveler and employee – I thought long about this dichotomy. I have asked airline pilots and flight attendants about their perceptions of airports, and not much has come out of this. Either you are interested in this history or not, and it does not matter if you are working or passing through there.

The same might be said about the passengers: Either they apprehend and appreciate the architectural efforts and art exhibits or they do not. The difference is the passive or active spectatorship. It is a choice. In my case, I choose to be an emancipated spectator of airport architecture.

---

330 http://english.visitkorea.or.kr/enu/ATR/SI_EN_3_1_1_1.jsp?cid=609933: The east wing's location is on the third floor departure area, only 5 m away from gate 24, next to the sign. The west wing's location is on the third floor departure area, about 5 m in front of gate 40, across from the coffee shop. The "Walk of the Royal Family" takes place in the Duty Free Area, 3rd Floor Passenger Terminal Public Area, 4th Floor Korean Cultural Street.

331 Ahmed Sarbutu, "Expression und Funktion. Das TWA Terminal von Eero Saarinen in New York." in: *Archithese* 5.02 September/Oktober, Heft 5, Jg. 32, Zürich 2002, p 32–35

The auratic effect of airport architecture has been demonstrated in its various stages – through the synesthetic effects of viewership and travel, through architecture that appeals to the senses, through interior design and consumption as well as through theatrical connotations.

The aura of the airport in times of high crisis, as we have been experiencing in the last couple of years, beginning with the impact on control and punishment since 9/11 and culminating in the current refugee crises, has changed into a more political aura.

From my perspective of the traveler in airports, I sense a shift away from the phantasmagorias on display and passive spectatorship that seduces to laziness and consumption. I sense a more humanitarian and altruistic future in terms of airport aura.

Part of it has to do with the discussion surrounding Norman Foster's droneport project for Africa. How will droneports affect the traditional airports? In emerging economies in Africa we will see a complete change of perspective in respect to macroeconomic and colonial history: where the economy of the country is centralized around one or two cities, the droneports will function well as a form of connectivity. They will create new hybrid places, that is, modular and temporary for social affairs.

The drones will supply rural areas with vital supplies while providing new spaces of social theater for the local inhabitants. Of course, this will not happen in megacities. But the paradigm shift of this droneport project lies on the rural, on the possibilities to improve and contribute to regions that are so opposite to the generic cities and their megastructure airports. Norman Foster believes that within a decade the footprint of the droneport will be bigger than his built airports up to date. The droneports remind me of Frank Lloyd Wright's ideas for his Broadacre City: The personal aerators that service the countryside. The appropriation of airport space for altruistic use is only just beginning.

One of the questions of what happens with actual airport design in terms of connectivity to the city center can be answered by Kasarda's aerotropolis model. Some aerotropolises are successful, interconnected infrastructure, such as Amsterdam's Schiphol Airport where Microsoft operates in the center of the Schiphol triangle, as well as Dubai where the city literally grew around the airport. Most European airports and those in Asian metropoles have a modern railway connection to the city center. But mostly, the aerotropolis model of turning a greenfield airport into new urban development is not satisfactory as there are many empty structures there – the area around Incheon Airport, Songdo, is far from completed and fully operational, even after 18 years of trying, due in part to the severe economic crisis.

Since the early days of aviation, airport designers have aspired to put the airport in the city and to use the airport to curb the economy around the city. In the early 1920s, European architects and visionaries suggested combining the airport with existing typologies such as amusement venues and railway stations – as attempted by Antonio Sant'Elia around 1912 for the Stazione Aeroplani in Milano. In the United States they were merging airports with new typologies such as supermarkets, parking lots, and golf courses – such as Kansas Fairfax Airport in the 1930s.

Airport architecture has come full circle since its inception: It is astonishing how current airport architects and their workshops on the airport of the future (Curtis W. Fentress holds these workshops with an international competition every two years) are returning to Sant'Elia's and Le Corbusier's early airport-in-the-city-center ideas. The outcome of these future airport design competitions is very alluring and very futuristic, with vertical aircraft taking off from airports above city centers or in between skyscrapers. We are still far away from this future, but definitely going there.

The following is a summary of three interviews I conducted with architects:

In 2013 I interviewed Paul Senzaki of the Jerde Partnership (now Jerde Architects) at their headquarters in Venice Beach, California. Jerde have not designed airports, but are renowned for their retail design. Jon Jerde had started out as an architect of public and retail places, known for the Horton Plaza in downtown San Diego, The Mall of America in Bloomington, Minnesota, and the Universal City Walk at Universal Studios Los Angeles. One of his outstanding designs is that of Roppongi Hills in Tokyo. Roppongi Hills is a multi-mix development of corporate offices, retail, entertainment, and public plaza, completed in 2003. In the center of the complex stands the 54-story-high Mori Tower, named after Japanese building tycoon Minoru Mori (constructed by Jerde and Kohn Pedersen Fox).

Paul Senzaki told me how the Jerde Partnership creates a public place that integrates the history of the city: By using retail and the local idiosyncracies, like using water and color schemes for locations by the sea (their San Diego and Fukuoka outdoor malls). This kind of design gives the place character. In the case of Roppongi Hills, Minoru Mori wanted an emphasis on the pedestrian. And Jon Jerde remembered having visited Saint-Paul-de-Vence in his younger years and being impressed by its historic center which can only be reached on a winding cobble stone way. Jerde projected this vision onto the winding pedestrian walkways which are slowly sloping around the center of Roppongi Hills into the Mori Tower, flanked by retail and dining.

This is the legend and aura behind the place-making company of Jerde.[332]

In 2015 I interviewed Roald Sand, the Oslo-based architect and airport planner at Nordic Architecture who co-designed the New Istanbul Airport in 2016 (re-named into Istanbul Grand Airport), about how they express their design philosophy. He mentioned that architects had understood that one dimensional focus on retail was no longer enough to attract the travelling public, hence his company's philosophy has always been to plan for the human being. Making the airport simple, understandable, and calm were top priorities.

The sense of direction and minimizing turns and level changes in the passenger flows give the users more control (in this patronizing environment). The sense of place lies in the design itself, with the quality of the architecture shown in the shaping of the building and the detailing and choice of materials – with natural materials giving it warmth and letting it age with dignity. Roald Sand sees the travellers as individuals and not as a mass, even though air travel has become as common as bus travel was decades ago. The meaning of the airport is efficient processing for some and a fulfillment of dreams for others. The humanistic approach to design will in most cases meet all travelers.

As to the sense of place design, the roof of Istanbul International Airport was inspired by the domes of historical buildings in Istanbul and the colors and light of Turkey.[333]

Between 2012 and 2015 I had the chance to talk to Curtis Fentress on a few occasions. He told me during my first interview at his company's headquarters in Denver, that as a young architect he got his formation by training at I.M. Pei's architectural firm in New York. Pei loved "strong forms" and was influenced by Mies and Le Corbusier. This was the best school according to Fentress: as he had no Master's degree, he considers his time working for Pei as his unofficial Master's degree.

Contextual regionalism and sense of place are Fentress' design philosophies. For Incheon Airport he studied Korean art and Asian architecture. He studied roof

332 Interview with Paul Senzaki of The Jerde Partnership, Venice Beach California, April 15, 2013
333 Interview with Roald Sand of Nordic Architecture, September 18, 2015

forms and learned that in the Korean home the central garden is in the building and that Koreans like to sit in their garden. He spent three months in Korea prior to commencing the creative process of building, learning about the culture and the catenary curve roof which is so typical of Korean architecture. He favors Frank Lloyd Wright and Saarinen's organic architecture to the technological supermodernist megastructure airports of our times. Thus comes his love of the sense of place design, the regional surroundings and the history of the place.[334]

What transpires is that each and every architect tries to create a humanizing experience.

Airports are still a work in progress. This theme is ongoing, so there is no conclusion here. Except that airport aura is what we bring into it, our emotions, expectations and our experiences – "a room into which we wander, we make our own".[335]

Airport aura is the sum of our emotions in a multi-sensory architectural setting, be they positive or negative.

---

334 Interview with Curtis Fentress, at his company's headquarters in Denver, 15 September 2012

335 Giuliana Bruno, Atlas of Emotions, p 209: The movement of tender cartography is a course along which geography itself is made into a room of one's own, "a room into which we wander, we make our own", writes Giuliana Bruno in her Atlas of motions. The voyage in this interior enacts a particular global tour.
This is an ode on Virginia Woolf's feminist essay on women in literature, titled A Room of One's Own. Giuliana Bruno writes about women, gender and geography by giving the example of Isabella d'Este's studiolo which housed a terrestrial and celestial globe. Bruno writes about the imaginative voyage one takes when one enters this particular cartography room. Bruno's essay is about female empowerment throughout the ages, but its quintessence is about the power of the imagination, regardless of gender, that creates your own room and space.

8 Illustration Credits

Figure 1: Kona International Airport, Big Island, Hawaii, photograph by Lilia Mironov

Figure 2: „Reporting from the Front", Biennale di Architettura 2016, Venice, photograph by Lilia Mironov

Figure 3 & 4: Finland Pavilion at Biennale di Architettura 2016, Venice, photograph by Lilia Mironov

Figure 5: Impressions from „Reporting from the Front", Danish Pavilion, Biennale di Architettura 2016, Venice, photograph by Lilia Mironov

Figures 6 & 7: „The Proposal of Droneports for Africa by Lord Norman Foster", Biennale di Architettura 2016, Venice, photograph by Lilia Mironov

Figures 8 & 9: „The Proposal of Droneports for Africa by Lord Norman Foster", Biennale di Architettura 2016, Venice, photograph by Lilia Mironov

Figure 10: „The Proposal of Droneports for Africa by Lord Norman Foster", Biennale di Architettura 2016, Venice, photograph by Lilia Mironov

Figure 11: Temporary Refugee Housing at Berlin Tempelhof Airport, 2016, Photograph by Gordon Welters ©

Figure 12: Grand Entrance (by car, what else in LA) to Los Angeles International Airport, LAX, by Lilia Mironov

Figures 13 & 14: Maglev Train entering Longyang Road Station and Shanghai Pudong Airport, by Lilia Mironov

Figure 15: Hong Kong International Airport Chek Lap Kok, photo courtesy of Foster+Partners ©

Figure 16: TWA Flight Center, Eero Saarinen, Photograph by Nick Sherman: https://search.creativecommons.org/photos/6c57e082-9361-4019-9e08-5cf67e06e612 License: *CC BY-NC-SA 2.0*

Figure 17: Kansai International Airport, Osaka, Renzo Piano. Photograph courtesy of Sky Front's © RPBW – Renzo Piano Building Workshop Architects © Fondazione Renzo Piano (Via P. P. Rubens 30A, 16158 Genova, Italy)

Figure 18: Denver International Airport, Curtis Fentress, photograph courtesy of Denver International Airport

Figure 19: Incheon Airport, Seoul, photograph by Lilia Mironov

Figure 20: Drawing courtesy of Dr. John Kasarda

Figure 21: Space debris / space-junk, as simulated in a computer image by NASA, courtesy of the NASA Orbital Debris Program Office https://commons.wikimedia.org/wiki/File:Debris-GEO1280.jpg License: Public domain

Figure 22: French Concession Area in Shanghai: http://www.chinahighlights.com/travelguide/china-hiking/shanghai-hiking.htm

Figure 23 & 24: Atrium lobby of the Hyatt Regency San Francisco by the Embarcadero, photograph by Lilia Mironov

Figure 25: Atrium / Great Hall of Tom Bradley International Terminal, Los Angeles International Airport, photograph by Lilia Mironov

Figure 26: "Vista" – view onto Downtown Chicago from the window of a Swiss Airbus 330, photograph by Lilia Mironov

Figure 27: View onto Beijing Capital Airport from the left cockpit window of a Swiss Airbus 340, photograph by Lilia Mironov

Figure 28: Diorama of a Buffalo in Nebraska, Durham Museum, Omaha, photograph by Lilia Mironov

Figure 29: Photograph of horse-drawn train, the first Mumbles Railway, Wales, photograph courtesy of the Richard Burton Archives, Singleton Park Library, Swansea, Wales

Figures 30 & 31: Photographs from the exhibition on Promontory, Utah. Exhibition at Durham Museum, Omaha, Nebraska, photograph by Lilia Mironov

Figure 32: Union Pacific "4-6-0 Ten Wheeler Steam Locomotive" built in 1890, Durham Museum, Omaha, Nebraska, photograph by Lilia Mironov

Figure 33: Wells Fargo Mail Service Carriage, Durham Museum, Omaha, Nebraska, photograph by Lilia Mironov

Figures 34 & 35: Durham Museum (Union Station), Omaha, Nebraska, photographs by Lilia Mironov

Figure 36: Madison Wisconsin Dane County Regional Airport, arrivals hall, courtesy of Alliiance Architects

Figure 37: St. Pancras Station, London, present day, photograph courtesy of Hugh Llewelyn
https://search.creativecommons.org/photos/ba7ef772-eba2-45b4-9eff-9583b6232c00
License: *CC BY-SA 2.0*

Figure 38: Chhatrapati Shivaji Terminus, formerly Victoria Station, Bombay, photograph courtesy of Francesco Bandarin, © UNESCO
http://whc.unesco.org/en/list/945/gallery/
License: http://whc.unesco.org/en/licenses/6

Figure 39: Chhatrapati Shivaji International Airport, Mumbai, India, photograph by Lilia Mironov

Figures 40 & 41: Grand Central Terminal, Manhattan, present day, photographs courtesy of Professor Luis Carranza

Figure 42: Pennsylvania Station, 1962, photograph by Cervin Robinson, Library of Congress
http://www.loc.gov/pictures/resource/hhh.ny0411.photos.119996p/
License: https://www.loc.gov/rr/print/res/114_habs.html

Figures 43 & 44: Oculus, Santiago Calatrava, Ground Zero, New York (2016), photographs by Lilia Mironov

Figure 45: First flight of the Brothers Wright, in Kitty Hawk, North Carolina, December 17, 1903, photograph by John T. Daniels
https://www.loc.gov/pictures/item/00652085/
License: No known restriction on publication

Figure 46: Stazione Aeroplani nella Città Nuova, Antonio Sant'Elia, 1912, drawing courtesy of Musei Civici di Como

Figure 47: Broadacre City, Frank Lloyd Wright 1932, Drawing 5825.004
photograph Copyright © 2019 Frank Lloyd Wright Foundation, Scottsdale, AZ. All rights reserved. The Frank Lloyd Wright Foundation Archives (The Museum of Modern Art | Avery Architectural & Fine Arts Library, Columbia University, New York)

Figure 48: Lloyd Wright's entry contribution to the Lehigh Portland Cement Company's competition on American Airport Designs, 1929. Photograph courtesy of Eric Lloyd Wright

Figure 49: Cover of the book American Airport Designs, 1929

Figure 50: Architectural model of Zentralflughafen Tempelhof, Ernst Sagebiel, photograph ca. 1937, courtesy of Library of Congress
https://www.loc.gov/item/2002721913/
License: No known restrictions

Figure 51: Flughafen Berlin Tempelhof in operation in 1984 during show day, photograph courtesy of Jose Lopez Jr. Luftaufnahme vom Flughafen Berlin-Tempelhof am Tag der offenen Tür 1984
https://commons.wikimedia.org/wiki/File:Flughafen BerlinTempelhof1984_crop.jpg
License: (TSGT Jose Lopez Jr., US Air Force. Public Domain)

Figure 52: Ford Dearborn Airport, Michigan, by Albert Kahn, 1927. Photograph courtesy of Don Harrison
https://www.flickr.com/photos/upnorthmemories/9678290415/in/photolist-fKeLy8-jkQWpb-pM-wuS8-bjvs7g-jkQoK8-a2dREh-a2aYzz-bX49aK-bjvtc8-fLpLD9-ospfGR-yeRx6Z-LsEEf7-pMinXJ-fLpNxG-hZejMY-fLpMKN-fL8aai-56oE48-fLpMZU-8mimyt-9mvY5N-4Wjoio-fL8a1P-fLpM7W-fL8aWp-fL8cnM-fLpMi3-fLpMCw-rtSA7n-fL8ciZ-fL8ame-fL8cB6-fLpLPN-fL8a66-fLpLLA-2b1tG7Y-KA4Wny-GeysCJ-2gGaYY4-2gGahg6-2gGahcy-2gGah97-2gGaYFF-2gGagT2-fLpN8A-fL89Sz-fLpLpW-fLpMmw-fLpNtE
License: CC BY-NC-ND 2.0

Figure 53: Pan Am International Airport, Miami, Delano & Aldrich, 1929. Photograph courtesy of Florida Memory
https://commons.wikimedia.org/wiki/File:PanAm_Key-West_terminal.jpg
License: In accordance with the provisions of Section 257.35(6), Florida Statutes, "Any use or reproduction of material deposited with the Florida Photographic Collection shall be allowed pursuant to the provisions of paragraph (1)(b) and subsection (4), provided that appropriate credit for its use is given."

Figure 54: Fairfax Kansas Airport, Kansas City 1929, vintage postcard

Figure 55: Grand Central Terminal, Glendale, California (1928), photograph courtesy of San Diego Air and Space Museum Archives
https://en.wikipedia.org/wiki/File:TWA_DC-1.jpg
License: GNU Free Documentation License referring to San Diego Air and Space Museum Archives Commons project Public Domain (No copyright restrictions): San Diego Air and Space Museum Archives

Figure 56: Liverpool Speke Airport, now the Crowne Plaza Liverpool John Lennon Airport Hotel. Photograph courtesy Chris J. Wood
https://commons.wikimedia.org/wiki/File:Crowne_Plaza_Liverpool_John_Lennon_Airport_Hotel_Airside.jpg
License: CC BY-SA 3.0

Figure 57: Ville Contemporaine, 1922, Le Corbusier, courtesy © FLC / 2019, ProLitteris, Zurich

Figure 58: *Naked Airport* sketch, Le Corbusier, 1946, courtesy © FLC / 2019, ProLitteris, Zurich

Figures 59 & 60, left: La Guardia Airport, Aldrich & Delano 1939, photograph courtesy of Historic American Engineering Record, Library of Congress
License: https://www.usa.gov/government-works/

Figure 61: Terminal City Map, New York International Airport, courtesy of Morten S. Beyer Papers, Accession 2007-0060, National Air and Space Museum, Smithsonian Institution
License: National Air and Space Museum, Smithsonian Institution Washington, Permission No.: 19-BK-309

Figure 62: TWA Flight Center, Eero Saarinen, sketch, courtesy of Library of Congress, Prints & Photographs Division, HABS NY-6371
https://commons.wikimedia.org/wiki/File:Trans_World_Airlines_Flight_Center_-_HABS_NY-6371_-_00013a.jpg
License: When reusing please credit: Library of Congress, Prints & Photographs Division, NY-6371

Figure 63: Gateway Arch, St. Louis, Missouri; Eero Saarinen, photograph courtesy of Bev Sykes
https://commons.wikimedia.org/wiki/File:St_Louis_Gateway_Arch.jpg
License: This file is licensed under the Creative Commons Attribution 2.0 Generic license.

Figure 64: TWA Flight Center, Interior, 1964; photograph courtesy of Balthazar Korab, Library of Congress, Prints & Photographs Division, LC-DIG-krb-00604
https://www.loc.gov/rr/print/res/598_kora.html

Figure 65: Eero Saarinen perfecting his model of the TWA Flight Center, photograph courtesy of Library of Congress, Prints & Photographs Division, Balthazar Korab Archive at the Library of Congress, LC-DIG-krb-00576
https://www.loc.gov/rr/print/res/598_kora.html

Figure 66: Hong Kong International Airport Chek Lap Kok, Norman Foster, Main Hall, photograph by Lilia Mironov

Figure 67: Korea Traditional Cultural Experience Center in Incheon Airport, Seoul, 200. Fentress Architects, photograph by Lilia Mironov

Figure 68: Kinetic Rain sculpture, Singapore Changi Airport, photograph courtesy of Choo Yut Shing
https://www.flickr.com/photos/25802865@N08/8239828700/in/album-72157666800632515/
License: CC BY-NC-SA 2.0

Figure 69: Singapore Changi Airport, Butterfly Garden, photograph courtesy of Dr. Raju Kasambe
https://commons.wikimedia.org/wiki/File:Butterfly_Garden_Changi_Airport_Singapore_by_Dr_Raju_Kasambe_DSC_5250_(2).jpg
License: CC BY-SA 4.0

Figure 70: Seoul Incheon Airport, musical performance space, photograph by Lilia Mironov

Figure 71: Seoul Incheon Airport, Korean Garden, photograph by Lilia Mironov

Figure 72: Bruno Taut's Glass Pavilion, 1914, photographer unknown
https://commons.wikimedia.org/wiki/File:Taut_Glass_Pavilion_exterior_1914.jpg
License: public domain because of age

Figure 73: Shanghai Pudong International Airport, Paul Andreu, 1999, photograph by Lilia Mironov

Figure 74: Seoul Incheon Airport, Fentress Architects, 2001, photograph by Lilia Mironov

Figure 75: Galleria Vittorio Emmanuele II, Milan, drawing before 1891, courtesy of Immanuel Giel
https://commons.wikimedia.org/wiki/File:MilanoGaleria-VittorioEmmanuele.jpg
License: Public Domain Mark 1.0

Figure 76: Galleria Vittorio Emmanuele II, Milan, courtesy of José Luiz Bernardes Ribeiro
https://commons.wikimedia.org/wiki/File:Glass_dome_-_Galleria_Vittorio_Emanuele_II_-_Milan_2014.jpg
License: CC BY-SA 3.0

Figure 77: Crystal Palace, Joseph Paxton. Sketch from 1851, courtesy of the public domain
https://commons.wikimedia.org/wiki/File:Crystal.Palace.Paxton.Plan.jpg
License: Public Domain Mark 1.0

Figure 78: Joseph Paxton's original sketch from 1850, pen and ink on pink blotting paper, mounted on a sheet of woven paper with a telegram form. Courtesy of Victoria and Albert Museum
http://collections.vam.ac.uk/item/O18167/the-great-exhibition-building-architectural-sketch-paxton-joseph-sir/
License: https://www.vam.ac.uk/info/va-websites-terms-conditions

Figure 79: Crystal Palace, Joseph Paxton, photographic print ca. 1860-1930. Courtesy of Library of Congress Prints and Photographs Division Washington
https://www.loc.gov/resource/stereo.1s08398/
License: No known restrictions on publication

Figure 80: Louis Haghe, color lithograph, 1851. Queen Victoria opens the Great Exhibition in the Crystal Palace in Hyde Park, London
https://commons.wikimedia.org/wiki/File:Crystal_Palace_-_Queen_Victoria_opens_the_Great_Exhibition.jpg
License: Public Domain Mark 1.0

Figure 81: Kansai International Airport, Osaka, Renzo Piano. Photograph courtesy of Terence Ong
https://commons.wikimedia.org/wiki/File:Kansai_International_Airport,_Restricted_Area_2.JPG
License: GFDL, CC-BY 2.5

Figure 82: Kansai International Airport, Osaka, Renzo Piano. Photograph courtesy of © RPBW – Renzo Piano Building Workshop Architects© Fondazione Renzo Piano (Via P. P. Rubens 30A, 16158 Genova, Italy) © KIAC © Kawatetsu

Figure 83: Kansai International Airport, Osaka, Renzo Piano. Photograph courtesy of Shinkenchiku-sha Co., Ltd © RPBW – Renzo Piano Building Workshop Architects © Fondazione Renzo Piano (Via P. P. Rubens 30A, 16158 Genova, Italy)

Figures 84 & 85: Bangkok Suvarnabhumi Airport, photograph by Lilia Mironov

Figure 86: Bangkok Suvarnabhumi Airport, photograph by Lilia Mironov

Figure 87: Bangkok Suvarnabhumi Airport, photograph by Lilia Mironov

Figures 88 to 90: Bangkok Suvarnabhumi Airport, "Scene of the Churning of the Milk Ocean", photographs by Lilia Mironov

Figure 91: Le Bon Marché à Paris, photograph ca. 1900, courtesy of Archives Moisant-Savey
https://de.wikipedia.org/wiki/Datei:Le_Bon_Marché_à_Paris_(1875).jpg
License: Public Domain Mark 1.0

Figure 92: Carson Pirie Scott Building, Chicago, Illinois. Ca. 1900. Louis Sullivan, architect. Present day photograph by Chris Smith
https://search.creativecommons.org/photos/37ddf532-d565-4b59-8079-ae1ce94ebd49
License: CC BY-NC-SA 2.0

Figure 93: West Edmonton Mall, "Europa Boulevard", Edmonton, Canada, photograph courtesy of Dylan Kereluk
https://commons.wikimedia.org/wiki/File:Shops_in_WEM.jpg
License: CC BY 2.0

Figure 94: Great Hall of Tom Bradley International Terminal, Los Angeles International Airport, Fentress Architects 2013, photograph by Lilia Mironov

Figure 95: Floorplan of the Baths of Diocletian, Rome. Drawing by Rodolfo Lanciani between 1893–1901 https://commons.wikimedia.org/wiki/File:Baths_Diocletian-Lanciani.png
License: Public Domain Mark 1.0

Figure 96: Terme di Antonino Caracalla, Rome, drawing by Ridolfino Venuti (1705–1763) courtesy of the Biblioteca General Antonio Machado, Sevilla https://commons.wikimedia.org/wiki/File:Terme_di_Antonino_Caracalla (19910165745).jpg
License: CC BY 2.0

Figure 97: Pennsylvania Station, print in the New York Tribune, 1904, courtesy of the Library of Congress New-York tribune. [volume], July 17, 1904, Image 47 https://chroniclingamerica.loc.gov/lccn/sn83030214/1904-07-17/ed-1/seq-47/
License: No known restrictions on reproduction.

Figure 98: Istanbul New Airport; Nordic, Grimshaw and Haptic Architects, 2018, photograph courtesy of Nordic / Grimshaw / Haptic_Produced by MIR

Figure 99: Snapshot of dancing couple, Incheon Airport, Seoul, photograph by Lilia Mironov

Figures 100 & 101: Chinggis Khan International Airport and Ulaanbataar, Mongolia, photographs by Lilia Mironov

Figure 102: LAX Los Angeles International Airport, Theme Building, William Pereira architect, 1961, photograph by Lilia Mironov

Figure 103: Oriental Pearl Tower and office building; Shanghai World Financial Center, Jin-Mao Tower and Shanghai Tower, photograph by Lilia Mironov

Figure 104: Panopticon, 1843, Jeremy Bentham sketch courtesy of The Works of Jeremy Bentham https://commons.wikimedia.org/wiki/File:Panopticon.jpg
License: Public Domain Mark 1.0

Figure 105: Postcard of Interior view of Illinois State Penitentiary, Stateville, Joliet. 1923 https://prisonphotography.org/2010/08/21/stateville-prison-joliet-il-art-object/
License: Copyright expired

Figures 106 & 107: Newark Airport, Star Alliance Lounge, photographs by Lilia Mironov

Figure 108: Denver International Airport, Great Hall from upper lever. Fentress Architects, 1995, photograph by Lilia Mironov

Figures 109 & 110: HSBC (Hong Kong and Shanghai Bank) Headquarters, Hong Kong Island, 1986 Norman Foster, architect, photographs by Lilia Mironov

Figure 111: Hajj Terminal at King Abdulaziz International Airport, Jeddah, Saudi Arabia, photograph by Yousef Madari https://commons.wikimedia.org/wiki/File:Haj_terminal.jpg
License: public domain

Figure 112: Hajj Terminal at King Abdulaziz International Airport, Jeddah, Saudi Arabia. Interior view. Photograph by Sasikan https://commons.wikimedia.org/wiki/File:King_Abdulaziz_International_Airport_(JED),_Jeddah_Saudi_Arabia_-_panoramio_(1).jpg
License: CC BY 3.0

Figure 113: Olympiastadion München, Frei Otto, architect. 1972. Photograph by Fritz Geller-Grimm https://commons.wikimedia.org/wiki/File:Olympia_stadion_fg01.jpg
License: CC BY-SA 2.5

Figure 114: Denver International Airport study, photograph taken by Lilia Mironov during visit of the headquarters of Fentress Architects in Denver, 15 September 2012.

Figure 115: Denver International Airport, photograph by Lilia Mironov

Figure 116: Singapore Changi Airport, *The Jewel*, by Moshe Safdie Architects, photograph courtesy of Matteo Morando
https://commons.wikimedia.org/wiki/File:JewelSingaporeVortex1.jpg
License: This work is free and may be used by anyone for any purpose.

Figure 117: Seoul Incheon Airport, The Walk of the Royal Family, photograph by Lilia Mironov

Figure 118: Freitag Flagship Store, Zurich, 2006 Annette Spillmann & Harald Echsle, photograph courtesy of Spillmann Echsle Architekten

Figure 119: House of Switzerland, Sochi Winter Olympics 2014, Annette Spillmann & Harald Echsle, photograph courtesy of Spillmann Echsle Architekten

Figure 120: Construction Drawing of Droneports, courtesy of Foster+Partners © and the Norman Foster Foundation

Figure 121: Visualization of Droneports, courtesy of Foster+Partners © and the Norman Foster Foundation

Figure 122: Visualization of Droneport Interior, courtesy of Foster+Partners © and the Norman Foster Foundation

Figure 123: De Young Museum, San Francisco, 2005 Herzog & de Meuron, photograph by Lilia Mironov

Figure 124: Spiral Jetty, Great Salt Lake. Robert Smithson. Photograph courtesy of Ian Longton
https://search.creativecommons.org/photos/126e4b7b-9279-4de7-b09a-8fc2e88d96c5
License: CC BY-NC-ND 4.0

Figures 125 & 126: Spaceport America, Norman Foster, 2014, courtesy of Nigel Young, Foster + Partners

Figures 127 & 128: Terminal 1, Aéroport Charles de Gaulle, Paris. Paul Andreu architect, 1974. Photographs by Lilia Mironov

Figure 129: *Slipstream* by Richard Wilson, Heathrow International Airport Terminal 5, photograph courtesy of Richard Wilson

Figure 130: *Mustang*, by Luis Jiménez, outside Denver International Airport, photograph by Lilia Mironov

Figure 131: Hamad International Airport, Doha, with Lamp Bear by Urs Fischer. HOK Architects, 2014, photograph Tim Griffith/Courtesy of HOK

Figure 132: Chhatrapati Shivaji International Airport, Delhi, SOM. Photograph by Lilia Mironov

Figures 133, 134 & 135: Art Installations in Mumbai Chhatrapati Shivaji International Airport, photographs by Lilia Mironov

Figures 136 & 137: Mudras in Arrivals Hall at Indira Gandhi International Airport, Delhi. Photographs by Lilia Mironov

Figure 138: Beijing Capital Airport, interior color schemes, photograph courtesy of Absorbb
https://search.creativecommons.org/photos/d397458f-59e8-4495-a378-30bec450fa83
License: CC BY-NC-ND 2.0

Figure 139: Beijing Capital Airport, interior, photograph courtesy of Pascal Sun
https://commons.wikimedia.org/wiki/File:Beijing_capital_airport_terminal3.JPG
License: CC BY 3.0

Figure 140: Grand Opéra Paris, Charles Garnier. Photograph courtesy of Benh Lieu Song
https://commons.wikimedia.org/wiki/File%3AOpera_Garnier_Grand_Escalier.jpg
License: CC BY-SA 3.0

Figures 141 & 142: Great Hall, Los Angeles International Terminal, Fentress Architects 2013, photographs by Lilia Mironov

Figure 143: Seoul Incheon Airport, Fentress Architects 2001. Photograph by Lilia Mironov

9 Bibliography

Adorno, Theodor W. 1983. *Prisms.* Cambridge: MIT Press.

Allen, Barbara L. "On Performative Regionalism." *Architectural Regionalism: Collected Writings on Place, Identity, Modernity and Tradition,* ed. Vincent B. Canizaro, Princeton Architectural Press 2007.

Andreu, Paul. 1998. *Fifty Airport Terminals,* Paris: Serge Salat.

Angélil, Marc. 2002. "Terminal Space. Gedanken zur zeitgenössischen Architektur." *Archithese* 32 (5.02), p 8–13.

Arendt, Hannah. 1958. *The Human Condition.* Chicago: The University of Chicago Press.

Art+Com. Kinetic Rain. Retrieved: November 2 2016. https://artcom.de/en/project/kinetic-rain/.

Augé, Marc, *Non-Places.* 2008. University of Michigan: Verso.

Awad, Salma. 2013. "Delayed Doha airport gets $6.8m giant teddy bear." Arabian Business. Retrieved October 29 2014. https://www.arabianbusiness. com/delayed-doha-airport-gets-6-8m-giant-teddy-bear-531018.html#.WRy351L5yDU.

Bachelard, Gaston. 1969. *The Poetics of Space.* Boston: Beacon Press.

Belcher, David A. Luis Jiménez, New York Times, Retrieved: 15 June 2016. https://mobile.nytimes. com/2006/06/15/arts/design/15jimenez.html.

Benjamin, Walter. 2007 (1968/55). *Illuminations.* Translation: Harry Zohn. New York: Schocken Books.

Benjamin, Walter. 1982. *The Arcades Project.* Translation: Howard Eiland and Kevin McLaughlin. Cambridge, MA: The Belknap of Harvard University Press.

Benjamin, Walter. 2008. *The Work of Art in the Age of Its Technological Reproducibility, and Other Writings on Media.* Cambridge, MA: Belknap Press of Harvard University Press.

Bennett, Tony. 1988. "The Exhibitionary Complex." *New Formations* (4): 73–102.

Berczeller, Paul. 2004. *The Guardian.* 6. September. Retrieved: 23. September 2016. https://www.theguardian. com/film/2004/sep/06/features.features11.

Berger, Horst. 2005. *Light Structures – Structures of Light: The Art and Engineering of Tensile Architecture.* Bloomington, IN: AuthorHouse.

Best, Ulrich. 2014. "The Debate about Berlin Tempelhof Airport, or: A Lefebvrean Critique of Recent Debates about Affect in Geography." In *Urban Revolution Now,* by Lukasz Stanek, Christian Schmid and Ákos Moravánszky, 283–300. Farnham: Ashgate Publishing Limited.

Bhabha, Homi. 1994. "Signs Taken for Wonders: Questions of Ambivalence and Authority under a Tree outside Delhi, May 1819." In *The Location of Culture,* by Homi Bhabha, 102–122. London.

Black, Archibald. 1930. *Lehigh Portland Cement Company, American Airport Designs: Containing 44 prize winning and other drawings from the Lehigh Airports competition, the first national contest for designs of modern airports held in the United States.* New York: Taylor, Rogers & Bliss.

Bredella, Nathalie. 2009. *Architekturen des Zuschauens: Imaginäre und reale Räume im Film.* Bielefeld: transcript Verlag.

Bruchansky, Christophe. *Heterotopia of Disneyworld.* Retrieved: August 19 2016. www.bruchansky.name.

Burckhardt, Lucius. 2017. *Landschaftstheoretische Aquarelle und Spaziergangswissenschaft.* Martin Schmitz Verlag.

Bruno, Giuliana. 2002. *Atlas of Emotions: Journeys in Art, Architecture and Film.* London: Verso.

Butler, Judith, and Gayatri Chakravorty Spivak. 2007. *Who sings the Nation-State? Language, politics, belonging.* London: Seagull.

Caesar, Catherine. 2013. "Long Read: The Cultural Politics of Air Travel: Art at Dallas Fort Worth Airport,

Then and Now." *might be good*. Austin, TX, Retrieved: 15 September 2016. http://www.fluentcollab.org/mbg/index.php/interview/index/181/116.

Carlson, Marvin. 1989. "The iconic stage." *Journal of Dramatic Theory and Criticism*, Spring: 3-18.

Carlson, Marvin. 2004. "What is Performance?" In *The Performance Studies Reader*, by Henry Bial, 70–75. New York: Rourtledge.

Cassirer, Ernst. 2006. "Mythischer, ästhetischer und theoretischer Raum." In *Raumtheorie. Grundlagentexte aus Philosophie und Kulturwissenschaften*, by Jörg Dünne and Stephan Günzel, 485–500. Frankfurt am Main: Suhrkamp.

Castells, Manuel, and Peter Hall. 1994. *Technopoles of the World: The Making of Twenty-First-Century Industrial Complexes*. New York: Routledge.

Cavallo, Roberto. 2008. *Railways in the Urban Context: An architectural discourse*. Delft: Technische Universiteit Delft.

Certeau, Michel de. 2008. "Praktiken im Raum (1980)." In *Raumtheorie. Grundlagentexte aus Philosophie und Kulturwissenschaften*, by Jörg Dünne and Stephan Günzel, 343–353. Frankfurt am Main: Suhrkamp-Taschenbuch Wissenschaft.

Changi Airport – Airport Experience. Retrieved: 27 September 2016. http://www.changiairport.com/en/airport-experience/attractions-and-services/kinetic-rain.html.

Chatwin, Bruce. 1998. *The Songlines*. London: Vintage.

Crawford, Margaret. 1992. "The World in a Shopping Mall." In *Variations on a Theme Park. The New American City and the End of Public Space*, by Michael Sorkin, Editor: Michael Sorkin, 3–30. New York.

Dittrich, Elke. 2005. *Ernst Sagebiel: Leben und Werk. 1892–1970*. Berlin: Lukas Verlag.

Doesburg, Theo van. 2003. "Der Wille zum Stil." In *Architekturtheorie im 20. Jahrhundert*, by Akos Moravanszky and Katalin Gyöngy, 61–64. Wien: Springer Verlag.

Dolff-Bonekämper, Gabi. 2000. *Berlin-Tempelhof, Liverpool-Speke, Paris-Le Bourget: Années 30 Architecture des aéroports*. Paris: Éditions du patrimoine.

Dover Museum. Bronze Age Boat. Retrieved: April 12 2016. http://www.dovermuseum.co.uk/bronze-age-boat/bronze-age-boat.aspx

Durham Museum Omaha, The History of Union Station, Retrieved: 15 May 2017. https://durhammuseum.org/our-museum/history-of-union-station/.

Easterling, Keller. 2004. *Enduring Innocence: Global Architecture and Its Political Masquerades*. Cambridge, MA: MIT Press.

Easterling, Keller. 2014. *Extrastatecraft: The Power of Infrastructure Space*. London: Verso.

Easterling, Keller. 2011. "The Action is the Form." In *Sentient City: ubiquitous computing, architecture, and the future of urban space*, by Mark Shepard et. al., 154–158. New York: MIT Press.

Ekeberg, Jonas. 2003. "Spaces of Conflict." *New Institutionalism*.

Fentress, Curtis, Christoph Heinrich, Donald Albrecht, Gillian Fuller, and Tibbie Dunbar. 2012. *Now Boarding: Fentress Airports and the Architecture of Flight*. Denver: Denver Art Museum in association with Scala Publishers.

Fernandes, Naresh. "Cities in motion: why Mumbai's new air terminal has gone off the rails." *The Guardian*, Retrieved: September 29 2014. https://www.theguardian.com/cities/2014/feb/20/cities-in-motion-mumbai-air-terminal-rails

Fezer, Jesko, Schmitz, Martin. 2012. *Lucius Burckhardt Writings. Rethinking Man-made Environments. Politics, Landscape & Design*. Wien: Springer Verlag.

Fischer, Thomas. 1994. *Kansai International Airport passenger terminal building Process: Architecture*.

Fischer-Lichte, Erika. 2004. Ästhetik des Performativen. Frankfurt am Main: Suhrkamp.

flydenver.com. *flydenver.com*. Retrieved: 14 February 2016. http://www.flydenver.com/about/art_culture/permanent.

Foster, Norman. *Foster and Partners. Droneports.* Retrieved: 27 October 2016. http://www.fosterandpartners.com/projects/droneport.

Foster, Norman. Foster and Partners. *Foster and Partners Chek Lap Kok Airport.* Retrieved: 28 October 2016. http://www.fosterandpartners.com/projects/chek-lap-kok-airport/

Foster, Norman. 2000. „Reinventing the Airport" 1996, in: *Kat. Foster On Foster ... Foster on,* ed. David Jenkins, Munich.

Foucault, Michel. 1995 (1975). *Discipline & Punish. The Birth of the Prison.* New York: Vintage Books Random House.

Foucault, Michel. 1997. "Of Other Spaces: Utopias and Heterotopias." In *Rethinking Architecture: A Reader in Cultural Theory,* by Neil Leach, Editor: Neil Leach, 330–336. New York City: Routledge.

Foucault, Michel. 1991. *The Production of Space.* Editor: Donald Nicholson-Smith. Oxford: Blackwell Publishing.

Frampton, Kenneth. 1983. "Towards a Critical Regionalism. Six Points for an Architecture of Resistance." In *The Anti-Aesthetic. Essays on Postmodern Culture,* by Hal Foster, 16–30. Port Townsend: Bay Press.

Friemert, Chup. 1984. *Die Gläserne Arche. Kristallpalast London 1851 und 1854.* München: Prestel Verlag.

Giedion, Siegfried. 2015. *Raum, Zeit, Architektur.* Basel: Birkhäuser.

Gordon, Alastair. 2004. *Naked Airport. A Cultural History of the World's most Revolutionary Structure.* Chicago: University of Chicago Press.

Habermas, Jörgen. 1989. *The Structural Transformation of the Public Sphere – An Inquiry Into a Category Of Bourgeois Society.* Cambridge: The MIT Press.

Hannah, Dorita. 2008. *Event-Space: Theater Architecture & the Historical Avant-Garde.* Editor: Department of Performance Studies. New York: New York University.

Haptic Architects, I*stanbul Grand Airport,* Retrieved: 18 May 2017. https://hapticarchitects.com/work/istanbul-airport-istanbul-turkey/.

Harries, Karsten. 1990. "Theatricality and Re-Presentation." *Perspecta 26, The Yale Architecture Journal,* 21–40.

Herzog, Jacques, and Pierre de Meuron. *Herzog & de Meuron.* Retrieved: 18 September 2016. https://www.herzogdemeuron.com/index/projects/complete-works/151-175/173-de-young-museum.html.

Hobhouse, Hermione. 2002. *The Crystal Palace and the Great Exhibition. Art, Science and Productive Industry. A History of the Royal Commission for the Exhibition of 1851.* London: Continuum.

Hughes, Stephen. 1990. *The Archeology of the Early Railway System: The Brecon Forest Tramroads. Royal Commission on Ancient and Historical Monuments in Wales.*

Ibelings, Hans. 2002. *Supermodernism. Architecture in the Age of Globalization.* Rotterdam: NAi Publishers.

Icon Eye: Interview Norman Foster. 9 August 2011. Retrieved: 16 September 2016. http://www.iconeye.com/architecture/features/item/9300-interview-norman-foster.

Jahn, Helmut; Sobek, Werner; Schuler, Matthias. 2007. *Suvarnabhumi airport: Bangkok, Thailand.* Ludwigsburg: Avedition.

Jenkins, David. 2008. *Foster 40 / Norman Foster.* Munich: Prestel.

Jerde, Jon Adams. 1998. *The Jerde Partnership International. Visceral Reality.* Milano: Arca.

Kasarda, John, and Greg Lindsay. 2010. *Aerotropolis: The Way we'll live next.* New York: Farrar, Strauss and Giroux.

King, Shorter Clement. 1908. *The Brontës: Life and Letters.* New York: New York Hodder and Stoughton.

Kipfer, Stefan, and Kanishka Goonewardena. 2014. "Henri Lefebvre on Colonization: From Reinterpretation to Research." In *Urban Revolution Now: Henri Lefebvre in Social Research and Architecture,* by Lukasz Stanek, Christian Schmid and Akos Moravanszky, 93–112. Farnham: Ashgate Publishing Limited.

Klonk, Charlotte. 2009. *Spaces of Experience. Art Gallery Interiors from 1800 to 2000.* New Haven: Yale University Press.

Klonk, Charlotte, Niklas Maak, and Thomas Demand. 2011. "The white cube and beyond." *Tate Etc.* 21.

Kolarevic, Branko. 2005. "Towards the Performative in Architecture." In *Performative Architecture: Beyond Instrumentality*, by Branko Kolarevic and Ali M. Malkawi, 204–213. New York: Spon Press.

Koolhaas, Rem. 2002. "Junkspace." *October* (MIT Press) 100 (Spring): 175–190.

Koohlaas, Rem. *Navigating Modernization.* Retrieved: 6 November 2016. http://oma.eu/lectures/navigating-modernization.

Koolhaas, Rem. 1995. *S, M, L, XL.* Rotterdam: The Monacelli Press.

Korein, Simone. 2002. „Landen unter Zelten. Skidmore, Owings & Merrill, Haj Terminal, Jeddah" *Archithese*, May: 36-37.

Korein, Simone. 2002. „Toroid und Welle. Renzo Piano: Kansai International Airport." *Archithese*, September: 42–45.

Kröncke, Meike, Kerstin Mey and Yvonne Spielmann, Hrsg. 2007. *Kultureller Umbau: Räume, Identitäten, und Re/Präsentationen.* Bielefeld: transcript Verlag.

Kröniger, Birgit. 2007. *Der Freiraum als Bühne. Zur Transformation von Orten durch Events und Inszenierungen.* Frankfurt: Peter Lang Verlag.

Kuhnimhof, Tobias, and Gebhard Wulfhorst. 2013. "The Reader's Guide to Mobility Culture." In *Megacity Mobility Culture*, by ifmo Institute for Mobility Research, 55–64. Heidelberg: Springer.

Kuhnimhof, Tobias, and Irene Feige. 2013. "What is Mobility Culture?" In *Megacity Mobility Culture*, by ifmo Institute for Mobility Research. Heidelberg: Springer.

La Biennale Architettura. 2016. *La Biennale.* Retrieved: 29 October 2016. http://www.labiennale.org/en/architecture/exhibition/national-participations/.

Lahiri, Tripti. 2010. The Wall Street Journal: Q&A: Delhi Airport's Hands Scultpure. Retrieved: 29 November 2016. https://blogs.wsj.com/indiarealtime/2010/07/28/qa-delhi-airports-hands-sculpture/.

Le Corbusier. 1987. *Aircraft: „L'avion accuse ...".* reprint from 1935. London: Trefoil.

Le Corbusier. 1979. *Le Corbusier: Städtebau (Urbanisme).* Editor: Hans Hildebrandt. Stuttgart: Deutsche Verlags-Anstalt.

Le Corbusier. 1946. *Oeuvre complète.* Bd. Vol. 4. Zürich: Boesinger.

Le Corbusier. 1987. *The City of Tomorrow and its Planning.* reprint of 1929 edition. New York: Dover Publications.

Le Corbusier. 2007. *Toward an Architecture.* Translation: John Goodman. Los Angeles: Getty Research Institute.

Leach, William. 1993. *Land of Desire: Merchants, Power, and the Rise of a New American Culture.* New York: Vintage Books.

Leatherbarrow, David. 2005. "Architecture's Unscripted Performance." In *Performative Architecture: Beyond Instrumentality*, by Branko Kolarevic and Ali M. Malkawi, 5–20. New York: Spon Press.

Lefebvre, Henri. 1991 (1974). *The Production of Space.* Translation: Donald Nicholson-Smith. Oxford: Blackwell Publishing.

Lefebvre, Henri. 2014. *Toward an Architecture of Enjoyment.* Editor: Lukasz Stanek. Minneapolis: University of Minnesota Press.

Liscombe, Rhodri Windsor, and Michelangelo Sabatino. 2016. *Canada: Modern Architectures in History.* London: Reaktion Books.

Löw, Martina. 2000. *Raumsoziologie.* Berlin/ Frankfurt am Main: Suhrkamp Verlag.

Lucae, Richard. 1869. „Über die Macht des Raumes in der Baukunst." *Zeitschrift für Bauwesen*, 294–306.

Lynch, Patrick. Santiago Calatrava's Oculus, *Archdaily.com.* Retrieved: 29 Septeber 2016. http://www.archdaily.com/795158/santiago-calatravas-oculus-opens-to-the-sky-in-remembrance-of-9-11.

Marinetti, F.T., Mino Somenzi, and Angiolo Mazzoni. 1934. "Futurist Manifesto of Aerial Architecture." *Sant'Elia 2*, 1. Feb.

Matsumasa, Teiji. 1994. Kansai International Airport passenger terminal building, Renzo Piano, *Process: Architecture*; no. 122.

McCartney, Scott. Airports for Art Lovers, *Wall Street Journal*. Retrieved: 16 September 2016. http://www.jimcampbell.tv/news/AirportsForArt-Lovers_WSJ_Article_Graphics.pdf.

McLuhan, Marshall. 1962. *The Gutenberg Galaxy. The Making of Typographic Man*. London: University of Toronto Press.

Meeks, Carroll L.V. 1975. *The railroad station: An architectural history*. New Haven: Yale University Press.

Merin, Gili. Crystal Palace, *Archdaily.com*. Retrieved: 23 September 2015. http://www.archdaily.com/397949/ad-classic-the-crystal-palace-joseph-paxton/.

Merleau-Ponty, Maurice. 2006. „Das Auge und der Geist." In *Raumtheorie. Grundlagentexte aus Philosophie und Kulturwissenschaften*, by Jörg Dünne and Stephan Günzel, 180–188. Frankfurt am Main: Suhrkamp Taschenbuch Verlag.

Merleau-Ponty, Maurice. 2002 (1945). *Phenomenology of Perception*. London: Routledge Classics.

Merleau-Ponty, Maurice. 1968. *The Visible and the Invisible*. Editor: Claude Lefort. Translation: Alphonso Lingis. Evanston: Northwestern University Press.

Möntmann, Nina, *Kollektive Handlungsräume: Ein Blick auf die politischen Perspektiven neuer Gemeinschaften*. University of Bern Sixth Lecture of the project's (The Interior) lecture series. Lecture 4 December 2013.

Moore, Rowan. 2018. "'Disneyland for adults': John Portman's dizzying interior legacy". *The Guardian*. Retrieved: 22 March 2019. https://www.theguardian.com/cities/2018/oct/22/disneyland-for-adults-john-portman-dizzying-interior-legacy.

Moos, Stanislaus von. 2003. In *Die Internationalität der Eisenbahn 1850–1970*, by Monika Burri, Kilian Elsasser and David Gugerli, 47–70. Zürich: Chronos-Verlag.

Mumford, Lewis. 1938. *The Culture of Cities*. New York: Routledge/Thoemmes Press.

2016. *Museum of Flight Seattle*. Aircraft. Retrieved: 16 September 2016. http://www.museumofflight.org/Site/aircraft/.

The Economist. 2018. Bilbao Effect. Retrieved: 22 September 2016. http://www.economist.com/news/special-report/21591708-if-you-build-it-will-they-come-bilbao-effect.

National Gallery. JMW Turner: Rain, Steam and Speed. Retrieved: 15 September 2015. https://www.national-gallery.org.uk/paintings/joseph-mallord-william-turner-rain-steam-and-speed-the-great-western-railway.

Negri, Antonio, and Michael Hardt. 2000. *Empire*. Harvard: Harvard University Press.

Nicholson, Louise. Mumbai Airport, *Apollo Magazine*. Retrieved: 22 February 2016. http://www.apollo-magazine.com/art-airport-terminal-2-mumbai/.

Nicolai, Bernd. 2015. „Kristallbau und Kristalline Baukunst als Architekturkonzepte seit der Romantik." In *Kristallvisionen in der Kunst*, by Matthias Frehner and Daniel Spanke, 43–51. Bern: Kerber Verlag.

Norberg-Schulz, Christian. 1980. Genius Loci: Towards a Phenomenology of Architecture. New York: Rizzoli.

O'Callaghan, Timothy J. 1993. *Henry Ford's Airport, and Other Aviation Interests 1909–1954*. Ann Arbor, Michigan: Proctor Publications.

Oldenberg, Ray. 1989. *The Great Good Place: Cafes, coffee shops, bookstores, bars hair salons and other hangouts at the heart of the community*. New York: Marlowe & Company.

Pallasmaa, Juhani. 2016. "Dwelling in Light: Tactile, Emotive and Life-Enhancing Light." *Daylight and Architecture Magazine by Velux* 26.

Pallasmaa, Juhani. 2005. *The Eyes of the Skin: Architecture and the Senses*. Chichester: Wiley & Sons.

Panofsky, Erwin. 1980. „Die Perspektive als ‚symbolische Form'". In *Aufsätze zu Grundfragen der Kunstwissenschaft*, by Erwin Panofsky, 99–167. Berlin: Volker Spiess.

Pawlyn, Michael. 2011. *Biomimicry in Architecture*. London: RIBA.

Pearman, Hugh. 2004. *Airports: A Century of Architecture*. London: Laurence King.

Perey, François. 1908–1918. "Les Premiers Hommes-Oiseaux." In *A Passion for Wings, Aviation and the Western Imagination*, by Robert Wohl. New Haven, Connecticut: Yale University Press.

Perur, Srinath. Chhatrapati Shivaji Terminus, Mumbai's iconic railway station – a history of cities in 50 buildings. *The Guardian*. Retrieved: 15 September 2016. https://www.theguardian.com/cities/2015/apr/21/chhatrapati-shivaji-terminus-cst-mumbai-railway-station.

Pevsner, Nikolaus. 2010. *Visual Planning and the Picturesque*. Editor: Mathew Aitchinson. The Getty Research Institute Publications Program.

Piano, Renzo, Teiji Matsumasa, Noriaki Okabe, Shinichi Okumura, and John Thackara. 1994. *Process Architecture: Kansai International Airport. Renzo Piano Building Workshop*. Editor: Noriaki Okabe. Tokyo: Process Architecture.

Platt, Craig. Shanghai Maglev Train, *Traveller*. Retrieved: 14 December 2016. http://www.traveller.com.au/400kmh-and-counting-on-board-the-worlds-fastest-train-15izo.

Pope, Alexander. 2007 (original 1744). *Epistles to several persons*. Ann Arbor: University of Michigan Library.

Qatar Museums. *Airport Art Installations*. Retrieved: 14 February 2016. http://www.qm.org.qa/en/project/airport-installations.

Rancière, Jacques. 2009. *The Emancipated Spectator*. Translation: Gregory Elliott. London: Verso.

Read, Gray, and Marcia Feuerstein. 2013. *Architecture as a Performing Art*. London: Taylor & Francis.

Rolt, L.T.C. Richard Trevithick, *Encyclopedia Britannica*. Retrieved: 16 September 2016. https://www.britannica.com/biography/Richard-Trevithick.

Roseau, Nathalie. 2012. *Aerocity: Quand l'avion fait la ville*. Marseille: Parenthèses.

Rossi, Aldo. 1984. *The Architecture of the City*. Oppositions Books.

RSA. *The Royal Society of the Arts*. Retrieved: 14 February 2016. https://www.thersa.org/about-us/archive-and-history/.

Said, Edward. 2003. *Orientalism*. London: Penguin.

Sant'Elia, Antonio. 2009. "L'architettura futurista: Manifesto". In: *Futurism: an anthology*. Ed. Rainey, Lawrence; Poggi, Christine; Wittman, Laura. New Haven: Yale University Press.

Santala, Susanna; Albrecht, Donald; Pelkonen, Eeva-Liisa; Scully, Vincent; Lipstadt, Hélène. 2006. *Eero Saarinen: Shaping the Future*. Exhibition Catalogue, Helsinki.

Sarbutu, Ahmed. 2002. „Expression und Funktion. Das TWA Terminal von Eero Saarinen in New York." *Architehese*, Sep/Oct: 32–35.

Schittich, Christian, Gerald Staib, Matthias Schuler, and Werner Sobek. 2007. *Glass Construction Manual*. 2nd revised and expanded edition. München: Birkhäuser – Verlag für Architektur Edition Detail.

Schivelbusch, Wolfgang. 2000. *Geschichte der Eisenbahnreise: Zur Industrialisierung von Raum und Zeit im 19. Jahrhundert*. Frankfurt a.M.: Fischer Taschenbuch Verlag.

Schlichting, Kurt. 2001. *Grand Central Terminal: Railroads, Engineering and Architecture in New York*. Baltimore: The Johns Hopkins University Press.

Schmid, Christian. 2014. "The Trouble with Henri: Urban Research and the Theory of the Production of Space." In *Urban Revolution Now: Henri Lefebvre in Social Research and Architecture*, Editor: Lukasz Stanek, Christian Schmid and Ákos Moravánszky, Translation: Christopher Findlay, 339. Farnham, Surrey: Ashgate.

Schmitz, Stephanus. 2009. "Identity in Architecture – A Construction?" In *Constructing Identity in Contemporary Architecture. Case Studies from the South*, by Stephanus Schmitz, Editor: Peter Herrle and Stephanus Schmitz. TU Berlin: Schriften der Habitat Unit, Fakultät Planen Bauen Umwelt, TU Berlin.

Schultz, Anne-Catrin. 2008. *Skidmore, Owings & Merrill, International Terminal, San Francisco International Airport.* Stuttgart: Edition Axel Menges.

Scully, Vincent. 2011. *Eero Saarinen: Shaping the Future.* Ed. Albrecht, Donald; Pelkonen, Eeva-Liisa. New Haven: Yale Universtity Press.

Skidmore, Owings, Merrill (SOM). Changi Airport. Retrieved: 17 October 2016. http://www.som.com/ projects/changi_international_airport__terminal_3.

Skidmore, Owings, Merrill (SOM), Hajj Terminal, Retrieved: 11 October 2016. http://www.som.com/ projects/king_abdul_aziz_international_airport__hajj_ terminal__structural_engineering.

Slater, Don. 1987. *Consumer Culture and Modernity.* Cambridge: Polity.

Sloterdijk, Peter. 2013. *In the World Interior of Capital: Towards a Philosophical Theory of Globalization.* Translation: Wieland Hoban. Cambridge: Polity Press.

Smith, Paul. 2000. *Annés 30 Architecture des aéroports: Berlin, Liverpool, Paris.* Paris: Editions du Patrimoine.

Smithson, Robert. *Robert Smithson Selected Writings.* Retrieved: 29 September 2014. https://www.robertsmithson.com/essays/provisional.htm.

Sophia, Mary. Dubai Duty Free. Retrieved: 31 October 2016. http://gulfbusiness.com/dubai-duty-free-named-worlds-largest-airport-retailer/#.VI6bK9KUe-4.

Sparke, Penny. 2010. *Interiors: Design/Architecture/Culture.* Editor: Anne Massey and John Turpin. Bd. Vol 1.

Sparke, Penny. 2008. *The Modern Interior.* London: Reaktion Books.

Sparke, Penny. 2010. "The Modern Interior: A Euro-American paradigm." *Interior Spaces in Other Places.* Brisbane: Queensland University of Technology. 1–6.

Spillman, Annette, and Harald Echsle. *Spillmann Echsle Architekten.* Retrieved: 14 October 2016. http://www.spillmannechsle.ch/wp/?p=140.

Stierli, Martino. 2011. "The Architect as Ghost-Writer: Rem Koolhaas and image-based urbanism." In *Postmodernism: Style and Subversion, 1970–1990,* by Glenn Adamson and Jane Pavitt, 137. London: V&A

Publishing. TWA Hotel. Retrieved: 22 July 2019. https://www.twahotel.com/hotel.

Taut, Bruno. 1914. „Glashaus: Werkbund-Ausstellung Cöln 1914." *Offizieller Katalog der Deutschen Werkbund-Ausstellung, Cöln 1914, Mai bis Oktober* (Cöln: Mosse) 122.

Teyssot, Georges. 2008. „Architektur als Membran." In *Explorations in Architecture Teaching, Design, Research,* by Urs Staub, 166. Basel: Birkhäuser.

Teyssot, Georges. 2011. „Traumhaus. L'intérieur comme innvervation du collectif." In *Spielraum: Walter Benjamin et l'architecture,* by Libero Andreotti et. al., 21–49. Paris: Editions de la Villette.

Thomas-Emberson, Steve. 2007. *Airport Interiors. Design for Business.* Chichester: Wiley & Sons.

Trunz, Helmut. 2008. *Tempelhof Flughafen im Herzen Berlins.* München: GeraMond.

Tsai, Eugenie. 2004. "Robert Smithson: Plotting a Line from Passaic, New Jersey, to Amarillo, Texas." *Robert Smithson.* Los Angeles: University of California Press, 12. September.

Tschumi, Bernard. 1994. *Event-Cities.* The MIT Press.

Tschumi, Bernard. 1976. *Manhattan Transcripts.* New York: Wiley & Sons.

Tzonis, Alexander. 2003. "Introducing an Architecture of the Present. Critical Regionalism and the Design of Identity." In *Critical Regionalism. Architecture and Identity in a Globalized World,* Editor: Liane Lefaivre and Alexander Tzonis. University of Michigan: Prestel.

Ursprung, Philip. 2006. „Phantomschmerzen der Architektur: Verschwindende Körper und Raumprothesen." in: *Kritische Berichte.* Bd. 34, No 2, p 17–28.

Ursprung, Philip. 2014. "Presence: The Light Touch of Architecture." In *Sensing Spaces,* by Kate Goodwin and Philip Ursprung, Editor: Vicky Wilson and Tom Neville, 39–53. London: Royal Academy Publications.

Ursprung, Philip. 2001. „Weisses Rauschen. Elisabeth Diller und Ricardo Scofidios Blur Building und die räumliche Logik der jüngsten Architektur." *Kritische Berichte.* Bd. 29, No 2, p 5–15.

V, Manju. "Mumbai Airport," *The Times of India*. Retrieved: 26 October 2014. https://timesofindia.indiatimes.com/city/mumbai/Mumbai-airports-T2-to-double-as-largest-museum/articleshow/28414398.cms.

Veblen, Thorstein. 2009. *The Theory of the Leisure Class*. New York: Dover Publications.

Venturi, Robert, and Denise Scott Brown. 2004. *Architecture as Signs and Systems*. Cambridge, MA: Belknap Press of Harvard University Press.

Venturi, Robert and Denise Scott Brown. 1977. *Learning from Las Vegas*. Cambridge: The MIT Press.

Visit Korea. Incheon Airport. Retrieved: 30 Octoeber 2016. http://english.visitkorea.or.kr/enu/ATR/SI_EN_3_1_1_1.jsp?cid=609933.

Wagner, Monika. 1994. „Die erste Londoner Weltausstellung als Warnehmungsproblem." *Ferrum: Nachrichten aus der Eisenbibliothek, Stiftung der Georg Fischer AG*, 31–38.

Wainwright, Oliver. "HSBC History." *The Guardian*. Retrieved: May 22 2016. https://www.theguardian.com/cities/2015/may/28/hong-kong-hsbc-hq-bank-history-cities-50-buildings.

Wainwright, Oliver. "Richard Wilson's Slipstream." *The Guardian*. Retrieved: 17 October 2016. http://www.theguardian.com/artanddesign/2014/apr/23/richard-wilson-slipstream-heathrow-installation.

Ward, David. 2002. "The Guggenheim Effect." *The Guardian*. Retrieved: 30 October 2016. https://www.theguardian.com/society/2002/oct/30/urbandesign.architecture2.

Weinstein, Beth. 2013. "Turned Tables: The Public as Performers in Jean Nouvel's Pre-Performance Spaces." In *Architecture as Performing Art*, by Marcia Feuerstein and Gray Read, 163–176. London: Routledge.

Wilhelmer, Lars. 2015. *Transit-Orte in der Literatur. Eisenbahn – Hotel – Hafen – Flughafen*. Bielefeld: transcript.

Wolfe, Tom. 1981. *From Bauhaus to Our House*. New York: Farrar Straus Giroux.

Wright, Frank Lloyd.1932. *The Disappearing City*. New York: William Farquhar Payson.

Yau, Wilson. 2014. "The Crystal Palace." *British Architectural Library, RIBA*. London.